Public Opinion and Interest Groups in American Politics

Donated by
The Public Interest Institute
to The Heartland Institute
2016

PUBLIC OPINION AND INTEREST GROUPS IN AMERICAN POLITICS

David H. Everson
Sangamon State University

Franklin Watts
New York / London / Toronto / Sydney

Also by David H. Everson
American Political Parties

Library of Congress Cataloging in Publication Data

Everson, David H., 1941–
Public opinion and interest groups
in American politics.

Includes bibliographical references and index.
1. Public opinion — United States
2. Pressure groups — United States.   I. Title
HN90.P8E93   303.3'8'0973   81–23139
ISBN 0–531–05642–2   AACR2

Franklin Watts
730 Fifth Avenue
New York, New York 10019

Copyright © 1982 by David H. Everson
Printed in the United States of America
All rights reserved
5 4 3 2 1

Contents

	Figures	vi
	Tables	vi
	Preface	ix
Chapter 1	Three Views of Democracy	1
Chapter 2	Pluralism and Interest-Group Theory	21
Chapter 3	American Political Parties: The Pluralist Reality, the Majoritarian Ideal, and Party Cycles	41
Chapter 4	The Citizen as Rational Activist	57
Chapter 5	The Fragmentation of American Politics	73
Chapter 6	The Mass Media and Political Fragmentation	95
Chapter 7	A Conservative Trend?	119
Chapter 8	The Group Bases of Opinion	141
Chapter 9	Group Voting Patterns	159
Chapter 10	Normal Policymaking	175
Chapter 11	Reaganomics: Nonincremental Change?	191
Chapter 12	The Future of American Politics	217
	Bibliography	233
	Index	239

Figures

Figure 2-1	A Simple Pressure Group Model	**36**
Figure 5-1	Turnout in Presidential and Off-Year Elections, 1920–1978	**84**
Figure 7-1	Should Government Guarantee a Job and a Good Standard of Living?	**123**
Figure 7-2	Support on Comprehensive Health Care	**124**
Figure 7-3	Power of Federal Government	**126**
Figure 7-4	Internationalism versus Isolationism	**128**
Figure 7-5	Foreign Assistance	**129**
Figure 7-6	Attitudes toward Defense Spending, 1972–1976	**130**
Figure 7-7	Busing to Achieve School Integration	**133**
Figure 7-8	Favor Desegregation or Segregation	**134**
Figure 7-9	Liberal to Conservative Index	**137**
Figure 9-1	A Model of Group Influence	**161**

Tables

Table 1-1	Degrees of Political Organization	**4**
Table 1-2	The Constitution Through Pluralist and Majoritarian Eyes	**7**
Table 1-3	Goals and Implications of Pluralist, Majoritarian, and Classical Theories	**9**
Table 1-4	Summary of Three Theories	**16**
Table 4-1	Classical Image Versus Average Citizen	**62**
Table 4-2	Classical Image Versus Average Citizen (1970's)	**68**
Table 5-1	Most Trusting Minus Most Cynical, 1958–1978	**77**
Table 5-2	Indicators of Party Decline: Electorate, Organization, Government	**78**

VII Tables

Table 6-1	Carter Job Ratings (October 1979 to March 1980)	97
Table 7-1	Defense Spending before and after Iran and Afghanistan Crises	131
Table 7-2	Public Sentiment on the Death Penalty, 1953–1981	135
Table 8-1	Relationship of Social Status and Response to Power of Federal Government, 1964	143
Table 8-2	Class Differences on Social Welfare Issues, 1964–1976	144
Table 8-3	Changes in Social Welfare Attitudes by Education and Occupation, 1964–1976	145
Table 8-4	Change in Social Welfare Attitudes of Black versus White Americans, 1964–1976	147
Table 8-5	Internationalism by Race, Education, and Occupation, 1960, 1976	148
Table 8-6	Attitudes toward Desegregation by Status, 1964, 1976	149
Table 8-7	Attitudes toward School Desegregation by Status, 1964, 1976	150
Table 8-8	Self-placement on Liberal/Conservative Scale by Status Groups, 1972, 1976	152
Table 8-9	Equal Role for Women by Social Groups, 1978	153
Table 9-1	Changes in Party Identification of New Deal Coalition Groups, 1964 and 1976	163
Table 9-2	Contribution of Groups to Democratic Vote, 1952, 1972	164
Table 9-3	Percent Democratic among Status Groups, 1940 Presidential Election	168
Table 9-4	The New Deal Coalition and Democratic Presidential Voting, 1964, 1976	169
Table 9-5	Group Voting Patterns, 1952–1980	170
Table 12-1	Democratic Performance in Presidential Elections versus Turnout, 1972–1980	226

For J and L

I wish to acknowledge the assistance of several people in preparing this book. As usual, Jackie Wright has been a superlative typist as well as an adept translator of my atrocious handwriting. Beth Phillips did an extraordinary job of gathering and organizing the material for the case study in Chapter Ten. Every chapter and nearly every line of this book benefited from the critical analysis of Rita Harmony, to whom my gratitude is boundless for her patience, humor, sharp eye, and intelligence. She also co-authored Chapter Six.

Finally, as director of the Illinois Legislative Studies Center, I want to acknowledge Sangamon State University for providing the time and support to write while serving as director. Without an able staff, I could not have attempted to write this book.

David H. Everson
Sangamon State University
Springfield, Illinois

Preface

Ideally, this book should be read as a companion to my earlier *American Political Parties* (New York: New Viewpoints, 1980). That work examined American parties (and politics) from a responsible-parties perspective. The conclusions reached about the future of American politics in an era of party decline were not optimistic. In this book, the focus is less on parties and more on public opinion and interest groups, but many of the questions are the same. The central question is where the current trends in American politics are taking us. As the final chapter indicates, I continue to be apprehensive.

Inevitably, this book is colored by the fact that it was written in the fall of 1980 and the spring of 1981; that is, it is heavily influenced by the election of Ronald Reagan and the early days of his administration. Thus, one major theme of the book is an assessment of the extent of the swing to the right in American politics. My assessment, buttressed by data in Chapters Eight and Nine, is that the swing was real but more modest than some would claim and also in part a product of the shrinking of the electorate (Chapter Five). The Reagan election afforded a rare example of nonincremental change in American politics upsetting many expectations, including my own (Chapter Eleven).[1]

As is my custom, I have tried to approach the subject from the perspective of democratic theory. The initial chapter spells out three versions of democratic theory (classical, majoritarian, and pluralist). In the following three chapters, the implications of each of these for the interpretation of American politics are explored. Each perspective has had an important influence in American politics, particularly with respect to political reform.

---

[1] It would be instructive to compare my account of President Carter's efforts to get a comprehensive energy policy in 1977 with the success of President Reagan's budget fight in 1981 and to inquire: why the difference? See *American Political Parties* (New York: New Viewpoints, 1980), Chapter Nine. Clearly, one reason was the perception of a Reagan mandate.

Chapter Two lays out the interest-group theory interpretation of American politics and examines the critiques of that approach. Chapter Three looks at the role of political parties in American politics by contrasting pluralism and majoritarian views of parties. In addition, the concept of realignment is introduced. Chapter Four explores the notion of a "rational-activist" citizen, an outgrowth of the classical view of democracy. In combination, the first four chapters set the stage for an exploration of the two major issues of the book: how far has the fragmentation of American politics gone, and what are the likely consequences?

The next five chapters describe changes in American politics. I have relied heavily on secondary analysis of published data. Particularly helpful, as the sources cited for the tables will indicate, have been the journal *Public Opinion*, published by the American Enterprise Institute, and the *American National Elections Data Sourcebook*, published by the Harvard University Press (1980), which summarizes a wealth of data collected by the Center for Political Studies at the University of Michigan. These chapters explore the decline of party and the increasing fragmentation of American politics (Chapter Five), the role of the mass media in American politics (Chapter Six), change in public opinion in a conservative direction (Chapters Seven and Eight), and changes in party identification and voting by groups (Chapter Nine).

Chapter Ten moves in a somewhat different direction by spelling out the normal policymaking process in the United States as pluralist / incrementalist. The policymaking process is seen as a natural product of a fragmented system of authority and decentralized political institutions. Again, realignment is introduced as a corrective to normal politics. Chapter Eleven contrasts the early days of Reagan's administration with the pluralist / incrementalist model as an illustration of abnormal politics.

The final chapter considers the future of American politics and reaches some bleak conclusions. In essence, it is argued that despite the successes of the early Reagan administration, the deinstitutionalization of American politics is likely to resume and accelerate, leading to extreme difficulties in the policymaking process for both liberals and conservatives.

CHAPTER 1

THREE VIEWS OF DEMOCRACY

This is a book about American democracy in the midst of political change. The focus will be on the public, public opinion, and interest groups and how these affect public policy. To a degree, democracy means choice on matters of public policy. This implies that citizens have preferences and choose the policies they prefer. Two central questions concern the relationship of public policy and citizen preferences: how do citizen preferences about public policy get known by elites and what mechanisms are there for assuring governmental responsiveness? These in turn raise general issues of political organization, its types, functions, and consequences.

This chapter deals with democracy and organization. The connection is problematic. Indeed, an inevitable tension exists between the goals of democracy and the need for organizations such as political parties and interest groups that establish collective goals and carry out collective decisions.[1] Democracy cannot function without organization, yet organization may imperil such democratic values as participation. Different versions of democratic theory treat the issue of organization in quite different ways. The three views of democracy that will be the main subject of this chapter are the *classical*, the *majoritarian*, and the *pluralist*. The classical view stresses self-development, direct participation in decision-making, and community consensus. The majoritarian perspective stresses political institutions, such as political parties, that contribute to majority rule. The pluralist approach stresses the reconciliation of diverse interests in democracy and the protection of minority rights.[2]

A recurring tension between organization and democracy is revealed in two issues. The more fundamental one is this: does organization have any legitimate role to play in a democratic system? The subsidiary question is this: what forms of organization are compatible with what forms of democracy?

In order to get at the question of organization, we need to consider what we mean in general by democracy. One simple perspective is that public policy should be in accord, insofar as possible, with public opinion: democracy is the voice of the people expressed in governmental action (or inaction). There are, of course, many other views; some writers would regard this formulation as extremely naive and misleading.[3] It is useful, however, for pondering the role of organization in democracy. For example, can public opinion be expressed in the absence of political organization? Other questions follow: what is public opinion and what means are available for converting opinion into policy?

The various views of democracy influence the way we think about the problems of political organization. Having raised the question of organization as it relates to opinion and democracy, it seems reasonable to consider what the term means.

A Note on Political Organization

In a general sense, the term "organization" refers to human relationships that have a high degree of *stability, uniformity, formality,* and *generality*.[4] In addition, a psychological property of the members of organizations, *identification with the organization*, may be cited. Stability refers to the degree to which the organization enjoys an ongoing, regular existence rather than an ad hoc, discontinuous existence. Uniformity describes the degree to which patterns of interaction within the group have become patterned and predictable. Formality is the degree to which the organization has a customary, written, and rule-bound structure. Generality refers to the degree to which the characteristics of the organization are similar to the patterns of the larger society. Finally, identification means that the members of the organization self-consciously identify with one another as members of a group. Obviously, groups vary in the degree to which they possess these characteristics. The two major types of organizations dealt with in this book are interest groups and, to a lesser extent, political parties. They clearly possess the general characteristics of organizations. In contrast, a scattered collection of individuals who share a political sentiment—such as protection of wildlife—but do not communicate at all are far removed from being a political organization (although the potential is there). Nevertheless, many cases can have some, but not all, of the characteristics of a full-fledged organization. Table 1.1 provides some illustrations of the various possibilities.

Table 1.1 Degrees of Political Organization

Examples	Stability	Uniformity	Formality	Generality	Group Identification
National Rifle Association	High	High	High	High	High
Ad hoc neighborhood issue group	Moderate to Low	Moderate to Low	Low	Low	High
Public opinion on aid to Pakistan	Low	Low	Low	Low	Low

Political organizations are those whose major function is to translate group sentiment into government action. Of course, such groups may have other functions, such as fulfilling social needs for their members.

At this point, let us consider the implications of democratic theories for political organizations.

Pluralist versus Majoritarian Democracy

We will now discuss, briefly, the three versions of democracy.[5] All belong to the general family of democratic theories. However, each emphasizes a somewhat different aspect of democracy, and each has somewhat different implications for the role of political organizations.

Pluralism can be identified as the political theory of the American Constitution, which creates a pluralistic structure of government. Pluralism is often seen as a solution to problems inherent in democracy, or the presumed excesses of democracy. One such problem is that of "majority factions."[6] Majority factions threaten individual liberty and the rights of minorities. The solution to the problem is implied in the term "pluralist": namely, the political system disperses power in such a way that individual liberty and the interests of minorities are protected. One may observe that the pluralist version of democracy is curious in that it is negative. Pluralism concentrates on dispersion of power and the protection of minorities. We often associate democracy with majority rule and political equality. Consequently, pluralism is susceptible to the criticism that it is not very democratic.[7] Nevertheless, this view of democracy has had a powerful influence on and in the American political culture.[8]

American pluralism is based on the constitutional separation of powers, political decentralization, recognition of the inevitability (if not the desirability) of political factions (interests), and attention to the problem of intense minority interests in the society. The constitutional separation of powers helps to prevent hasty or ill-conceived majorities from preying on the rights of minorities. The American Constitution limits majorities as evidenced by its separation of powers, its difficult amendment processes, and its implied power of judicial review. Decentralization of governmental structure (federalism) serves the same objective as well as taking into account the diversity in the large nation-state. These diverse interests are bound, in a free society, to organize and pursue their particular objectives. The sheer number and variety of interests work to the advantage of the Madisonian-pluralist system because they impede the easy creation of majorities.[9] (The word "Madisonian" is used with reference to James Madison, one of the fathers of American pluralist thought; see Chapter Two.) If any majority is difficult to create, majorities inimical to the rights of others will likewise be difficult; especially, the interests of intense minorities need to be taken into account. In extreme forms, pluralism may insist on some form of a veto group or "concurrent majority" providing protection for minorities.[10] This amounts to governing by the consensus of the affected interests.

As indicated, pluralism may seem to turn democracy on its head in terms of its concern for minority interests. Nevertheless, the moderate version of pluralism, illustrated in the American Constitution, is republican and is ultimately responsive to majority wishes. The intent of pluralism is, however, limited, not absolute, democracy.

Majoritarian democratic theory stands in sharp contrast to pluralism and conflicts with it directly on several basic points. The majoritarian view has two dominant, interrelated goals: majority rule and political equality. In national political systems, majoritarian democracy must be realized through representative institutions such as legislatures. The realization of majoritarian goals in nation-states seems to require the following: centralization of political authority, nationalization (by that is meant the treatment of issues on the basis of national interests) of major issues, and insistence on egalitarian political procedures. Centralization of political authority is required for majoritarianism because centralization allows for effective translation of national interests (as defined by national majorities) into public policy. The same argument applies to the nationalization of political issues. Local diversity and opposition should not be allowed to prevent needed action by national majorities. Political insitutions and procedures should reflect faithfully the norm of political equality; no special interests, whatever their intensity, should weigh more heavily in the political process than others.

The contrast between the pluralist and majoritarian views of democracy can be seen in terms of how they view important American political institutions:

Table 1.2 The Constitution Through Pluralist and Majoritarian Eyes

	Pluralist position	Majoritarian position
More representative institution	Congress	President
Preferred method of presidential selection	Indirect—electoral college	Direct election of President
Amendment of Constitution	Difficult	Easy
Judicial review	Necessary	Undesirable
Separation of powers	Desirable	Undesirable

A pluralist would normally prefer Congress as a representative institution because the Congress is elected from local constituencies and (more or less) faithfully represents all the national diversity. In addition, Congress is strewn with minority protection devices, whereas the Senate is an extreme manifestation of *unequal* weighting of interests (each state, regardless of the size of its population, has two senators). In contrast, a majoritarian prefers the presidency because the President is elected from a national constituency, can claim a national mandate, and (if the electoral college did not intervene) would be elected by a system in which every vote counted equally. The *pluralist*, on the one hand, would defend the electoral college because it weighs various interests (small states, large states) unequally and because it supports federalism.[11] The *majoritarian*, on the other hand, would much prefer the egalitarian direct popular election of the President (as long as there were safeguards, such as a runoff to ensure that the winner actually had a majority.) The pluralist would prefer that the Constitution be difficult to amend, to protect minority interests, and would favor prudent exercise of judicial review for the same reason. The majoritarian would take the opposite point of view on both questions. This brief section should indicate that the basic American constitutional structure is pluralist at its base. Pressure for change, reform, often comes from majoritarian perspectives that attack the "undemocratic" features of the constitutional order. Both share, however, the recognition that in nation-states, representative democracy is a necessity and participatory democracy is impossible.

Classical Theory

The third orientation to democracy, classical,[12] is distinctly different from both the pluralist and majoritarian perspectives. As we shall see, it shares some aspects with both. The primary goal is individual, direct participation in the decisions that affect the life of the individual. Political participation is necessary both for the full development of the individual and for building commitment to the polity and its decisions. Classical theory shares the passion for political equality of the majoritarian view of democracy. However, the classical view stresses, not majority rule, but rather a deliberative consensus as the preferred means of decision-making. The emphasis on individual participation and its benefits for individual development separates this view from either of the others. Moreover, the scope of the political world is enlarged in classical theory to include social, economic, and family decisions.[13] *Direct* participation in those decisions that affect individuals requires that one question the assumption that democracy and representative institutions are compatible. In the classical view, representation is inherently suspect. Consequently, the classical view implies a radical decentralization of political and social structure. This is true because the need for individual participation severely limits the size of the governing units.[14] In large units, time constraints preclude full participation.[15] As indicated previously, the expected outcome of mass participation in decision-making is a deliberative consensus. In this aspect, there is a convergence with pluralism where the expected outcome of a clash of interests is a political compromise.

To recapitulate, the three versions of democracy in terms of their major objectives and implications are:

Table 1.3 Goals and Implications of Pluralist, Majoritarian, and Classical Theories

	Pluralist	**Majoritarian**	**Classical**
Major goals	Guarding of minority rights; representative government in diverse societies	Majority rule; political equality	Individual participation in decision-making (for self-development); community consensus
Major implications	Separation of authority; decentralization of political units	Unification of authority; centralization of political processes	Radical decentralization of political units

There are few pure practicing classical democrats, majoritarians, or pluralists, but political reform movements often reflect these various perspectives. For example, the Progressive movement of the early part of this century resembled the classical point of view in its hostility to political organizations. Although elements of both pluralism and majoritarianism can be found in Progressive thought, the movement espoused the twin goals of direct democracy and decision-making by consensus.[16] In their hostility to organization, Progressives advocated reforms, such as the initiative and referendum, aimed at more direct popular participation in government, but they stopped well short of suggesting the radical decentralization required by pure classical theory. There was probably an inevitable contradiction between the goals of direct democracy and the nationalistic preferences of Progressives such as Theodore Roosevelt and Herbert Croly.

In the 1970s there was a drive for increased use of initiatives and referenda in the United States, a modest revival of some ideas advocated by the Progressives.[17] For example, in 1980 thirty-one initiated propositions appeared on the ballot in eighteen states as opposed to eighteen in ten states in 1960. There are, of course, innumerable local referenda in the United States each year. This form of direct democracy allows for individual participation in policy decisions without the necessity for decentralization, but mass participation in the discussion of alternatives is missing.

In the 1960s a student-led movement advocated radical decentralization of decision-making as part of a program of political and social democracy. The Port Huron statement of the Students for a Democratic Society said, in part, "we seek the establishment of a democracy of individual participation."[18] And although there was no direct connection, government antipoverty programs of the mid-1960s sought to achieve "maximum feasible participation" by citizens at the local community level.[19] And the late 1960s brought a wave of political reform in the United States, one aspect of which was the drive for more direct participation in the affairs of the political parties.

The point of these examples is that the value of individual participation is a potent and recurring one in American politics despite its apparent limited applicability in a large nation-state.

The majoritarian point of view is most clearly expressed in the writings of the proponents of "responsible political parties."[20] The advocates of responsible parties argue that reforms are needed to strengthen the national political parties in order to overcome the fragmentation of the American political system and the influence of special interest groups.

In 1950 a committee of the American Political Science Association issued a report calling for a more responsible party system in the United States.[21] That report stressed the need for stronger national party organizations, more cohesion within the parties, and (in a bow in the classical direction) more grass roots participation in the parties. This latter point had not been part of the program of responsible parties to that point.[22] The call for more responsible parties, on the British model with a parliamentary system of government, has been a recurring one in American political history. Recently Lloyd Cutler, adviser to President Carter, reiterated the plea.[23] So the majoritarian impulse is also strong in the United States. Nevertheless, pluralist political thought has usually been dominant.

The pluralist viewpoint usually has less of a reformist bent than either the classical or the majoritarian. In fact, the pluralist would generally oppose, or question the feasibility of, responsible parties.[24] The modern pluralist emphasizes the extent to which organized groups check and balance one another in the political struggle and contribute to political moderation and compromise. Pluralism seems to be an unconscious, but pervasive, value of the American political culture.

Functions of Political Organizations

Before turning to the impact of these ideas on the way parties and interest groups are evaluated, let us briefly consider the functions of political parties and interest groups in representative-competitive political systems. Political parties have three major functions: contesting elections, organizing the policymaking machinery of government, and educating the public. Parties, however imperfectly, link citizens to electoral and representative institutions. Parties organize elections around common symbols, select candidates, and conduct political campaigns in order to capture the government. For this function to be carried out, parties must be competitive. Single-party dominance will not suffice. Party also provides the glue that makes structuring a governing coalition possible. A governing coalition is a majority that makes policy (it may, of course, include both parties, but the core element is a party). Finally, parties perform a broadly educational role by formulating issues and programs so that the public can comprehend political conflict and make choices among competitors for offices that affect the content and direction of public policy.

Basically, interest groups help channel demands to government and provide an organized means of "educating" members and nonmembers. Interest groups may also, of course, mobilize votes for or against parties and candidates. But parties and interest groups are distinguishable from each other (even though there may be some ambiguous cases such as single-issue groups that attempt to become parties). A distinction may be made in terms of method: parties seek votes under a party label; interest groups do not. In addition, parties generally reflect broader sets of interests than do interest groups. Of course, this distinction does not always hold. From the point of view of democratic theory, however, this is the most important distinction: parties represent broader versus narrower concerns. Parties, especially American parties, have to balance the interests of a diverse set of members.

Public Opinion, Organization, and Public Interest

The three views of democracy discussed in this chapter have different implications for how organizations can (or should) link opinion and government policy in order to achieve the common good (public interest). Let us begin with pluralism.

13   Three Views of Democracy

There are two views of the public interest in pluralism. In one form in which pluralism is advocated as a check on the extremes of democracy, the public interest is identified with natural or inherent rights. In this view, factions (interests) may, and frequently do, pose grave threats to the common good. In the other form, which seeks to describe what actually happens in the political system, there is no objective reality to the public interest.[25] The "public interest" is achieved only through the pull and tug of the various competing interest groups. Nevertheless, both forms of pluralism recognize that opinion is expressed through the conflict between interest groups. Especially for the latter pluralists, whom we shall call interest-group pluralists, organized interest groups are the central actors in the political process.

From that perspective, one could argue that public opinion itself is a myth—that opinion is real (significant) only as it is expressed in the struggle of interest groups. As John Dickinson said, "The only opinion, the only one which exists, is the opinion, the will, of special groups."[26] This may explain why interest-group pluralists use terms such as "latent groups" to refer to general public opinion. It is only when latent groups become active that they are directly influential in the political system. It may be, however, that the public has indirect influence because public officials must take into account their responses to policy.[27]

In the pluralist view, political parties are important, but secondary, institutions. Their purpose is to aggregate diverse opinion—to build consensus. The major goal of the party in a pluralist system is to win elections: the overriding incentive is to mobilize votes to win office (for whatever purposes). Such parties stress public policy as a means rather than as an end and seek to build majority support from the diversity of interests in society. Such parties, in other words, seek to build a majority coalition that will allow them to capture office. These coalitions, in a large and diverse society, must be a bundle of compromises. In addition, such parties cannot permit the governing function (making public policy once control of office has been achieved) to dominate the electoral function. Therefore, the diversity of opinion reflected in the party during the election will carry over into the governing coalition, which must be a loose one.

Such parties in a pluralist system are consistent with a decentralized party system and weak party cohesion in governing. If we examine the fit of such parties and pluralism generally, we can see that the decentralized and weakly cohesive parties fit nicely into a decentralized, fragmented, and congressionally oriented system of government. It should be obvious that the party we have been describing has been strong in American political history. The two-party system in the United States has rested on such parties. Uniquely, American parties have been decentralized, minimally cohesive coalitions of diverse interests. American parties have been primarily oriented to elections. Therefore, policymaking in the United States has been less affected by parties than by the conflict of organized interest groups. It should also be obvious that the tension between the pluralist and majoritarian concepts of democracy is reflected in quite opposite opinions on the proper role, and power, of parties and interest groups.

If modern pluralism is receptive to interest groups and subordinates political parties to the electoral and aggregative functions, majoritarian democratic theory tends to distrust interest groups (which are, by definition, representative of minority interests) and to elevate political parties to a position of preeminence in terms of the organized representation of public opinion. Specifically, political parties of a particular type (as we noted earlier—"responsible") can serve to link majority positions on public policy to government action. Advocates of responsible parties see elections as a means to effective control of government and for education of the public to their policy positions. The primary purpose of the responsible party is effectively to organize the majority to take control of the government. Indeed, a responsible party is the institutionalized means by which majoritarian democracy could be realized in large representative systems. The responsible party receives a mandate to govern from an electoral majority. The pluralist party receives no such mandate. It receives an instruction to go on with the difficult process of majority coalition-building, based on the constellation of organized interests, after the election.

What is the classical view of opinion and organization? At the outset, it is hostile to the very idea of organization. In a participatory democracy, organizations or institutions have no positive functions. They serve only to perpetuate narrower interests and to subvert the popular will. Consequently, a purely classical position would severely restrict both parties and interest groups.

Few modern proponents of classical ideals have pushed their arguments quite that far, however. Rather, in the case of parties, they have called for more direct participation. The direct primary for nominating candidates was devised to foster "intraparty" democracy.[28] The rallying cry of the reformers has been to take the party out of the hands of the "bosses" and return it to the people. In the reformers' view, it is insufficient that parties, through interparty competition, provide a means of democratic control for citizens in elections. In many boss-dominated systems, two-party competition did not exist. Direct participation in the affairs of the party is vital to ensure democracy. The party serves as an arena for mass participation. Similar arguments for taking government out of the hands of the "interests" and for putting government back in the hands of the "people" have been made in support of the regulation of lobbying and campaign finance as well as the calls for referenda and initiatives. The impracticality of the classical ideal has led to a version of democracy in which partisanship and organized interest groups are allowed to play a role, but one that is greatly mitigated by regulation, reform, and modest efforts at direct participation. Few thinkers have allowed themselves to imagine a system with neither parties nor interest groups.

American Pluralism and Reform

The purposes of this chapter have been two. The first was to sketch three conflicting images of democracy. The second was to show how each has a different perspective on the role of political organization. The three versions and their implications for organization and reform are summarized as follows:

Table 1.4 Summary of Three Theories

	Pluralist	Majoritarian	Classical
Distinguishing features	Guarding of minority interests; representative government	Maximum majority rule and political equality	Maximum individual participation; community consensus
Implications for organization of public opinion	Interest groups as major political actors	Political parties as major political actors	Organization undesirable in democracy
Reform	No advocacy of major reforms	Responsible parties via constitutional change or strengthening party competition	Initiative, referenda, primaries, regulation of interest groups

As a direct consequence of the strife-torn 1968 Democratic convention, a reform movement was instituted in the Democratic party. There is no doubt that reform of the nomination process was, in many respects, justified. One intent of the reforms was to broaden active participation in party affairs, particularly on the part of women, minorities, and young people. (Expanding participation has been a constant theme in party reform throughout U.S. history.) The rationale was to bring the disaffected back into the party system by allowing them a meaningful role in the party. This is a subtheme of classical democracy—participation builds loyalty. There is also little doubt that the reforms did lead to greater participation (at least in a statistical sense) of women and minorities in the affairs of the Democratic party.[29] But whether the reforms actually strengthened the party is a subject for considerable debate.[30] Since its democratization, the faction-ridden Democratic party has suffered two disastrous presidential defeats, in 1972 and 1980, to the "unreformed"[31] Republican party.

The American political system has always been formally pluralist (whether the outcomes have been genuinely pluralist is a matter of dispute) and vulnerable to the criticisms of those who represent both majoritarian and classical perspectives. Reform movements have pushed the American polity in both directions. That is, majoritarians have sought reforms that would strengthen political parties and increase the competitiveness of the two-party system. Classical democrats have sought to weaken political parties. Majoritarians have sought to nationalize American politics. The tendency of classical theory is toward decentralization. Of course, sometimes reformers combine majoritarian and classical ideals, as in the drive for strong *and* democratic parties, without realizing the fundamental incompatibility of the two theories and objectives. While one certainly cannot say that the recent changes in American politics are due exclusively, or even primarily, to reform, it is certainly part of the story, especially with respect to the decline of parties. The Progressive movement started the decline of parties, and the reforms of the late 1960s and early 1970s in presidential selection hastened their decay. The hopes of the majoritarians for a more cohesive party system do not seem to have been realized. The United States seems to be moving away from a politics based on parties and elections and toward a politics of organized interest groups, even so-called single-issue groups. Is this a movement toward "excessive pluralism" or, perhaps, a necessary condition for the emergence of a more participatory democracy?

We have identified pluralism as the predominant American political theory. Pluralism leads directly to interest-group theory. The next chapter explores pluralist thought in more detail, examines how pluralism blends into interest-group theory, and then reviews the criticisms of both.

NOTES
CHAPTER ONE

[1] The strongest expression of these views asserts the impossibility of democracy in large organizations because organization begets oligarchy. See Robert Michels, *Political Parties: A Sociological Study of the Oligarchical Tendencies of Modern Democracy* (New York: Free Press, 1962).
[2] These three versions of democratic thought are alluded to by Leon D. Epstein, *Political Parties in Western Democracies* (New York: Praeger, 1967), pp. 15–18. (It should be noted that Epstein uses "individualist" for what I call the "classical" theory.)
[3] See, for example, Giovanni Sartori, *Democratic Theory* (New York: Praeger, 1965).
[4] David Truman refers to group patterns that have a high degree of stability, uniformity, formality, and generality as institutions. See *The Governmental Process* (New York: Knopf, 1951), p. 26.
[5] It should be understood that these brief discussions cannot begin to do justice to the complexities and subtleties of these three perspectives. For that, the obvious solution is to read the originals. It is useful, however, to consult Robert A. Dahl, *A Preface to Democratic Theory* (Chicago: University of Chicago Press, 1956) for an understanding of pluralist democracy (which he calls Madisonian democracy; see Chapter 1) and majoritarian democracy (which he calls populistic democracy; see Chapter 2). On the classical view, see Carole Pateman, *Participation and Democratic Theory* (Cambridge: Cambridge University Press, 1970).
[6] Such a faction is a majority of citizens "who are united and actuated by some common impulse of passion, or of interest, adverse to the rights of other citizens, or to the permanent and aggregate interests of the community." See Clinton Rossiter, ed., *The Federalist Papers* (New York: New American Library, 1961), p. 78.
[7] Of course, Madison argued in favor of republican—that is, representative—government as opposed to democracy; *Federalist*, pp. 81–82. For modern critiques of pluralism, see William E. Connolly, *The Bias of Pluralism* (New York: Atherton, 1969).
[8] Some writers refer to a set of ideas that are akin to and compatible with pluralism as Lockean liberalism. See Louis Hartz, *The Liberal Tradition in America* (New York: Harcourt, Brace and World, 1955). For an empirical assessment of these ideas in the American political culture, see Donald J. Devine, *The Political Culture of the United States* (Boston: Little, Brown, 1972).
[9] *Federalist*, pp. 82–84.

[10] The idea of a "concurrent majority" can be found in John C. Calhoun, *Disquisition on Government* (Indianapolis: Bobbs-Merrill, 1953).

[11] For advocacy of direct election of the President, see Neal R. Peirce, *The People's President* (New York: Simon & Schuster, 1968). For a defense of the electoral college based on the federalist argument, see Martin Diamond, *The Electoral College and the American Idea of Democracy* (Washington, D.C.: American Enterprise Institute, 1977).

[12] It should be reiterated here that there is no single *locus* for the classical democratic theory. Pateman relies on the writings of Jean Jacques Rousseau, John Stuart Mill, and G. D. H. Cole.

[13] Pateman, p. 106.

[14] This point is demonstrated by Robert A. Dahl in *After the Revolution* (New Haven: Yale University Press, 1970), pp. 85–88.

[15] Of course, one can argue that referenda allow direct participation. However, there is no guarantee of mass discussion and no solution to the problems posed by highly technical issues. It can be claimed that technological innovations, such as cable television and home computer terminals, will also allow for mass participation in decision-making. See Alvin Toffler, *The Third Wave* (New York: Bantam, 1980), pp. 427–31. What is missing from such formulations is any sense of the *pace* of decision-making in deliberative systems. It is not simply a matter of listening to both sides of a debate and making a choice. It is a matter of shaping alternatives and compromises throughout an entire process of decisions.

[16] For a summary of the Progressive perspective on political organization, see Judson L. James, *American Political Parties in Transition* (New York: Harper & Row, 1974), pp. 23–25.

[17] On the general subject, see David Butler and Austin Ranney, *Referendums* (Washington, D.C.: American Enterprise Institute, 1978). For a contemporary expression of the "democratic progressive" argument, see David P. Thelen, "Two Traditions of Progressive Reform, Political Parties, and American Democracy," in Patricia Bonomi et al., eds., *The American Constitutional System under Strong and Weak Parties* (New York: Praeger, 1981), pp. 37–63.

[18] Quoted in Arnold S. Kaufman, "Participatory Democracy: Ten Years Later," in Connolly, p. 203.

[19] For a critical analysis, see Daniel P. Moynihan, *Maximum Feasible Misunderstanding* (New York: Free Press, 1970).

[20] On "responsible parties," see Austin Ranney, *The Doctrine of Responsible Party Government* (Urbana: University of Illinois Press, 1954), and David H. Everson, *American Political Parties* (New York: New Viewpoints, 1980), Chapter 1.

[21] American Political Science Association, Committee on Political Parties,

"Toward a More Responsible Two-Party System," *American Political Science Review* 44 (Sept. 1950), Supplement.

[22]See, for example, E. E. Schattschneider, *Party Government* (New York: Holt, Rinehart & Winston, 1942).

[23]Lloyd N. Cutler, "To Form a Government," *Foreign Affairs* 59 (Fall 1980): 126–43.

[24]See Austin Ranney and Willmoore Kendall, *Democracy and the American Party System* (New York: Harcourt Brace Jovanovich, 1956).

[25]For example, David Truman says that "we do not need to account for a totally inclusive interest, because one does not exist," p. 51.

[26]Quoted by Glendon Schubert in *The Public Interest* (Glencoe, Ill.: Free Press, 1961), p. 141.

[27]See Robert A. Dahl, *Who Governs?* (New Haven: Yale University Press, 1961), p. 164.

[28]James, p. 94.

[29]The percentages of blacks and women delegates in Democratic party presidential conventions from 1968 to 1980 are as follows:

	1968	1972	1976	1980
Women	14%	36%	34%	50%
Blacks	6%	14%	11%	14%

These data are from Denis G. Sullivan et al., *The Politics of Representation* (New York: St. Martin's Press, 1974), p. 23; *Congressional Quarterly Weekly Report*, July 10, 1976, p. 1793; and Paul T. David, "The National Conventions of 1980," paper delivered at the 1980 Presidential Election Lecture Series, Legislative Studies Center, Sangamon State University, Sept. 17, 1980, p. 3.

[30]For a generally "pro-reform" perspective, see William Crotty, "Building a 'Philsophy' of Party Reform," paper prepared for delivery at the 1978 Annual Meeting of the American Political Science Association, New York, N.Y., August 31–Sept. 3, 1978. For a generally skeptical perspective, see Austin Ranney, *Curing the Mischiefs of Faction* (Berkeley: University of California Press, 1975).

[31]But see Charles Longley, "Party Reform and the Republican Party," paper prepared for delivery at the 1978 Annual Meeting of the American Political Science Association, New York, N.Y., August 31–Sept. 3, 1978.

ёCHAPTER

2

PLURALISM AND INTEREST-GROUP THEORY

Pluralism is one major variant of democratic theory. Of course, there is no single source of pluralist theory; it is a general set of ideas that embody both values and descriptions of political reality. Nevertheless, the core ideas of pluralism are clear: multiple interests exist in society; institutional arrangements should be constructed so that the interests of minorities are protected and so that democratic stability is preserved. Some of these ideas of pluralism have been incorporated into a theory of how political decisions actually get made in American politics; we shall refer to this theory as the *interest-group theory* of politics.

The purpose of this chapter is to summarize the ideas of the major pluralist theorists and their successors. In addition, we will examine the major criticisms of interest-group theory. In its most general sense, interest-group theory provides an explanation of how policy decisions are made, at least in American politics. In addition, various facets of interest-group theory deal with interest-group formation, the internal politics of groups, the determinants of group access to the political system, and the consequences of group conflict for political stability.

The precursors of interest-group theory were the political thinkers we have labeled pluralist. In order to see their impact on interest-group theory, we must examine their ideas in more detail.

Pluralism and interest-group theory are often treated as interchangeable. Nevertheless, they ought to be distinguished from each other.[1] Pluralism paved the way for conventional interest-group theory. Some aspects of classical pluralist thought, however, are in conflict with interest-group theory, and the thrust of classical pluralism is clearly different.

Classical pluralism is concerned with the tension between majority rule and individual liberty. Further, it is concerned with how diversity can contribute to democratic stability. Consequently, pluralist thought, albeit unintentionally, legitimizes the group as a major political actor. In different ways, James Madison, Alexis de Tocqueville, John C. Calhoun, and William Kornhauser exemplify various aspects of pluralist thought.[2]

James Madison, while decrying the "mischiefs of faction," developed a rationale for the creation of a large republic by arguing in the *Federalist Papers* that if you "extend the sphere and you take in a greater variety of parties and interests...you can make it less probable that a majority of the whole will have a common motive to invade the rights of other citizens; or if such a common motive exists, it will be more difficult for all who feel it to discover their own strength and to act in unison with each other."[3] In other words, the creation of a large republic would increase diversity (pluralism) and would decrease the opportunity for majority tyranny. This analysis provided a defense of the new Constitution, which created a stronger national political system.

Tocqueville, the French observer of the American scene in the 1830s, lamented the extraordinary hold that *majority opinion* had on the individual in the United States. In his masterful and sweeping account of American democracy Tocqueville anticipated the development of mass society, the welfare state, and totalitarianism, all fueled by the relentless appetite for social equality. In a long and remarkable passage, Tocqueville described the future shape of despotism: "That power is absolute, thoughtful of detail, orderly, provident, and gentle. It would resemble parental authority if, fatherlike, it tried to prepare its charges for a man's life, but on the contrary, it only tries to keep them in perpetual childhood...it daily makes the exercise of free choice less useful and rarer, restricts the activity of free will within a narrower compass, and little by little robs each citizen of the proper use of his own faculties. Equality has prepared men for all this...government then extends its embrace to include the whole of society. It covers the whole of social life with a network of petty, complicated roles that are both minute and uniform."[4] But he also saw a flourishing system of voluntary association and federalism that might prove to be defense against the rise of an all-powerful state.[5]

The extreme version of the pluralist position is that of John C. Calhoun of South Carolina. During the national debate over slavery and the status of the southern states prior to the Civil War, he argued for a theory of the "concurrent majority" by which he meant a series of (sectional) minority vetoes on national policy: "The necessary consequence of taking the sense of the community by the concurrent majority is...to give to each interest or portion of the community a negative on the others. It is this mutual negative among its various conflicting interests which invests each with the power of protecting itself, and places the right and safety of each where only they can be securely placed, under its own guardianship."[6] Calhoun reasoned that representative government in the United States would not survive if the interests of intense, dissenting minorities were not safeguarded.[7] In a system of concurrent majorities the need for a national consensus on policy would force needed compromise on policy.

William Kornhauser's more recent version of pluralism was heavily influenced by Tocqueville and Walter Lippman.[8] Kornhauser was concerned that modern liberal democracies were threatened from above by manipulative elites and from below by unruly masses. The experiences with fascist and communist movements in Europe in the 1930s much influenced contemporary theorists, who reasoned that theories of democracy must take into account the totalitarian potential of mass society. The crux of Kornhauser's argument is that pluralism, a flourishing system of intermediate associations, is necessary to avoid twin dangers: the excesses of mass movements and the manipulation of the masses by unscrupulous elites.[9] Pluralism provides a means to avoid the excesses of popular democracy by channeling the raw demands of the people through the moderating influence of group leaders. This process is aided if groups overlap in their memberships.[10] Groups also shield their members from direct manipulation by elites by providing interpretations of events and propaganda.

Classical pluralism (and its more recent manifestations) is thus concerned with the three major problems:

1. protecting the rights of minorities;
2. preserving political stability;
3. avoiding the extremes of mass society and totalitarian government.

Classical pluralism is a prescriptive theory, but it is based on empirical observation (such as Tocqueville's on the extent of equalitarian norms in the United States), assumptions about human nature, and projections of the dire consequences of excess democracy. The heart of classical pluralism is the desire for a mixed system of virtuous elites, voluntary associations, decentralized government, and public involvement in government.

Pluralism lays the groundwork for a sympathetic examination of the role of interest groups by showing that groups are both inevitable and necessary (if not always desirable) in society, by arguing that diversity can contribute to stability as opposed to unmitigated conflict, given the proper institutions (such as a federal system).

Group Theory I: Bentley

Group theory, nevertheless, has a quite different objective from normative pluralism. That purpose is a *scientific* understanding of how the political process works. In other words, group theory aims at measurement, description, explanation, and prediction of political phenomena. It does not, on its face, pretend to prescribe a form of government or to say that dispersion of power, per se, is desirable.

The father of group theory was Arthur F. Bentley. His work, *The Process of Government*,[11] was an effort to "forge a tool" for the scientific understanding of society. Bentley's work was published in the early part of this century. It was rediscovered by political scientists, especially David Truman, about the middle of this century.

To begin, it is important to know that Bentley rejected, as misleading and inadequate, any understanding of social, economic, or political life based on psychology or the use of ideas as causes. He scorned explanation by reference to ideas as "soul stuff," inherently subjective and unmeasurable: "we know nothing of 'ideas' and 'feelings' except through the medium of actions" (p. 177). Bentley also forcefully rejected explanations based on individuals, law, or all-inclusive interests. With respect to individuals, Bentley asserted that "the raw material we study is never found in one man by himself, it cannot even be stated by adding man to man.... The 'President Roosevelt' of history, for example, is a very large amount of official activity, involving very many people" (p. 176). Bentley insisted that the "raw material" for the study of politics involved, not individuals, but relationships among individuals and activity: "The 'relation,' i.e., the action, is the given phenomena, the raw material, the action of men with or upon each other" (p. 176). Moreover, Bentley condemned the formal (legal) study of government: "The raw material of government cannot be found in the law books.... It cannot be found in the 'law' behind the law books.... It cannot be found in the proceedings of constitutional conventions, nor in the arguments and discussions surrounding them.... It cannot be found in essays, addresses, appeals, and diatribes on tyranny and democracy" (p. 179). Finally, Bentley denied the reality of social wholes or the common interest: "On any political question which we could study as a matter concerning the United States... we should never be justified in treating the interests of the whole nation as decisive. There are always some parts of the nation to be found arrayed against other parts" (p. 220). Note that this is an empirically based objection to the idea of a common interest.[12]

As noted, Bentley was especially critical of explanations that rested on the assumption that the formal structure of government mattered very much. We must remember that much of the political science of the time was given over to such description. Bentley's point was that a social science rested on observation of activity. Bentley may seem extreme to us today, but he needed to clear away the underbrush of competing explanations in order to suggest his own method for studying society and politics scientifically. And his method depended on dealing with that which could be observed. Bentley was a forerunner of the political behaviorists[13] of the late 1950s and early 1960s in political science.

He believed that the group concept was the key to unlocking the mysteries of the political world: "When the groups are adequately stated, everything is stated. When I say everything, I mean everything" (pp. 208–9). Bently held that groups should not be defined by formal characteristics (such as organizational structure, membership lists) but by activity. No group is without its interest. The group interest is determined by activity. Groups "exist" in relation to one another—conflicting, cooperating, moving toward their interests as expressed by their activity. What we can observe is group activity, which includes propaganda, but we should understand groups by what they do, not by what they say they are doing.

According to Bentley, individuals do not "reason" about public policy questions; rather, public opinion reflects the conflict of group interests: "What a man states to himself as his argument or reasoning or thinking about a national issue is, from the more exact point of view, just the conflict of the crossed groups to which he belongs. To say that a man belongs to two groups of men which are clashing with each other; to say that he reflects two seemingly irreconcilable aspects of the social life; to say that he is reasoning on a question of public policy, these all are but to state the same fact in three forms" (p. 204). The hypothesis that individuals are "cross-pressured" by their group memberships was to become an important facet of later explanations of political behavior.[14]

In terms of understanding politics, there are three central propositions to Bentley's group theory:

1. Individuals "belong" to a nearly infinite variety of groups that "crisscross" one another. This crisscrossing effect leads to political moderation and compromise for both the individual and the group.[15]
2. There are broadly shared values in society, which Bentley called a "habit background," that help to regulate the intensity of group conflict.[16]
3. Public policy is the result of the collision and compromise

of group interests as expressed in activity. The essential role of government is passive—that of a "registration clerk," a scorekeeper.[17]

All these propositions are central to group theory as an explanation of the policymaking process in the United States. They suggest that policy is made by the clash of groups but within the boundaries of certain mutually agreed-upon restraints.

From the publication of *The Process of Government* until the next major theoretical advance, numerous useful descriptive works on interest groups in American politics were published. These include Peter Odegard's study of the Anti-Saloon League, E. E. Schattschneider's study of the policies of the tariff, and Oliver Garceau's study of the political life of the American Medical Association.[18] These works contributed greatly to the empirical understanding of the activity of groups in the American political system. There was a growing recognition of how important interest groups were in American politics. None of these case studies explicitly used the group framework outlined by Bentley.

Group Theory II: Truman

Central to the resurgence of the study of interest groups, and to the growing acceptance of an interest group/pluralist interpretation of American politics, was the publication in 1951 of David Truman's *The Governmental Process*.[19] Truman's work was inspired by Bentley; note the similarity between the two titles. Truman, however, made numerous fresh contributions to the conceptual and empirical study of American interest groups. He was able to take advantage of numerous advances in the social sciences that were made during the intervening years, including the development of social psychology and the wide application of survey research. While Bentley eschewed precise definitions of concepts ("who likes may snip verbal definitions in his old age, when his world has gone cracky and dry," p. 199), Truman made careful distinctions between various types of groups and introduced the concept of a potential group based on shared attitudes.[20] The use of this concept seemed to solve a central problem of group theory: on what basis do groups get formed? He developed an elaborate model of interest-group birth, growth, and development as well as the groups' "inevitable gravitation toward government."[21] Truman's model was based on the notion that disturbances such as depressions create shared interests that lead ultimately to interaction and group formation.

Truman paid careful attention to the problems of leadership and cohesion within groups. He expanded on Bentley's notion that crisscrossing groups make multiple group memberships (of an overlapping kind) a central aspect of group theory. He argued that the cohesion of groups was reduced by multiple group memberships and that group leadership had to function within the context of a "democratic mold" (Chapters V to VII). This notion is similar to Bentley's concept of a habit background.

Truman emphasized the key role of governmental structure in defining access to the political system: "The formal institutions of government...do not prescribe all the meanderings of the stream of politics. They do mark some of its limits...and designate certain points through which it must flow" (p. 322). He effectively argued that decentralized and fragmented American political structure allowed for multiple points of access. He also drew attention to the group ties within government and ties between government and groups outside government and examined the relationship of groups to public opinion and the role of groups in political parties and elections. He also explored the role of interest groups in the executive branch and in the judiciary (Chapters VIII to XV).

Truman developed a theory of the stability of the American political system based on his concepts of multiple group memberships and potential groups committed to the democratic rules of the game: "It is thus multiple memberships in potential groups based on widely held and accepted interests that serve as a balance wheel in a going political system like that of the United

States" (p. 514). But he also, in a much neglected section, explored the conditions that might lead to instability in American politics (pp. 516–24). He included the possible inability of latent groups to be activated in the case of threats to the rules of the game (p. 523).

David Truman's work differed from Bentley's in both style and substance. In style, it is less dogmatic; in substance, it makes ample use, as we noted earlier, of the social science that had developed during the intervening years. The picture Truman draws of the American polity is, in a general sense, a very recognizable one: American politics is based on the conflict of organized groups that operate in a framework of decentralized political structure and widely understood rules of the game, which, along with multiple group memberships, help to keep the system in balance and induce political compromises.

In its most general sense, the Bentley-Truman position can be summarized as follows: public policy is a temporary equilibrium of conflicting groups in society: "The balance of the group pressures is the existing state of society...government is the process of the adjustment of a set of interest groups" (Bentley, pp. 258–60).

But where does pluralism fit into a group theory of politics? The pluralist aspects of groups seem to entail the following assumptions:

1. that political interest groups are activated by environment disturbances;
2. that there are multiple points for group access to the political system;
3. that groups adhere (broadly) to the democratic rules of the game;
4. that groups engage in various forms of political compromise, given the realities of American politics;
5. that multiple group memberships contribute to compromise and political stability.

It is not too much to say that these assumptions, all of which are distinctly pluralist in character, had become the conventional interpretation of American politics by the late 1950s and early 1960s.[22]

Criticism of Interest-Group Pluralism

If the interest-group/pluralist interpretation of American politics was the accepted view of the 1950s and early 1960s, a series of logical, empirical, and value-based objections to group theory soon developed. At this point, we are going to treat interest-group theory with the broader ideas of pluralism in order to examine the ideas of those critics who do not always clearly separate the two.

One of the clearest and most compelling critiques of interest-group pluralism can be found in E. E. Schattschneider's *Semisovereign People*.[23] Several themes that he develops in that book form the basis for subsequent critiques of the pluralist perspective. One point he insists on is that, *contra* interest-group theory, there is a reality to the public interest. Schattschneider holds that the absence of unanimity is no sign that a public interest does not exist: "there is nearly always one dissenter at every hanging" (p. 24). The public interest is expressed in law. The law expresses the public interest when institutions, such as political parties, make legitimate majority rule possible. Schattschneider is an avowed majoritarian democrat. More significantly, he argues that the "pressure system" (his term for the conflict of organized interest groups) is a closed system, not an open and accessible one as suggested by the pluralist thinkers: "The problem with the pluralist heaven is that the choir sings with a strong 'upper class accent'" (p. 35). He argues that the pressure system is heavily stratified in the direction of elites and tilted toward conservative interests. This is a frequent contention of critics of pluralism.

This brings us then to a general, value-based charge against group theory: that it is inherently protective of the status quo. Critics contend that group theory is not a scientific explanation but a justification for the existing distribution of power in society. The basis for such an indictment is that the theory accepts the outcomes of the group struggle as inevitable (and right) but does not realize that the outcomes are predetermined by existing values, rules of the game, and the distribution of valued resources. Pluralism is not essentially *plural*: it benefits organized as opposed to unorganized interests, and it benefits defenders of the status quo as opposed to opponents.

One of Schattschneider's concepts, "mobilization of bias" (pp. 71–72), helps clarify this argument. He points out that many potential claims on government never even reach the decision stage of government; they are effectively screened out of consideration by the prevailing value systems and by the existing structure of power. Many interests are unorganized, latent. For example, where in American politics is there room for debate over nationalization of basic industry? It requires a genuine change in the "mobilization of bias," the existing structure of power supplemented by the value system, for unorganized or previously ineffective group interests to gain effective access to the political system. A sophisticated pluralist retort here would be to acknowledge the problem but still point to the potential for access. For example, when black Americans were effectively denied access to Congress by voting restrictions, there were still opportunities to press their claims through the courts. There are inequalities, but access is still widely available.[24] The system has sufficient "slack" to allow mobilization of unused resources.

Another criticism is made by some who concede the pluralist character of the process but deplore the *product*. These critics grant that interest groups influence the process of government and that the outcomes are patchwork compromises of the interests of the affected groups; they deny, however, that this produces good public policy. Policy that is acceptable to all interested parties is, in their view, likely to be flawed because it lacks direction, consistency, and coherence and ignores long-range considerations. It is, in short, ineffective, and that ineffectiveness ultimately undermines the legitimacy of those policies. These critics are also likely to believe in the reality of the public interest, which, in pluralism, is undermined by private groups.

Another sharp critic of interest-group theory, which he labels "interest group liberalism," is Theodore Lowi[25] His arguments are long and complex; only a few are sketched here. Lowi argues that pluralism has been perverted in that, as a public philosophy, it has permitted the delegation of authority for the implementation of public policy to be turned over to private groups who can then execute decisions without the constraints of public oversight and in defiance of the public interest. Pluralism in the making of law is right and necessary in a representative government. But governing, the execution of law, cannot be given away to private groups without corrupting the authority of government.

One of Lowi's chief criticisms of pluralism is that it "militates against the idea of a separate government."[26] By reducing the state to the conflict of organized groups (a charge that is more applicable to Bentley than to Truman), pluralism loses the capacity to deal with stable, effective, and legitimate administration of public policy, leaving the way open for excesses of interest-group liberalism.

The analysis of economic self-interest provides another set of criticisms of interest-group/pluralist thought. Mancur Olsen has argued that the basic explanation provided by interest-group theorists for the formation and maintenance of large, economically oriented interest groups, is flawed.[27] Olsen points out that such groups provide collective benefits (those that are indivisible; all share regardless of contribution). The fate of such large organizations does not rest on the contribution of particular individual members. The benefits provided to individuals will be forthcoming even if the individuals do not join. Therefore, it is economically irrational for any individual to join such an organization. We cannot leap, in other words, from shared interests to the formation and maintenance of an interest group. Such organizations must coerce membership (as in a union shop) or must provide *selective* inducements to join. This was a powerful criticism, for it seemed to undermine the very foundations of group theory. It should be repeated that the analysis does not apply to small groups or to noneconomic groups (such as groups that support causes which are not in the economic self-interest of members— e.g., anti–capital punishment).[28]

A landmark study of reciprocal trade legislation provides a final set of criticisms of interest-group theory. Raymond A. Bauer et al. concluded that a strong pressure-group model *overstated* the influence of interest groups in the policymaking process for a variety of empirical reasons.[29]

The Bauer et al. case study was, and remains, one of the most comprehensive and multifaceted inquiries into how public policy gets made in the United States. Several important qualifications of the conventional pressure-group model of the political process emerged. One was that the self-interest of groups, central to an understanding of groups in the political process, is ambiguous. For example, self-interest can be defined in the short run or in the long run. And how is self-interest defined when there are conflicts of value (pp. 472–75)? It is seldom the case in a complex issue (such as the tariff) that, for a firm or other interest group, only a single value would be at stake. Conflicting values must be weighed and balanced. A second qualification was that interest groups seldom operated with the timeliness, skill, and unlimited resources that group theory implies (Bauer et al., Chapters 21 to 23). Third, there was a circularity to the process of attempted influence on the part of interest groups: "We were further unprepared for the fact that most activities of pressure groups involved interaction with people on the same side" (p. 398). There was a strong tendency for the converted to talk to the converted. Finally, political decision-makers (congressmen) had a much more independent role to play in decision-making than interest-group theory, unqualified, would allow. The line of influence runs not only from interest group to decision-making but also vice versa (see Bauer et al., Chapters 29 to 34). Moreover, interests balance one another out, leaving legislators free to make their own decisions. In all, these findings raised serious enough questions that the authors could claim there was a mythology of pressure-group influence.

Nevertheless, their research was a case study of only a single policy area during a limited time span, as critics were quick to point out.[30] To the degree that the Bauer et al. critique was successful, it became a new "conventional wisdom"—that the influence of interest groups in the policymaking process had been overstated. This new "conventional wisdom" has recently been challenged by Michael T. Hayes, who has asserted that there is a "much greater role for organized interest groups in the legislative process than has commonly been assumed since the publication of *American Business and Public Policy*."[31] Hayes questioned the assumption of Bauer et al. that there are inevitably numerous interests involved in any given decision (freeing political decision-makers for decision) and that the legislative process is just one stage of the group struggle, one where decisions are often postponed (*Pressure Groups*, pp. 139–41). Hayes argued that "organized interest groups play a much greater role in the legislative process than is commonly understood...they possess considerable advantages over unorganized publics in obtaining tangible benefits from government...interest groups will often provide the only source of constituency cues available to the...representative, and their dominance of the distributive and self-regulatory arenas will typically be accepted as legitimate by Congressmen while provoking little challenge from deprived groups....Genuinely redistributive policies will be rare, as unorganized publics will be protected, if at all, only coincidentally, when policy matters are able to play off counterbalanced pressure groups."[32] While not rejecting the findings of *American Business and Public Policy*, Hayes suggests they have been oversimplified.

Restating Group Theory

After two decades of assault, what is left of interest-group theory? Let us consider the major proposition of group theory: public policy is a temporary equilibrium of the conflicting groups in society. The proposition is too vague to be very useful. It must be qualified in a number of significant ways. First, we must note that either "group" must be defined very broadly here (to include organized and unorganized groups, official groups as well as private groups, etc.) or the proposition is false. But if we define "group" that broadly, are we really saying anything very insightful? If everything is a group, then "group" explains everything, and nothing. It seems more likely that we must say that organized interest groups have a varying impact on public policy in the United States, depending on the type of issue.

The other propositions must also be modified on the basis of research:

1. Political interest groups are not generated "automatically" because there is an objective need or environmental disturbance.
2. There are multiple points of access, but access is unequally distributed.
3. The rules of the game help some groups and hinder others, and the democratic rules are not universally endorsed.
4. There is a need for compromise, but some groups have more leverage to extract favorable compromise than do others.
5. There is little evidence of the multiple group membership hypothesis.[33]

In short, a simplistic pressure-group model of the following sort cannot be sustained:

Figure 2.1 A Simple Pressure Group Model

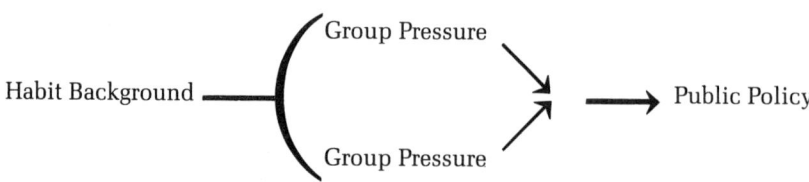

Actually, Truman never intended such a simple model.[34] The job of the political scientist is to consider the conditions under which interest groups influence public policy more or less.

Interest-group influence will be maximized to the degree that the decisions involve issues that are less salient to broader publics, relatively invisible, and routine. In these instances, interests (which include government interests) may simply reach accord on policy. To the degree that policy decisions are highly salient, highly visible, and nonroutine, other factors (beyond the balance of group interests) can be brought into play. One institution that theoretically could reduce the impact of interest groups is the political party. It is to the role of parties in American democracy that we now turn.

NOTES
CHAPTER TWO

[1]Earl Latham distinguishes between philosophical (classical) and analytical (descriptive) pluralists. He also notes that "fragments of pluralistic politics are to be found in the classics of American political philosophy, notably in Madison and Calhoun." See "The Group Basis of Politics: Notes for a Theory" in H. R. Mahood, ed., *Pressure Groups in American Politics* (New York: Scribners, 1967), p. 28.

[2]See Clinton Rossiter, ed., *The Federalist Papers* (New York: New American Library, 1961); Alexis de Tocqueville, *Democracy in America* (Garden City, N.Y.: Doubleday-Anchor, 1969); John C. Calhoun, *A Disquisition on Government* (Indianapolis: Bobbs-Merrill, 1953); and William Kornhauser, *The Politics of Mass Society* (Glencoe, Ill.: Free Press, 1959).

[3]*Federalist*, p. 83.

[4]Tocqueville, p. 692.

[5]Ibid., pp. 690–702.

[6]Calhoun, p. 28.

[7]Ibid., pp. 19–54.

[8]See Lippman, *The Public Philosophy* (New York: Mentor, 1955).

[9]See Kornhauser, *Politics of Mass Society*, Chapter 13: "what kind of social structure will meet these conditions of liberal democracy?... some pluralism is a sound arrangement which performs this function," p. 230.

[10]Lewis Coser, *The Functions of Social Conflict* (New York: Free Press, 1956), pp. 153–54.

[11]Arthur F. Bentley, *The Process of Government* (Cambridge, Mass.: Harvard University Press, 1967), hereafter cited in the text.

[12]As Bentley says, "we are out of the field of social science" (p. 220).

[13]For an introduction to the study of political behavior, see Heinz Eulau, *The Behavior Persuasion in Politics* (New York: Random House, 1963).

[14]See Paul Lazarsfeld et al., *The People's Choice*, 3rd ed. (New York: Columbia University Press, 1968), pp. 56–64.

[15]"And compromise—not in the merely logical sense, but in practical life— is the very process itself of the crisscross groups in action," Bentley, p. 208.

[16]"These are 'rules of the game' in existence, which form the background of the group activity," Bentley, p. 218.

[17]One statement of this position is that of Latham: "The legislature referees the group struggle, ratifies the victories of the successful coalitions, and records the terms of the surrenders, compromises, and conquests in the form of statutes," p. 41.

[18] Oliver Garceau, *The Political Life of the American Medical Association* (Cambridge, Mass.: Harvard University Press, 1941); Peter H. Odegard, *Pressure Politics: The Story of the Anti-Saloon League* (New York: Columbia University Press, 1928); E. E. Schattschneider, *Politics, Pressures and the Tariff* (New York: Prentice-Hall, 1935).

[19] David Truman, *The Governmental Process: Political Interests and Public Opinion* (New York: Knopf, 1951).

[20] I used Truman's classification in Chapter One. Truman's definition of a potential group: "On the basis of widely held attitudes that are not expressed in interaction... it is possible to talk of potential interest groups," (p. 35).

[21] For Truman's discussion of group formation, see *Governmental Process*, pp. 26–33 (for the theory) and pp. 66–104 (for examples). On the "inevitable gravitation to government," see pp. 104–06. Further references to this work will appear in the text.

[22] See, for example, a representative text by Robert A. Dahl, *Pluralist Democracy in the United States: Conflict and Consent* (Chicago: Rand McNally, 1967).

[23] E. E. Schattschneider, *Semi-sovereign People: A Realist's View of Democracy in America* (New York: Holt, Rinehart & Winston, 1960), hereafter cited in text.

[24] Dahl calls this perspective "dispersed inequality"; see his *Who Governs?* (New Haven: Yale University Press, 1961), pp. 85–86.

[25] See Theodore Lowi, *The End of Liberalism*, 2nd ed. (New York: Norton, 1979).

[26] Ibid., p. 36.

[27] Mancur Olsen, *The Logic of Collective Action: Public Goods and the Theory of Groups* (Cambridge, Mass.: Harvard University Press, 1965). Truman has provided a response to the Olsen critique in his introduction to the second edition of *The Governmental Process* (New York: Knopf, 1971) pp. xxviii–xxxi.

[28] In expanding Olsen's version of group membership, Terry Moe asserts that "people may join interest groups simply because they believe in group goals, because they enjoy going to meetings or because they think their contributions facilitate political success, and there is nothing irrational about their doing so." See "A Calculus of Group Membership," *American Journal of Political Science* 24 (Nov. 1980): 629.

[29] Raymond A. Bauer et al., *American Business and Public Policy: The Politics of Foreign Trade*, 2nd ed. (Chicago: Aldine-Atherton, 1972), hereafter cited in text.

[30] See Theodore J. Lowi, "American Business, Public Policy, Case Studies, and Political Theory," *World Politics* 16 (July 1964): 677–715.

[31] Michael T. Hayes, "The Semi-sovereign Pressure Groups: A Critique of Current Theory and an Alternative Typology," *Journal of Politics* 40 (1978): 159. For a more complete explication of Hayes's arguments, see his *Lobbyists and Legislators* (New Brunswick, N.J.: Rutgers University Press, 1981).

[32] Michael T. Hayes, "Interest Groups and Congress...," in Leroy N. Rieselbach, ed., *The Congressional System* (North Scituate, Mass.: Duxbury Press, 1979), p. 270.

[33] In addition to the other criticisms cited above, see Stanley Rothman, "Systematic Political Theory," *American Political Science Review* 44 (Mar. 1960): 15–33. On the failure of masses or elites to protect the rules of the game during the McCarthy era, see Peter Bachrach, *The Theory of Democratic Elitism* (Boston: Little, Brown, 1967).

[34] See Truman, *Governmental Process*, pp. 322–50.

CHAPTER 3

AMERICAN POLITICAL PARTIES: THE PLURALIST REALITY, THE MAJORITARIAN IDEAL, AND PARTY CYCLES

Political parties exist in all Western national democratic systems. Whether they are absolutely necessary or not is a debatable issue;[1] nevertheless, they are a fact of political life. Parties serve in the recruitment and nomination of candidates for political office and in the education of the public about political issues; they compete in elections and organize the government and represent the diverse interests in society. It should be apparent that parties are not the only institutions that can do these things. For example, the mass media may play a considerably more crucial role than parties in "educating" the public on political issues. Nevertheless, parties uniquely are the entities that organize and compete in elections in democratic systems. How they do this, and for what ends, is the critical question.

This chapter, in following the general theme of the book, concentrates on the contrasts between two types of parties: the pluralist and the majoritarian.[2] The distinction between the two is in priorities: the pluralist party focuses on winning office for pragmatic reasons and the majoritarian party on winning elections for policy reasons. Thus winning is the top priority for the pluralist party, while making policy is the incentive for the majoritarian party. In pluralist parties, policy is the means; in majoritarian parties, policy is the end.[3] In American politics, the pluralist type has been the norm; the majoritarian, a model.

Pluralist Parties

American political parties have been fundamentally—some would say incurably—pluralist in character. American parties have been primarily interested in winning elections and have served as "vast, gaudy umbrellas" encompassing a wide diversity of interests. The parties have traditionally been national coalitions of heterogeneous groups. Interparty contests have been less over ideology, principle, or program and more over control of office. The parties have been quite willing to adjust their principles to the temper of the times.

At this point, let us consider some salient characteristics of

American pluralist parties. First, as organizations, American parties have been notably *decentralized*.[4] Strong national parties have never been the rule in American politics. National party organizations control neither party nominations nor the policy direction of the party, but national party platforms are not meaningless.[5] Platforms do indicate roughly what a party would do in power.

State and local party organizations in the United States vary enormously in their vigor and strength, but no one doubts that the American party system is one that is built from the bottom up. Of course, this decentralization meshes well with the idea of a heterogeneous party, especially since the basis for that heterogeneity has been regional diversity. It is clear that the Massachusetts and Texas Democratic parties are quite different animals. The most frequently cited example, but by no means the only one, has been the presence of the more conservative southern wing of the Democratic party in the period since the New Deal. The southern Democrats have often, although not invariably, made alliance with conservative Republicans on policy issues.[6] As will be seen in Chapter Eleven, this alliance is not just a past phenomenon. The cooperation of conservative southern Democrats with the Reagan administration was a vital factor in passing the President's economic proposals in 1981. Recently there has been a modest resurgence of national party organizations realized in different ways in both major parties.[7] Nevertheless, the fundamental fact of decentralization remains the rule.

As noted, the parties have convened every four years to nominate presidential candidates. These nominations have normally been pragmatic in character; that is, the top spot has gone to someone widely believed to be both personally attractive and moderate in appeal. A classic example was the selection of "nonpolitical" Dwight Eisenhower over "Mr. Republican," conservative Robert Taft, in 1952. Nevertheless, there appears to be a trend toward serious, issue-based, even ideological challengers in the nominations. This may be related to the expansion of the primaries and the changing character of the activists in the parties.[8] In the main, however, American parties during presidential nominations have behaved as if winning were the major goal.

American parties have traditionally lacked cohesion in governing; that is, both majority and minority parties in government (in the legislature) have suffered frequent defections by their ranks on salient issues. There has been a steady decline in the cohesion of the parties in Congress in this century.[9] Interparty coalitions, such as the previously mentioned conservative coalition, have been relatively frequent. This lack of cohesion led James MacGregor Burns to formulate a theory of "four-party" politics in the United States (in the early 1960s). In his theory Burns postulated that there were two wings to each party: a presidential wing, which was more liberal, and a congressional wing, which was more conservative. The presidential wings were more liberal because of the pressures of national two-party competition and the need to appeal to minority and urban interests in the large states. The congressional wings were more conservative because of the lack of competition in local congressional districts and because of the more rural, more homogeneous, and more conservative nature of many of the districts.[10] Although Burns's thesis may still have some force, at least two changes have modified the conditions of American national politics. One is that population shifts, along with attitudinal changes, mean that a genuinely conservative presidential candidate can be nominated and elected, thus making the presidency a bastion of conservatism, under Ronald Reagan and to some degree under Richard Nixon.[11] The South and West are now more important in presidential politics than previously, and those regions are generally more conservative than the Northeast and the larger states of the Midwest. It is also the case that in the 1960s and 1970s more liberals secured positions of power in the Congress. Nevertheless, these changes have not really enhanced intraparty cohesion in Congress.

E. E. Schattschneider linked the decentralization of American parties and low cohesion in governing.[12] The needs of local parties and local constituencies, as opposed to the interests of national parties, have normally been paramount in the calculus of individual legislators because nomination and election were tied to those constituencies.

To fill out the picture, the American electorate was basically partisan in its makeup but nonideological and flexible enough to defect from party on the basis of broad-scale judgments about governmental performance and/or personalities. Americans have had a strong and stable sense of loyalty to one or the other of the major parties, and that loyalty has shaped individual and collective voting decisions. For the most part, departures from partisanship in voting have been on "valence" grounds: for example, that the government in power was inept or corrupt.[13] It should be noted that the more recent portrait of the American electorate has uncovered a "decline of party"[14] (see Chapter Five).

Decentralized parties, in combination with low cohesion in governing and a partisan but flexible electorate, allow for parties that contain diverse interests, and especially regional diversity; engage in intraparty bargaining over party decisions; and allow for multiple interpretations of party positions (ambiguity). Several studies document that the activists of the parties are an ideologically diverse group.[15] One chief virtue of pluralist parties has been their ability to facilitate compromise in the American political system.[16] The chief criticism has been that pluralist parties have been too unconcerned with developing and carrying out policy positions. It should be clear at this point that pluralist political parties fit nicely into the more general pluralist conception of politics. In this view, parties are part of a series of intermediate institutions standing between citizens and their government, and not at all the most important. The majoritarian critics of pluralism, in contrast, exalt the political party as the institution par excellence for achieving democracy.

Majoritarian Parties

Majoritarian political parties, most frequently called "responsible parties,"[17] contrast sharply with pluralist parties. One type of responsible parties, which might be called the "policy mandate"[18] school, has the following requirements:

1. In a responsible-parties system, the parties must present coherent policy differences to the electorate.
2. In a responsible-parties system, party policy must be determined democratically by the mass party organization.
3. In a responsible-parties system, the party in government is a team that must act cohesively.
4. In a responsible-parties system, the electorate must act in a programmatic manner in voting.

In a two-party system, then, responsible parties yield public policy consistent with the mandate given by a majority of the electorate. But a responsible-parties system is an ideal—a model— not fully realized in any political system. It is also possible to conceive of a responsible-parties system that is more pluralist in character—one that eschews intraparty democracy and is not based on the electorate giving a precise policy mandate. Such a system would depend on the cohesion of party elites. However, we will not deal with this notion of responsible parties here.[19]

The responsible-parties school is an old one in American politics. Reform in that direction was advocated by Woodrow Wilson and others around the turn of the century. And over the past forty years, numerous works have advocated reform in that direction. Often, the British party system seemed to be the implicit model for reformers.

The majoritarian critics of American (pluralist) parties have generally made the following points: American parties have been too decentralized, too uncohesive, too regionalized, and too expedient, and there has been a lack of two-party competition. Notice that the critics of American parties generally agree with pluralists on the basic description of American parties; the disagreements are over the consequences and the feasibility (or desirability) of reform.

To achieve responsible parties in the United States, reformers have suggested a number of steps. The most extreme of these is constitutional change: the establishment of some variation of parliamentary government.[20] A second route suggested has been the strengthening of national party organizations. (As noted above, some of these reforms have in fact been accomplished.) This in turn would lead to two effects favorable to party government: stronger (and more nationalized) two-party competition and more centralization in party decision-making. Finally, reformers advocate educating the public on the need for responsible parties, arguing that the major barriers are not legal but attitudinal. If the public could be convinced of the need for change, it would follow.

The critics of the responsible-parties school have unleashed a barrage against the reformers, on both normative and empirical grounds. One set of criticisms is of crucial importance here—that the American mass electorate has characterists incompatible with the requirements of responsible parties. In sum, these criticisms were as follows:

1. that the public lacks the information necessary for evaluating party performance;
2. that the public does not display notable policy orientation in voting;
3. that the public does not show the attitude consistency necessary for giving a programmatic mandate to parties.[21]

However, these same voter characteristics are certainly consistent with pluralist parties.

But in the mid-1960s research on voting behavior started to turn up findings more consistent with an electorate capable of supporting responsible parties.[22] In brief, that evidence suggested that voters were more policy-oriented, issue-consistent, and aware of party differences. In turn, these findings have been challenged on methodological grounds.[23] A reasonable conclusion is that the electorate has moved in a direction more consistent with responsible parties but is still far short of the requirements of the model.

Nevertheless, other recent developments are more favorable for responsible parties. Among these are:

1. the strengthening of national party organizations;

2. the increased nationalization of two-party competition in American elections;
3. the revitalization of the Republican party in 1978–1980;
4. the strengthening of the party leadership and party caucus in the U.S. House of Representatives.[24]

These four trends seem favorable for responsible parties because they should lead to stronger two-party competition nationally. Two-party competitiveness is absolutely essential for majoritarian democracy. One chief problem of the pluralist system has been the tendency toward one-party domination in states and localities. Strong two-party competition in congressional districts on national issues would force a degree of cohesion in the parties on roll calls. Of course, none of these developments is clear-cut in its meaning for responsible parties. For example, in Congress, signs of decentralization are as prevalent as those of the strengthening of party.[25] There are strong antiparty currents in American politics, and some issues, such as energy, still have a tremendous capacity to regionalize the conflicts in Congress.

Realignment?

The dispute between the defenders of pluralist parties and the advocates of majoritarian (responsible) parties has been partially eclipsed by the contemporary trends toward the decline of party. If the survival of parties is at stake, then the question of what kind of parties suddenly seems less urgent.

Of course, there have always been those who argued that American politics would be better off without parties. These sentiments are closely related to the classical view of democracy, a view that is suspicious of all political organization as potentially destructive of the public interest. Nonpartisan elections have been legislated at the local level in many communities in the United States.

The decline of party would mean that the electorate would be less bound to party ties in voting; that the results of elections, especially presidential elections, would be less predictable; that party organizations would disintegrate; and that party cohesion in the Congress would continue to decline. Party responsibility for policy, at a minimum in American politics during the best of times, would be nonexistent. The politics of individualism would flourish.

A different interpretation of contemporary trends is that the stage is being set for one of the periodic critical realignments in American politics: the current loosening of party ties creates the conditions for the mobilization of a new pattern of political support.[26] A realignment involves a reshuffling of partisan loyalties in the electorate, the creation of a new majority party, and the creation of a new issue agenda. In this view, American parties act in a majoritarian manner immediately following a critical realignment and gradually drift in a more pluralist direction until the next realignment.

A realigning election, or period, is a time when the policy agenda is transformed, when partisan political alignments are upset and then gradually recast and a new public philosophy is created. The prime example is that of the New Deal era, during which the agenda was changed with respect to the role of the national government in the economy, and as a result the Democrats, who advocated those changes, replaced the Republicans as the country's majority party. Liberalism became the dominant public philosophy. Early in the New Deal years, the political system was able to respond in an energetic way to the crisis because of the close cooperation between President and Congress. Franklin Roosevelt had received a large electoral majority in the 1932 election, although he certainly did not receive a positive mandate, and he also had an overwhelming Democratic majority in the Congress. In 1936 the electorate evidently approved of the Roosevelt program for recovery. Over time, however, the unity of the Democratic party subsided, and it became more and more difficult to create majorities for liberal policies. The full realization of the New Deal program had to wait until another exceptional set of circumstances produced the Lyndon Johnson landslide of 1964.

Some have speculated that the conditions of the mass electorate in the 1920s were similar to those of today—a large unmobilized electorate capable of being attracted to a party by a program and a widespread perception that the program had succeeded.[27] Thus the apparent decline of party could be an opportunity for realignment.

Since 1964 there has been periodic speculation that another major realignment was in the works. The 1980 election provided the best fuel for the belief that a new conservative majority is emerging in the United States. The following facts contributed to the speculation:

1. the substantial popular vote and spectacular electoral vote victory given to Ronald Reagan, an acknowledged conservative;
2. the seizure by the Republican party of control of the U.S. Senate for the first time since 1954;
3. the defeat of numerous liberal Democrats in races for the House (1980) and Senate (1978, 1980);
4. the prospect that the new Reagan administration did intend to carry out substantial alterations in policy direction at the national level;
5. the evidence of changes in public attitudes or moods on public policy (the feeling had died that big government was the answer to social and economic problems).

All these circumstances contributed to the sense that a new political era had dawned.[28]

Indeed, the Reagan victory could be seen as the culmination of a transforming era of American politics that began with the Goldwater defeat of 1964 and was continued by the Nixon victories of 1968 and 1972. The perceived excesses and failures of the Johnson administration triggered a conservative response that elected Nixon. In other words, a growing conservatism in national politics was derailed by Watergate. The Carter presidency was, in this view, an aberration. Two critical tests of this projected conservative realignment, then, will be the ability of President Reagan to move his policies through the Congress and the ability of the Republican party to seize control of Congress in 1982 and for the party to hold on to the presidency in 1984.

The realignment thesis, briefly described above, would suggest that American parties are behaving pretty much normally, alternating between normal pluralism and temporary responsibility induced by realignment.[29] In other words, realignments are necessary to produce responsible parties.

The sequence could be illustrated by the following simplified outline:

Pre-New Deal (unmobilized electorate)— decline of party—1920s	New Deal realignment and responsible parties— 1930s–1940s	Pluralist parties dominate— 1950s	Decline of parties— Mid-1960s– mid-1970s	Realignment and emergence of responsible parties— Mid-1970s– Early 1980s	Pluralist parties re-emerge— Middle to late 1980s

In this view, American politics moves from normal pluralism to party decline to realignment and back to pluralism in regular rhythms. But the evidence for such a theory is imperfect at best.[30] For example, it would be hard to claim that responsible parties have clearly emerged in the electorate or in the Congress as the 1980s began, although the Republican party acted with extremely high cohesiveness on the Reagan budget cuts (see Chapter Eleven). Rather, the parties still resemble pluralist institutions in many respects. Recent evidence of decay of parties would, in this view, be part of the larger cyclical pattern of American politics rather than an inevitable decline.

An Alternate Scenario

Of course, there is an alternate scenario that projects the decline of party, not as part of a cycle, but as a steady downward trend.

Some evidence for such a view is presented in a later chapter. From this perspective, for example, the recent successes of Republican presidential candidates in 1968, 1972, and 1980 have been personal or ideological rather than a response to the efforts of the Republican party. Presidential voting is divorced from subnational, especially congressional, voting.

Everett C. Ladd has argued that "the 1980 presidential contest...has all the markings of a primary...so weak have attachments to the parties and their candidates become that this general election has taken on primary-like properties...the evidence...suggests that neither party is likely to acquire majority status of the kind the Democrats enjoyed in the New Deal era and the Republicans held from McKinley to Hoover."[31]

The evidence for the decline of party is substantial.[32] If the interpretation of a continued decline is correct, then the pluralistic character of American parties would gradually become totally atomistic. The salient characterists of a *near* no-party system (or extremely weak two-party system) would seem to be the following:

1. extremely low voter turnout;
2. extreme volatility in presidential voting results;
3. extremely weak party cohesion in Congress;
4. frequent creation of ad hoc coalitions around specific issues;
5. growing influence of special-interest groups;
6. confusion, delay, and deadlock in the policymaking process;
7. pressure on the President to govern by unilateral or extraconstitutional means because of the electorate's demands to be effective.

The absence of strong two-party competition would reduce turnout. The lack of partisan loyalites would make the electorate susceptible to wide swings in preference from one election to another. Party loyalty in Congress would continue to decline, forcing the development of short-term coalitions around specific policies—a politics of strange bedfellows. The influence of interest groups would grow as party strength declined. The policymaking process would be more complex, arduous, and prone to stalemate, and the pressure on the executive would be enormous. In other words, the major features of a pluralist system would be exaggerated. The consequences of a continued decline of party are not benign. Such a politics could be labeled "hyperpluralistic."

This chapter has presented two models of political parties. The pluralist party fits nicely with pluralist political theory and interest-group politics. It also, unquestionably, fits the reality of American political history better than does the majoritarian party. The majoritarian party has been an ideal—for some—a method for achieving majoritarian democracy. The method is dependent on competition between strong and cohesive political parties. The model may result from an American misreading of how the British political system has operated.[33] In any event, there are nearly always reformers in the United States who seek to move American parties in a more responsible direction. As many have noted, however, the creation of responsible parties in the United States is a formidable, perhaps even an impossible, task.

Enter the theory of realignment, which postulates that a realignment may accomplish what reform cannot—the creation of a broad-scale and effective change in national policy direction. Later, we will consider whether the Reagan election in 1980 signaled a Republican/conservative realignment similar to the Roosevelt/Democratic one in the 1930s.

The important message of this chapter is that American political parties have, as a rule, been pluralistic in nature: decentralized, lacking cohesion, coalitions of diverse interests, motivated to winning elections. There has been an excellent fit between the parties, the formal structure of government, and the socioeconomic and cultural diversity of the society. In a two-party structure, it is difficult to see how the parties could have been much different. Now the parties appear to be changing. There are pulls in the direction of both disintegration and realignment. Realignment has been the characteristic response to intractable political problems. Disintegration is also possible. We may yet learn what it is like to try to govern a nation-state without political parties.

NOTES
CHAPTER THREE

[1] See the discussion by Leon D. Epstein, *Political Parties in Western Democracies* (New York: Praeger, 1967), pp. 13, 97.

[2] Ibid., pp. 15–17.

[3] As Anthony Downs expresses the distinction: "parties formulate policies to win elections, rather than win elections to formulate policies." *An Economic Theory of Democracy* (New York: Harper & Row, 1957), p. 28.

[4] The classic texts make this point emphatically. See Austin Ranney and Willmoore Kendall, *Democracy and the American Party System* (New York: Harcourt Brace, 1956), p. 488, and V. O. Key, Jr., *Politics, Parties and Pressure Groups*, 4th ed. (New York: Thomas Y. Crowell, 1958), p. 346.

[5] See Gerald M. Pomper with Susan S. Lederman, *Elections in America*, 2nd ed. (New York: Longman, 1980), especially Chapters 7 and 8.

[6] For a recent analysis see David W. Brady and Charles S. Bullock, III, "Coalition Politics in the House of Representatives," in Lawrence C. Dodd and Bruce I. Oppenheimer, eds., *Congress Reconsidered*, 2nd ed. (Washington, D.C.: Congressional Quarterly, 1981), pp. 186–203.

[7] For a discussion see the essays in *Party Renewal in America*, Gerald M. Pomper, ed. (New York: Praeger, 1980).

[8] For a discussion, see Jeane J. Kirkpatrick, *Dismantling the Parties* (Washington, D.C.: American Enterprise Institute, 1978).

[9] See David Brady et al., "The Decline of Party Strength in the House," *Legislative Studies Quarterly* 4 (Aug. 1979): 381–407.

[10] James MacGregor Burns, *The Deadlock of Democracy* (Englewood Cliffs, N.J.: Prentice-Hall, 1963).

[11] Of course, some members of the "congressional wing" of the Republican party, such as Jesse Helms of North Carolina, may be still more conservative than the President for the broad reasons suggested by Burns.

[12] E. E. Schattschneider, *Party Government* (New York: Holt, Rinehart & Winston, 1942), pp. 131–32.

[13] For the standard view of the American electorate, only briefly summarized here, see Angus Campbell et al., *The American Voter* (New York: Wiley, 1960).

[14] Norman Nie et al., *The Changing American Voter* (Cambridge, Mass.: Harvard University Press, 1979), especially Chapter 4.

[15] See Samuel J. Eldersveld, *Political Parties* (Chicago: Rand McNally, 1964), pp. 218–19, and John Kessel, *Presidential Campaign Politics* (Homewood, Ill.: Dorsey Press, 1980), pp. 64–84.

[16] For this perspective, see Edward C. Banfield, "In Defense of the American Party System," In Robert A. Goldwin, ed., *Political Parties, U.S.A.* (Chicago: Rand McNally, 1964), pp. 21–39.

[17] For a discussion of the concept, see Austin Ranney, *The Doctrine of Responsible Party Government* (Urbana: University of Illinois Press, 1954).

[18] The purest example is a report issued by the American Political Science Association in 1950; see "Toward a More Responsible Two-Party System," *American Political Science Review* 44 (Sept. 1950), Supplement.

[19] See David H. Everson, *American Political Parties* (New York: New Viewpoints, 1980), Chapter 1.

[20] See Charles Hardin, *Presidential Power and Accountability* (Chicago: University of Chicago Press, 1974).

[21] For a full-scale critique of the mandate school of responsible parties, see Evron Kirkpatrick, "Toward a More Responsible Two-Party System," *American Political Science Review* 65 (Dec. 1971): 965–90.

[22] Gerald Pomper, "From Confusion to Clarity: Issues and American Voters, 1956–1968," *American Political Science Review* 66 (June 1972): 415–28.

[23] Michael Margolis, "From Confusion to Confusion," *American Political Science Review* 71 (Mar. 1977): 31–43.

[24] Point 1 is covered by Gerald Pomper in "The Decline of Partisan Politics," in Louis Maisel and Joseph Cooper, eds., *The Impact of the Electoral Process* (Beverly Hills: Sage, 1977), pp. 31–32. Point 2 can be found in Pomper, "Toward a More Responsible Two-Party System? What, Again?" *Journal of Politics* 33 (Nov. 1971):923. Point 3 is well summarized by M. Margaret Conway in "Political Party Nationalization, Campaign Activities, and Local Party Development," paper prepared for delivery at the Midwest Political Science Association Meeting, Cincinnati, Ohio, Apr. 16–18, 1981, especially pp. 4–13. The final point can be found in Lawrence C. Dodd and Bruce I. Oppenheimer, "The House in Transition: Change and Consolidation," in Dodd and Oppenheimer, eds., pp. 50–57.

[25] Dodd and Oppenheimer, p. 57.

[26] On the general notion of realignment, see James Sundquist, *Dynamics of the Party System* (Washington, D.C.: Brookings, 1973).

[27] Paul Allen Beck, "Youth and the Politics of Realignment," in Edward C. Dreyer and Walter A. Rosenbaum, eds., *Political Opinion and Behavior*, 3rd ed. (North Scituate, Mass.: Duxbury, 1976), pp. 366–73.

[28] Richard M. Scammon and Ben J. Wattenberg, "Is This the End of an Era?" *Public Opinion*, Oct./Nov. 1980, pp. 2–12. This article was actually written before the election, and the authors underestimated the size of the Reagan/conservative win (as did nearly everyone).

[29] The idea that realignments can create temporary conditions resembling responsible parties is found in Walter Dean Burnham, *Critical Elections and the Mainsprings of American Politics* (New York: Norton, 1970), p. 137.

[30] For evidence that supports the emergence of responsible parties in Congress during a realigning period, see David W. Brady, "Critical Elections, Congressional Response and Clusters of Policy Changes," *British Journal of Political Science* 8 (Jan. 1978): 79–89.

[31] "Realignment? No. Dealignment? Yes." *Public Opinion*, Oct./Nov., 1980, p. 55.

[32] See Norman H. Nie et al., *The Changing American Voter* (Cambridge, Mass.: Harvard University Press, 1979), Chapter 4.

[33] David Butler, "American Myths about British Parties," *Virginia Quarterly Review* 31 (Winter 1955): 45–56.

CHAPTER 4

THE CITIZEN AS RATIONAL ACTIVIST

Classical democracy is impossible in the large nation-state. The simple reason is that the requirements for participation and full discussion cannot be met. Nevertheless, the classical ideal is the basis for concepts of what citizenship means in a democratic society. In this chapter we will spell out the abstract requirements of democratic citizenship—the so-called rational-activist model—examine the various facets of public opinion, see how these fit the model, and explore some alternate concepts of democracy.

The Rational-Activist Model

The rational-activist model is an attempt to transfer the classical model to national political systems. The assumption is that the good citizen in a small participatory democracy is also the good citizen in a nation. The rational-activist citizen "is expected to be politically informed, involved, rational, and, above all, active."[1] Those requirements flow from the notion that public policy should be constructed, rationally, through mass participation and deliberation. Of course, the need for representative institutions in nation-states means that most participation is indirect. The most frequent and visible form of participation is voting in elections for representatives. Therefore, the empirical scrutiny of the degree to which citizens live up to the model has been directed to voting behavior.

The model of the rational-activist citizen would specify three paramount conditions that must be fulfilled:

1. a high level of information on public affairs;
2. a high level of participation in politics, especially, but not confined to, voting;
3. a high level of issue orientation in voting.

To these three characteristics, which may be regarded as relating directly to policy, may be added a fourth:

4. a high level of commitment to the democratic rules of the game.²

In short, democratic citizens must be *informed, participatory, issue oriented,* and *committed to democratic procedures.*

Research on the mass electorate raised doubts about its qualifications for democratic citizenship, doubts that in turn caused revisions in democratic theory.

The Nonrational, Nonactivist Citizen

Survey research, which began on a major scale in the 1950s, quickly turned up a portrait of the electorate that was substantially at odds with the classical ideal.

Political information

One of the clearest findings generated by survey research was that the level of political information of the mass electorate was abysmally low. One analyst of public opinion asserted that it "would be astonishing if we should discover that many people had anything more than the sketchiest information about the performance of their Representative or Senators."[3] The data confirm that guess. For example, half of or fewer than half of voters knew the name of their representative, and even fewer had any significant information about his performance.[4]

More generally, virtually every public opinion study of political information turned up astonishing gaps in the public's knowledge of even elementary political facts. As illustrations, substantial numbers of the public did not (as shown by various surveys) know that mainland China was communist; nor did they know the names of their mayor, the vice-president of the United States, or of the secretary of state of the United States; nor did they realize that there are two senators from every state. An astonishing 60 percent evidently were prepared to believe that the Soviet Union was a member of NATO.[5] Many more people can identify entertainment figures, even fictional ones, than can recognize important political figures. None of these questions involves any reasoning or subtlety about public affairs—just simple factual information.

Consider how important information is to the theory of an activist public. At root, there is the rationality assumption: that behavior rests on deliberation, reasoning about public policy issues. But how much reasoning can there be in the absence of elementary political facts? How can one discuss policy toward the Far East if one cannot distinguish China from Taiwan?

Political participation

If evidence of the poverty of mass political information was damaging to the rational-activist model, the findings on participation were virtually equally devastating. A typical set of findings was that more than 70 percent of the population was relatively or completely inactive in politics.[6] Even voting in presidential elections was an act engaged in by only about six eligible Americans in ten. Moreover, political participation was clearly related to socioeconomic status: those of higher status tend to participate more in politics.[7] This observation became an important part of the revision of democratic theory to be discussed below.

The low level of participation of most Americans raised more doubts about the model of rational activism. If substantial proportions of citizens fail to exercise their duty to participate, what does this say about the quality of mass democracy, especially if those of lower status are less likely to participate?

Issue orientation in the electorate

A third component of the rational-activist model is that voters cast their votes on the basis of the issues of elections (as opposed to blind partisanship, personality, or some other "irrational" basis). The evidence on information among voters may suggest the findings on issue orientation. In *The American Voter*, a landmark study of the American electorate in the 1950s, the authors found only a "modest articulation between party policy and voter response." They found, for example, that only somewhere between 20 and 40 percent of the electorate were in a position to vote on the basis of specific issues. Evidence seemed to indicate overwhelmingly that partisan identification and the personality of the candidate counted for much more in American voting behavior than did issues.[8]

Commitment to the democratic rules of the game

By the 1950s evidence had been available for some time that abstractions about democracy were widely endorsed by Americans but that specific applications of the rules did not elicit similar agreement. A summary of the earlier studies generalized that:

> The great majority of the public reveal a strong devotion on a broad or abstract level, to the basic principles of liberty and equality.... On a variety of surveys an almost unanimous lip service has been paid to the fundamental principles of liberty and equality. But again, when we drop to the level of specifics, the majorities fall off. Repeated surveys have shown that one American in four would not permit the Socialist party to publish newspapers, and one in three would not allow newspapers to criticize our form of government.[9]

There followed a set of studies that substantiated these findings. The landmark study found that fewer than 60 percent of Americans would permit free speech for socialists, atheists (40 percent), or communists (30 percent).[10] In addition, this study found that community leaders were more tolerant of the expression of unpopular ideas than was the general public. Several other pieces of research corroborated the basic findings and added that there was greater consensus on specific applications of the rules of the game among citizens with more education and among the politically active.[11]

In all, the empirical research seemed conclusive: the classical image of the democratic citizen was not realized in any respect in the mass public.

Table 4.1
Classical Image versus Average Citizen

	Classical image	"Average" citizen, 1950s
Political information	Highly informed	Fragmentary
Political participation	Highly participant	Infrequent, beyond voting
Issue orientation (voting)	Highly issue-oriented	Little issue voting
Commitment to democratic rules	Highly committed	High on generalities, low on specifics

An early voting study concluded that "requirements commonly assumed for the successful operation of democracy are not met by the behavior of the 'average' citizens."[12]

Democratic Elitism

Prior to the survey findings just discussed, other theorists had raised questions about the reality of representative democracy. These theorists, often called "elitists,"[13] called attention to several severe problems in conventional democratic theories. They called into question the rationality of mass publics and pointed to their normal state of apathy. They pointed out the important role of myth and symbol in governing and the tendency of small, organized groups (elites) to manipulate these ideas and to dominate decision-making. In effect, the elitists argued that anything resembling the rational-activist model of representative government was a cruel illusion. The discovery that American citizens did not, in fact, live up to the democratic ideal forced several scholars to revise the concept of how democracy actually worked in nation-states. This revision also incorporated the elitist criticism.

One resolution of the dilemma induced by the empirical findings was to suggest that it was the politically active who had the characteristics necessary for the maintenance of a democratic system. Democracy could be seen as a competition between elites, via interparty competition and elections. These elites were assumed to have a strong commitment to the democratic rules of the game. Access to the elite structure was assumed to be relatively open. Underlying the political structure of elite competition was assumed to be a flourishing system of social pluralism. There was assumed to be enough slack in the system so that the mass public could mobilize on specific issues. Finally, it was assumed that elites anticipated and were responsive to the preference of the public.[14]

Such a system would be decidedly imperfect from the classical perspective. It could, however, be regarded as a realistic readjustment of democratic requirements, given the actual characteristics of most citizens. But it is not surprising that partisans of the classical view responded strongly and negatively to "democratic elitism."[15] One telling point was that elites did not always seem committed to the rules of the game, as Watergate seemed to prove. The partial reinstatement of the classical model of rational activism, however, awaited changes in the findings and interpretations of survey research.

In addition to democratic elitism, theorists of public opinion pointed to portions of the public, called "attentive publics,"[16] who had the characteristics of good citizens on particular issues, presumably because of sociological characteristics (education), self-interest on the issue, or location in the social structure. Presumably, elites would be responsive to attentive publics.

The Rational-Activist Citizen (Partially) Restored

In recent years, some aspects of the rational-activist view of citizenship (as a realizable goal) have been restored, largely through empirical, survey-based research, although some new interpretations of data have also been involved.

Political information

There is no claim that citizens are vastly better informed than they were once believed to be. There is, however, some modification of the position that voters are basically ignorant. As W. Lance Bennett has pointed out, "The trouble is, we have never really studied what kinds of information people actually use in their daily lives."[17] The implication is that information varies with salience and with the quality of political information presented.

It seems reasonable to assume that the more important an issue is to an individual, the more information he or she will have on that particular question. Indirect support for this supposition is found in a study of issue salience by David E. RePass. In contrast to earlier research, which found the public unable to distinguish political party differences on issues, he reported that "the public does perceive party differences on those issues that are salient to them."[18] It may also be true that public knowledge varies with the degree of emphasis given a particular issue by political elites and the mass media. We know, for example, that ideological evaluations of politics increase in the public when ideological candidacies appear.[19]

More specifically, recent studies have uncovered more useful public information about, for example, congressional candidates than previous work suggested. Thomas E. Mann has reported that the "first task was to discover what the public knows about the congressional candidates. The conventional wisdom is that it knows very little. My investigation...led me to conclude that the public is more aware of congressional candidates than we have believed."[20] For example, Mann found that, although voters could not *recall* the names of incumbents, they could *recognize* their names and "most had a positive or negative response."[21] Public information does not approach the classical ideal, but neither is the public mind a vacuum on the issues it cares about.

Political participation

In the realm of participation, the revisionism has been more thoroughgoing. One point stands out in the revision: many more people engage in at least some forms of political participation than the early studies suggested. The path-breaking study by Sidney Verba and Norman H. Nie reports that earlier researchers "may have seriously underestimated the amount of political participation in America and its degree of dispersion."[22] This underestimation resulted from two related problems: the assumption that all forms of political participation were highly correlated and the failure even to consider some forms of participation. It had previously been assumed that political participation was unidimensional.[23] That is, if one performed the most difficult acts of participation, then one also performed all of the less difficult ones, and if one did not do the least difficult acts, then one did not do the harder ones. Verba and Nie demonstrated that political participation was at least partly multidimensional. Moreover, they looked at forms of participation not generally examined. One example is "particularized contacting"—that is, contact by an individual citizen with a government official. "Contacting" turns out to be "a unique mode of activity."[24] The citizen, for example, decides the agenda for the contact.

The upshot of the newer conceptualization and research has been to expand the notion of participation and to show that a substantial proportion of Americans are at least somewhat active. Verba and Nie found, for example, that nearly half of the population had performed at least one of the six most difficult political acts.[25]

A focus on voting and a unidimensional concept of political participation resulted in a conclusion that the bulk of the American public was relatively inert politically. Now that picture has been altered. Although voting participation (in presidential elections) continues to decline (see Chapter Five), other forms of participation have been uncovered, and the extent of mass activity seems to have been underestimated. This does not mean the United States is a hotbed of participatory democracy, but it does mean that the simple division into political activists and inert mass is inaccurate.

Issue orientation in the electorate

Whereas previous research had shown little issue orientation in the electorate, studies of the 1964, 1968, and 1972 presidential elections found a marked upsurge in issue voting.[26] The favored explanation of these changes was that the voting choices, particularly in 1964 and 1972, permitted (even encouraged) issue-oriented behavior on the part of the electorate. In other words, the electorate is typically about as rational as its choices allow it to be. As V. O. Key, Jr., once wrote, "in the large the electorate behaves about as rationally and responsibly as we should expect, given the clarity of the alternatives presented to it and the character of the information available to it."[27] In turn, these new findings have been challenged on a variety of methodological grounds.[28] No one claims that the electorate now achieves the classical ideal in terms of issue voting. Rather, it is argued that voters are more rational than previously supposed and moved by salient issues when alternatives are presented.

Democratic rules of the game

As mentioned, research on mass devotion to the democratic rules of the game did not yield encouraging results. That same research, however, showed a relationship between education and a commitment to the rules. Therefore, as levels of education have increased, it might be expected that tolerance of political dissent would also. More recent research has concluded that tolerance of communists, socialists, and atheists has increased significantly since the 1950s: "The conclusion most often reached is that the electorate has become more politically tolerant in the last twenty years."[29] It has also been demonstrated that, with education controlled, political elites are no more tolerant than their mass counterparts.[30] While tolerance of political dissent is far from perfect, at least in terms of some political deviants the reach of the democratic rules of the game has been extended.

It is certainly provocative that these separate findings on information, participation, issue orientation, and commitment to the rules of the game have changed in a direction that would suggest a more favorable portrait of the mass electorate in terms of democratic citizenship. This portrait, at best, is still far short of the classical idea. It suggests that rational citizens respond to the extent and quality of polical stimuli in terms of information, participation, and issue orientation and that increased education is having its predicted impact on political tolerance.

Much of the recent research is controversial (for example, has issue voting increased or not? has tolerance increased or not?). Nevertheless, if we assume some accuracy to the present picture, we can contrast the ideal and two versions of reality—the old and the new:

Table 4.2
Classical Image versus Average Citizen (1970s)

	Classical image	Average citizen (1950s view)	Average citizen (1970s view)
Political information	Highly informed	Uninformed	Informed on salient issues
Political participation	Highly participant	Infrequent, beyond voting	Not unidimensional; many participate beyond voting
Issue orientation	Highly issue-oriented	Little issue voting	Issue voting depends on choices
Commitment to rules of game	Highly committed	High on generalities, low on specifics	Growing commitment

Rousseau would still be unhappy with the 1970s version.

No realistic theory of popular democratic control could be based on the ideals of a classical citizen: fully informed, highly active, issue-oriented, and fully committed to the rules of the game. Even those whose profession is politics cannot fully live up to these ideals. The response to the discovery that the public actually was far from the ideal was probably extreme—to place the full burden of democratic maintenance on political elites.

This resolution neglected the realities that exist for elites as well. For example, sharp divisions on intense issues may strain elite commitment to the rules of the game.

Democracy could not function if there were no truth to the classical ideal; it cannot all be myth. However, the ideal places too great an emphasis on the positive aspects of citizenship. A reformulation would recognize that the essence of democracy is not popular direction of policy but popular ability to render a negative judgment on existing policy and to change leadership. In order to be able to achieve this, the electorate must have sufficient information to reach a judgment about how things are going and who is responsible. Moreover, there must be an opportunity to participate. And the rules of the game must protect normal political conflict.

NOTES
CHAPTER FOUR

[1] Norman R. Luttbeg, "Political Linkage in a Large Society," in *Public Opinion and Public Policy* (Homewood, Ill.: Dorsey Press, 1968), p. 4.

[2] This requirement was added because of the need to keep political conflict within acceptable boundaries. For a statement of the position, see Robert A. Dahl and Charles E. Lindblom, *Politics, Economics and Welfare* (New York: Harper & Row, 1953), pp. 294–99.

[3] V. O. Key, Jr., *Public Opinion and American Democracy* (New York: Knopf, 1961), p. 494.

[4] Also see Donald E. Stokes and Warren E. Miller, "Party Government and the Saliency of Congress," in Angus Campbell et al., *Elections and the Political Order* (New York: Wiley, 1966), pp. 199–200, on public knowledge of control of Congress.

[5] Summarized in Robert S. Erikson and Norman R. Luttbeg, *American Public Opinion* (New York: Wiley, 1973), p. 25, Table 2-1.

[6] Julian L. Woodward and Elmo Roper, "Political Activity of American Citizens," *American Political Science Review* 44 (Dec. 1950): 872–75.

[7] Fred J. Greenstein, *The American Party System and the American People*, 2nd ed. (Englewood Cliffs, N.J.: Prentice-Hall, 1970), p. 19, figure 2.

[8] Angus Campbell et al., *The American Voter* (New York: Wiley, 1960), pp. 182–83, Chapters 3, 6, 7.

[9] Herbert Hyman and Paul B. Sheatsely, "The Current Status of American Public Opinion," in Daniel Katz et al., eds., *Public Opinion and Propaganda* (New York: Dryden, 1954), p. 41.

[10] Samuel A. Stouffer, *Communism, Conformity, and Civil Liberties* (Garden City, N.Y.: Doubleday, 1955), pp. 28–46.

[11] James W. Prothro and Charles M. Grigg, "Fundamental Principles of Democracy," *Journal of Politics* 22 (1960): 276–94; and Herbert McClosky, "Consensus and Ideology in American Politics," *American Political Science Review* 58 (June 1964): 361–82.

[12] Bernard R. Berelson et al., *Voting: A Study of Opinion Formation in a Presidential Campaign* (Chicago: University of Chicago Press, 1914), p. 307.

[13] The three leading elite works are R. Michels, *Political Parties* (Glencoe, Ill.: Free Press, 1915); G. Mosca, *The Ruling Class* (New York: McGraw-Hill, 1939); and V. Pareto, *The Mind and Society* (New York: Harcourt Brace, 1935).

[14] A good short summary of the democratic elitist position can be found in Lester M. Milbrath, *Political Participation* (Chicago: Rand McNally, 1965), pp. 149–53. Perhaps the most completely developed position is that of

Robert A. Dahl, *Who Governs?* (New Haven: Yale University Press, 1961), pp. 305–25.

[15] See, among many, Jack Walker, "A Critique of the Elitist Theory of Democracy," *American Political Science Review* 60 (June 1966): 285–95.

[16] See Donald J. Devine, *The Attentive Public* (Chicago: Rand McNally, 1970).

[17] W. Lance Bennett, *Public Opinion in American Politics* (New York: Harcourt Brace Jovanovich, 1980), p. 90.

[18] David E. RePass, "Issue Salience and Party Choice," *American Political Science Review* 65 (1971): 394. Emphasis deleted.

[19] Norman H. Nie et al., *The Changing American Voter*, enlarged ed. (Cambridge: Harvard University Press, 1979), pp. 110–22.

[20] Thomas E. Mann, *Unsafe at any Margin* (Washington, D.C.: American Enterprise Institute, 1978), p. 101.

[21] Ibid., p. 30.

[22] Sidney Verba and Norman H. Nie, *Participation in America* (New York: Harper & Row, 1972), p. 40.

[23] Milbrath, p. 18.

[24] Verba and Nie, p. 64.

[25] Ibid., p. 35.

[26] Nie, *Changing American Voter*, pp. 156–73.

[27] V. O. Key, Jr., *The Responsible Electorate* (New York: Vintage, 1966), p. 7.

[28] Among many, see David E. RePass, "Comment: Political Methodologies in Disarray: Some Alternative Interpretations of the 1972 Election," *American Political Science Review* 70 (Sept. 1976): 815.

[29] John C. Pierce and John L. Sullivan, "An Overview of the American Electorate," in Pierce and Sullivan, eds., *The Electorate Reconsidered* (Beverly Hills: Sage, 1980), p. 25. For an example of research suggesting higher levels of tolerance, see David G. Lawrence, "Procedural Norms and Tolerance: A Reassessment," *American Political Science Review* 70 (1976): 99. Also see John L. Sullivan et al., "An Alternative Conceptualization of Political Tolerance," *American Political Science Review* 73 (1979): 784. This article explicitly compares the Stouffer study (1954) with 1977 findings and shows increases in tolerance that average 25 to 30 percent on tolerance of atheists and communists. However, this article also criticizes the new research for specifying the content of the measures of tolerance and because "the questions asked invariably referred to specific groups, generally of a leftist persuasion" (785). Using content-controlled measures, the authors conclude that "intolerance has not necessarily declined much over the past 25 years, but merely has been turned toward new targets" (792).

[30] Robert W. Jackman, "Political Elites, Mass Publics and Support for Democratic Principles," *Journal of Politics* (Aug. 1972): 765.

CHAPTER 5

THE FRAGMENTATION OF AMERICAN POLITICS

In the first four chapters we laid the theoretical groundwork for the analysis of public opinion in contemporary American politics, emphasizing the pluralist character of American government and political parties. We explored the nature of the mass public in terms of democratic citizenship. In addition, we noted the tensions between pluralism and the other versions of democracy, majoritarian and classical. We also examined the criticisms of interest-group pluralism and its stepchild, democratic elitism. All this was preparatory to an examination of contemporary American politics. Assuming that the general label of pluralist is still somewhat accurate, what trends in American politics can we discern?

Commentary on American politics these days emphasizes change, and the tone of much of that commentary is negative or pessimistic.[1] While continuity in American politics remains an important aspect of a comprehensive view, it has been change, and not benevolent change, that has caught the eye of most observers.

One of the most negative evaluations of the policymaking capacity of American government comes from futurist Alvin Toffler: "In the United states we find an almost total paralysis of political decision-making in connection with the life-and-death questions facing society...the U.S. political machinery still spins helplessly on its axis, unable to produce anything remotely resembling a coherent energy policy. This policy vacuum is not unique. The United States also has no comprehensive (or comprehensible) urban policy, family policy, technology policy."[2]

The President's Commission for a National Agenda for the Eighties, in the report, "The Electoral and Democratic Process in the Eighties," addresses a number of problems that are virtually a constant refrain in contemporary comment on American politics: declining confidence in American political institutions, declining voter turnout, the fragmentation of American government and the decline of political parties in the United States, and the increased influence of interest groups in Washington. The panel asserts that "the trends in and influences on the executive branch, the Congress, the federal courts, the political parties, and the various interest groups have produced a fragmentation of the political process that makes effective governmental action to meet the major problems of the eighties more difficult."[3] In a similar view, James Sundquist has recently called attention to several interrelated trends that he believes have, in combination, weakened the competence of the American national government. These trends include the decline in confidence of Americans in their national government, party disintegration, haphazard presidential selection, rejection of presidential leadership, limitations on congressional leadership, and deterioration of administrative competence.[4] Although each of the problem areas identified by Toffler, the panel, and Sundquist might be disputed, the overall pattern is one of increased fragmentation of American politics and a consequent inability of American government to act competently with respect to a range of serious problems.

The nation faces serious issues, such as inflation and energy needs, that seem to require long-range, coherent, and consistent policy direction and administration. The political trends that have been identified presumably undermine the capacity of government to deal with these policy problems.

In this chapter we describe and examine several of those trends, which have changed the American political system in the past twenty years. The changes may have negative consequences, or they may not, but at minimum they shape the content and direction of the American political system. Therefore, it is important to understand these changes in order to comprehend the role of public opinion and organization in American politics.

Political Cynicism

The first change to be examined in this chapter is the decline of confidence of American citizens in their government. An important foundation for a democratic political system is a widespread sense that its political institutions are legitimate and effective.[5]

In a democracy, some skepticism about government and officials is healthy, but the corrosive effects of a pervasive cynicism can eat away at the capacity of government to perform effectively. Widespread expectations that government is corrupt or ineffective can be a cause of government failure, a kind of self-fulfilling prophecy.

Since the mid-1960s events, widespread perceptions of government failure, and actual government failures have served to undermine public confidence in American national government. These events included the Vietnam War, civil disorders, and Watergate. The perceptions included the widespread belief that the "war on poverty" of the 1960s created more problems than it solved. The government failures included the inability of either Democrats or Republicans to check inflation. It is worth noting that there has been a nearly universal decline in confidence in basic American institutions,[6] but government has been a prime victim. As Sundquist has noted: "Every poll that has been designed to measure the confidence of the American people in their government has shown a precipitous decline in that confidence since the mid-1960s."[7] Sundquist, of course, believes that this cynicism contributes to governmental incompetence.

Since the advent of large-scale survey research, a series of questions concerning public trust in government has been asked by scholars at the Interuniversity Consortium for Political Research at the University of Michigan. These questions concern the integrity of government officials and their competence. In the late 1950s such trust was relatively high. Since then there has been a dramatic erosion of the levels of such trust. One simple measure of the change is the proportion of those giving the "most trusting" responses minus the proportion of those giving the "most cynical" responses. Table 5-1 gives those proportions for selected years. The table clearly shows the epic changes that have occurred. By 1978 cynics outnumbered trusting Americans by 2½ to 1. There is a considerable dispute about the meaning of these changes and their significance for the political system.[8] At one extreme, some argue that such a decline seriously weakens the capacity of

Table 5.1 Most Trusting Minus Most Cynical, 1958-1978 (percent)

	1958	1964	1970	1974	1978	Total change
Proportion of most trusting	58	61	38	24	19	−39
Proportion of most cynical	11	19	36	50	52	+41
	+47	+42	+2	−26	−33	80

SOURCE: Warren E. Miller, "Misreading the Public Pulse," *Public Opinion*, Oct./Nov. 1979, p. 11, fig. 1.

American government to function effectively. At the other, the change is seen as more superficial, reflecting fashions in opinion, not serious indicators of a collapse of support for the political system. Some argue that decline in confidence is related to the actual occupants of office rather than to the institutions or the system.[9] It is worth noting that a major change in indicators of public confidence in government has taken place in roughly the same period when political parties and voting turnout have also declined. We turn now to those trends.

The Decline of Party

The decline of party has become a central concern of American political science and a frequent topic in the mass media. The literature, both academic and popular, is now vast. Many articles and books report a variety of indicators of party decline. Much of the literature has described and attempted to explain weakening party loyalty in the electorate. Table 5-2 summarizes the variety of clues cited as evidence of partisan decline in the electorate. It also indicates the evidence for organizational and legislative party decline.

There is a general sense that parties have weakened across the board. The most important aspect of change, or at least the one that has received the most attention, has been the decline of party in the electorate as indicated by voter alienation from parties and increased volatility in voting behavior in the electorate. In the main, the "decline of party" refers to the behavior and responses of voters. The indications of a decline of party in the electorate

Table 5.2 Indicators of Party Decline: Electorate, Organization, Government

Party-in-electorate	Party organization	Party-in-government
Negative attitudes toward parties	Replacement of party organizations in campaigns by candidate-centered organizations (based on technology and media)	Decentralization of power (House)
Growth in numbers of independents in electorate	Loss of control of nominations by party organizations (expansion of presidential primaries)	Declining party cohesion (long-term)
Decline in voter turnout	Atrophy of local party organization	Power of incumbents (reelection)

Party-in-electorate	Party organization	Party-in-government
Increased ticket splitting and decreased influence of party identification in voting (increased partisan defection	Rise of single-issue groups and increased influence of political action committees (PACs)	Decreased impact of President on legislative party
Increased influence of issues and/or candidate images on voting choices		
Unpredictability (volatility) of vote		

SOURCES: See notes 10, 12.

include expressions of negative judgments about parties, growth in the percentages of self-declared independents in the electorate, increases in ticket splitting and in partisan defection by voters, and the growing unpredictability of the outcome of elections, especially presidential elections. All these changes seem to spell an electorate that increasingly relies on something other than blind partisanship in making voting choices. (The reader may wonder whether this is not a positive development. The possible negative consequences of the decline of party are taken up below.)

As V. O. Key, Jr., pointed out long ago, political parties are divided into three distinct elements.[11] In recent writing, less empirical attention has been given to party organizational decline, although it is often asserted, and even less to party decline in the legislature.[12] Almost no explicit attention has been given to links between changes in one aspect of parties and changes in the other areas. For example, do declining party loyalties in the electorate have effects on legislative party cohesion? If the effects of party decline did not show up ultimately in the policymaking process, the significance of such changes would be much less. It would also seem important to discover whether there is a common source of party decline. Is the decline, for example, a product of the technological changes and growth of the mass media in society, both of which seem to make some of the traditional functions of parties obsolete? Is it a function of the changed education composition of the electorate? Or is it a temporary product of political conditions?

The significant consequence of the decline of party is that it also weakens the capacity of government to function effectively. The American system of government is formally divided and naturally fragmented; it requires some centralizing force to make it capable of working. Historically, party has been a means of some centralization and coherence of policy. The collapse of party threatens the capacity of government to act decisively.

There has, of course, arisen a literature that counters or qualifies the party-decline thesis. An early expression of the counter position asserted that "instead of the demise of political parties, we conclude that in many instances broader and more systematic management, financial and program approaches are instilling new vigor into party bodies."[13] It is clear that this quotation refers to parties *as organizations* and, indeed, much of the "party renewal" literature deals with national party organizations,[14] which have undergone a sort of rebirth.

In the 1980 elections it was clear that a revitalization of the Republican party had taken place at the grass roots under the leadership of national committee chairman William Brock, indicating that indeed it was possible to restructure parties in the media age. It had been just a short time since Watergate precipitated another round of death-of-the-Republican-party worries. Another skeptic of party decline has noted that "those who gather data often fasten their gaze on some one aspect—a reduction in the number of strong partisans in the electorate or a change in party rules—and then generalize from those data to 'political parties' as a whole."[15] Trends in party development (decline or revitalization) in one area may be independent of trends in another area, or the impact of change in one area may be delayed in its appearance in another.[16] The decline of party in the electorate is regarded by some as less substantial than is often asserted. The evidence is clear that presidential voting remains heavily partisan in character.[17]

Despite these reservations about the extent and seriousness of party decline, there seems little doubt that it does exist and it does have consequences. Organizational weakness, partisan decomposition of the electorate, and the lack of discipline and coherence of legislative parties can be found at all levels in the United States. Moreover, as suggested in Table 5-2, party decline may be linked to the drop in voter turnout in the United States. Let us now consider that trend.

The Decline of Voter Turnout

Along with the decomposition of the party in the electorate, one of the most widely noted contemporary trends in American politics is the fall in voting turnout in presidential and congressional elections. Figure 5-1 traces the pattern of recent decline, including the 1980 election. Some writers have connected this drop directly to the weakening of parties and party competition. Walter Dean Burnham has, for example, argued that "the disappearance of party as a meaningful vehicle for calculating utilities is likely to result not only in increasing abstention generally, but also [in increasing] abstention among those who already vote least."[18] Burnham holds that parties provide cues to self-interest in voting. Thus weakened party competition may reduce turnout. Competitive parties stimulate turnout because they have the capacity to mobilize voters and because the stakes of politics are clearer to the less advantaged when there is a partisan struggle.[19] Historically, Burnham has traced the dramatic slide in national turnout after the presidential election of 1896 to the withering of party competition that followed.[20] Even earlier, the death of the Federalist party in the second decade of the nineteenth century created a "crisis of participation"[21] in which the absence of two-party competition clearly reduced voter turnout. In some areas where the Federalists withdrew from the partisan struggle, participation fell by as much as 50 percent. In addition, studies of nonpartisan local politics generally report higher turnout in partisan as opposed to nonpartisan cities.[22]

Of course, similar findings can be cited from the one-party South. There are ways in which nonpartisan, one-party, and enfeebled two-party politics are similar. In each, party labels and the efforts of party organizations have little or nothing to do with outcomes. Voters must structure their decisions on some basis other than partisanship. Of course, turnout in southern (one-party) general elections was, historically, extraordinarily low. Turnout in the decisive primaries, however, was also lower than general election turnout in competitive two-party systems.[23] Personal or factional competition did not substitute for institutionalized two-party competition.

Several aspects of the contemporary drop in voting participation are intriguing. One is that the decline has persisted in the face of numerous sociological countertrends.[24] Income and educational levels have risen appreciably. In addition, legal restrictions on participation have been reduced. The expansion of the electorate by the Twenty-sixth Amendment to include eighteen- to twenty-year-olds undoubtedly contributed to the decline (particularly in 1972), but that change cannot account for all of the total drop.[25] The voting rates of eighteen- to twenty-year-olds are appreciably below those of older age groups, thereby pulling down the overall rate of participation in 1972. If we examine the decline by states, we find that it has been more severe in northern, urban, industrial states. For example, while national turnout in presidential elections declined 10 percent from 1960 to 1980, the decline in Illinois, California, and New York was nearly double that.[26] In contrast to the rest of the nation, turnout has doubled in the South since 1948.[27] This is, of course, a substantial reversal of previous tendencies and may be related to increases in party competitiveness in the South.

A recent paper concluded that there are four major reasons for the decline in voter turnout in presidential elections from 1960 to 1976: "the changing age composition of the electorate [the most important]...a growing public feeling of political inefficaciousness...[the fact that] people have become less reliant on the more intellectually demanding medium of newspapers [and]...the increase in avowed independents and the decline in intense partisans.[28] This latter point is, of course, consistent with the suggestion that party decline and turnout decline are linked.

As noted, voting turnout has declined in both presidential (1960-1980) and congressional (1966-1978) elections. Figure 5-1 places the contemporary falloff in the context of patterns of "surge and decline"[29] since 1920. It is clear that the recent drop is only one of three low points experienced between 1920 and 1978. This is an important point: the recent decline is not novel. Therefore, one could argue that in the normal course of events it will turn upward.

Voting participation in national elections since 1920 has surged and declined in apparent response to political stimuli, particularly two-party competitiveness. The turnout surge in the 1930s came as a result of a critical realignment that ended a period of Republican hegemony stretching virtually back to 1896. The weakness of two-party competition was most evident in the 1920s, a decade that resembled the present period in terms of the lack of partisan commitment in the electorate.[30] The New Deal and its aftermath substituted Democratic for Republican dominance, and turnout fell off again (doubtless also influenced by the bipartisanship of the war period). The close, partisan 1948 election produced extremely low turnout. A very attractive Republican presidential candidate, Dwight Eisenhower, in 1952, however, increased Republican competitiveness, especially in the South. Ultimately, the Eisenhower victories were to be more personal

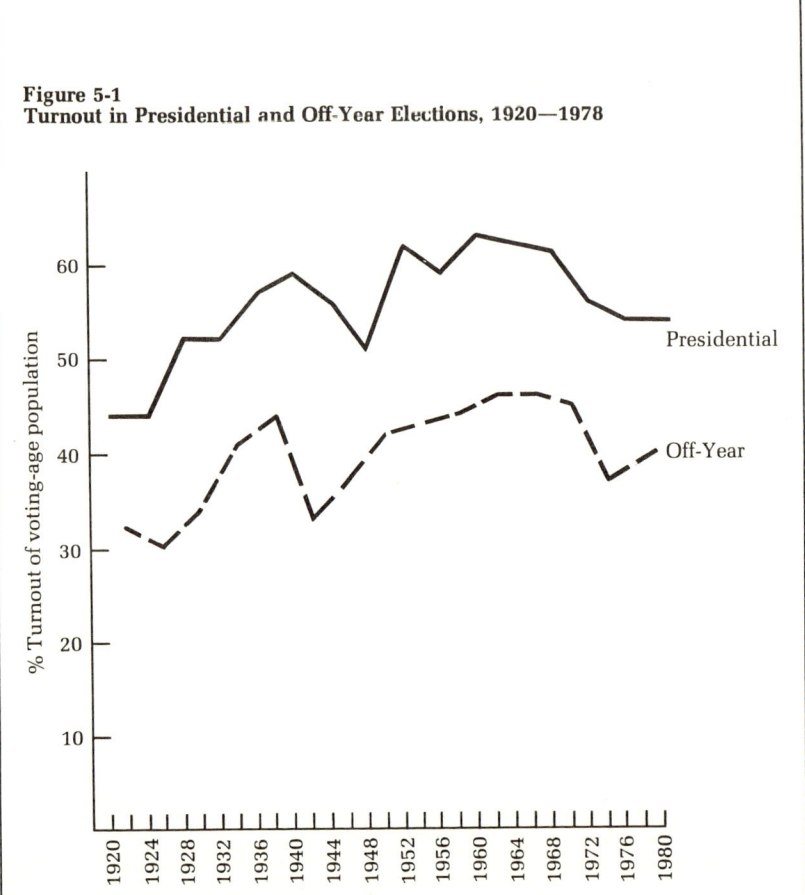

**Figure 5-1
Turnout in Presidential and Off-Year Elections, 1920—1978**

SOURCES: William J. Crotty and Gary C. Jacobson, *American Parties in Decline* (Boston: Little, Brown, 1980), p. 7; Martin Plissner and Warren Mitofsky, "What If They Held an Election and Nobody Came?" *Public Opinion,* Feb./Mar. 1981, p. 50.

than party-oriented, and the competitiveness of the Republican party at the congressional level slipped back again. The contests for the presidency since 1952 have become less and less partisan.

The resurgences in turnout in the 1930s and 1950s followed rather closely after periods of low turnout. In the modern period, attractive presidential candidates could temporarily boost turnout. In the absence of an unforeseen strengthening of two-party competition, however, it seems likely that the turnout rates will approach 50 percent in presidential elections and as low as 30 percent in off-year elections.[31]

As with all of these changes, a definite counterposition at least qualifies the thesis. Those who minimize the fall in voter turnout generally make several points. One of the strongest is that turnout figures for the United States (in comparison with those of European nations) are misleading because of difficult registration procedures and mobility. In addition, others point to the cyclical nature of turnout in the United States and to the fact that much of the current decline can be explained by population changes.[32]

As one form of political activity—voting—is declining (in terms of rates of participation), another—organized interest group activity—seems to be expanding. It is to this trend that we now turn attention.

The Resurgence of Interest Groups

At a time when political trust, political parties, and voter turnout have all declined in American politics, there has been an evident resurgence, not as readily quantifiable, in the amount, variety, and intensity of interest-group activity. One familiar political science proposition would predict that weak political parties lead to or tend to coexist with strong pressure groups. American political parties have never been overwhelmingly strong or centralized. American politics has always been a politics of groups, organized and unorganized. Such groups have attempted to find access to the various decentralized and fragmented areas of American government. Nevertheless, there appears to have been an expansion of interest-group activity, and perhaps influence, in American politics. In part, this may be a natural response to the greatly enlarged role of the national government: "As Americans came in recent decades to accept an enlarged mission for government, the federal establishment greatly expanded and thousands of new lobbies sprang up. The various interest groups actually found the traditional dispersion of authority much to their liking.[33]

Whatever the cause, there are several indications of a resurgence of interest groups. One is the expansion of the number and activity of "single-issue" groups.[34] Such groups are, of course, not completely new in American politics. In fact, M. Ostrogorski (in a critique of parties in the United States around the turn of the century) advocated single-issue politics *as a reform*: "Is not the solution demanded by the problem of parties an obvious one? Does it not consist in discarding the use of permanent parties with power as their end, and in restoring and reserving to party its essential character of a combination of citizens formed specially for a particular political issue."[35] There have always been groups devoted intensely to single issues such as Prohibition. The distinguishing feature of single-issue politics is that political evaluations are determined by absolute positions on particular issues rather than a balanced or mixed judgment based on a range of issues. For example, pro-life groups have frequently evaluated candidates solely on the basis of their positions on abortion. As a second example, pro-ERA women at the Democratic National Convention in 1980 forced adoption of a plank withholding party funds from candidates who did not support ERA. The President's commission asserts that "the uncompromising positions of single-issue groups often provoke divisive and time-consuming Congressional debates, making it more difficult to find acceptable compromises among groups and to attend to other legislative business."[36] Traditional interest groups operate with a much more flexible, long-term, and compromising outlook.

A second indication of the resurgence of interest groups has been the proliferation of political action committees (PACs). PACs are organizations formed by interest groups for the purpose of political education and raising money to distribute to political candidates. Several of the more prominent PACs (the AFL-CIO's Committee on Political Education, the American Medical Association's AMPAC) are longstanding. Recently, however, the PAC concept has been adopted by more and more groups ranging from business to environmental to religious. According to the Federal Election Commission, the sheer number of PACs more than doubled between 1974 and 1979.[37] More recently, data reported by M. Margaret Conway show a quadrupling of PACs between 1974 and 1980 with a more than tenfold increase in business PACs.[38] In addition, so-called New Right and even Christian Right organizations have created PACs.[39] Such groups were widely perceived to have had influence in the 1980 presidential and congressional elections. PACs have become increasingly active in congressional elections, contributing large sums of money, especially (although not exclusively) to incumbents.[40]

A third development on the interest-group front has been the growth of groups loosely labeled "public-interest" groups. Much of the public-interest movement was initiated by the consumer-oriented activities and successes of Ralph Nader, and many of its actions were carried out by public-interest lawyers in courts of law. A prominent example of a public-interest group is Common Cause,[41] founded in 1968. Common Cause was founded as a political reform organization interested in issues such as campaign finance reform. A typical sentiment expressed by the organization is the following: "Over and over we see special interest groups pushing for legislation which serves their narrow interests at the expense of the broader national interest."[42] So-called public-interest groups have been concerned with environmental and consumer issues, political reform, and other such causes. Although "public interest" is a "downright ambiguous expression,"[43] the core of the idea is that the members of the organization do not benefit narrowly (in terms of their economic self-interest) from the policies they support. Of course, all groups believe, or at least state, that the policies they favor are in the broader interest. Nevertheless, it seems clear that some broad distinctions can be made on the grounds that the policy "will not selectively and materially benefit the membership or activists of the organization.[44]

Interest groups are active in all realms of government—legislative, executive, bureaucratic, and judicial. But the upsurge in the activity of interest groups has paralleled a fragmentation of authority in the Congress.[45] Part of the story has, indeed, been the decline of party-in-government. In addition, the capacity of Presidents to influence Congress has declined somewhat, and the leadership in Congress has become increasingly decentralized. With the dependency of congressmen on campaign contributions, and with the conflicts between single-issue groups and between public and special-interest groups, it is no wonder that some observers have begun to believe that the system is perfectly designed for delay, stalemate, incoherence, and domination by strong interest groups. It has been asserted that the "single-issue groups are finding that Congress itself is badly fragmented, a near perfect arena for their efforts."[46]

None of these changes in the role of interest groups represents entirely new developments in American politics. American politics has normally been characterized by decentralization of political power and relatively strong interest groups. Nevertheless, being unable to be absolutely precise on the extent of change, it seems clear that there has been a resurgence of interest groups in American politics. What does this mean for the future of American politics?

The Impact of Change

Four changes in American politics have been reviewed in this chapter. The purpose has been to set the stage for what follows. These changes are:

1. the decline in the American people's confidence in the national government;

2. the decline in political parties, especially in the electorate;
3. the decline in voter participation;
4. the increase in the role of interest groups in American politics.

It seems that these changes form a pattern; they fit together. The first three suggest a detachment of Americans from their political institutions. Nevertheless, the fourth suggests a redirection of political energy into organized political activity. The causes of these changes would appear also to be linked. In essence, they are of two broad types:

1. long-term historical trends, such as technological changes and rising levels of education, which probably tend to rob institutions of their functions and to qualify the "automatic" legitimacy accorded political institutions;
2. specific events such as the Vietnam War or Watergate, that shake citizen confidence in institutions.

The costs of these changes lie in the areas indicated by Toffler, the President's commission, and Sundquist—the incapacity of government to make and implement effective policy. The fragmentation of government is exacerbated by the weakness of political parties, by the lack of trust in government, by the lack of legitimacy of political leaders selected by dwindling proportions of the electorate, and by the increased power and intransigence of organized interest groups. All these trends make the construction of effective governing coalitions difficult. If the essence of effective policy is coherence and direction, then the increased fragmentation of American politics and the inability to construct governing coalitions means that policies will be indecisive and drifting.

Moreover, there may be an ideological tilt or bias to the changes in that they favor conservative political values over liberal ones. In an earlier volume I wrote, "The fragmentation of the national policymaking process, the emphasis on interest-group politics and the weakening of political participation and electoral politics may lead to an ideological tilt...to the Right, especially in terms of social welfare politics. The fragmentation of the process makes it difficult to move broad-scale liberal legislation through Congress. The significance of interest-group politics is that it favors organized as opposed to unorganized interests....The bias of the organized system of interest-group politics underrepresents those who benefit from 'Old-Liberal' policies....In short, the much discussed move to the Right...may be a partial consequence of the decline of parties."[47] These words were written before the election of a conservative President in 1980 and before the efforts to cut back on social programs. It should be noted, in addition, that entrenched interests are there to defend many of these programs, such as Social Security.

It would be unfair, however, simply to indicate the cost of change; there are also possible benefits. One has certainly been the expression of, and indeed the influnce of, interests (such as those of consumers), which have historically had little impact on the policymaking process. To a degree, access to the system of interest-group pluralism has been expanded. The desirability of interest-group politics as means of democratic representation, however, does not depend solely on the degree to which all affected interests are organized and can get access to the political system. It also depends on the capacity of such a system to produce effective and legitimate policies. As we have seen, there are severe doubts about the American political system in those realms. It is as if the virtues of pluralism have turned into excesses.

NOTES
CHAPTER FIVE

[1] In a review of one of those commentaries, Anthony King noted that "the foreign reader of this volume must be struck by the atmosphere of gloom and uncertainty pervading it." *American Political Science Review* 74 (1980): 1091.

[2] Alvin Toffler, *The Third Wave* (New York: Bantam, 1980), p. 393.

[3] President's Commission for a National Agenda for the Eighties, Report of the Panel on the Electoral and Democratic Process, *The Electoral and Democratic Process in the Eighties* (Washington, D.C.: Government Printing Office, 1980), p. 11.

[4] James L. Sundquist, "The Crisis of Competence in Our National Government," *Political Science Quarterly* 95 (1980): 183–208.

[5] For an early statement of this perspective, see Seymour Martin Lipset, *Political Man: The Social Bases of Politics* (Garden City, N.Y.: Doubleday-Anchor, 1963), Chapter 3.

[6] *Electoral and Democratic Process*, p. 2., table 1.

[7] Sundquist, pp. 183–84.

[8] See Arthur H. Miller, "Political Issues and Trust in Government: 1964–1970," and the "Comment" by Jack Citrin as well as the "Rejoinder" by Miller in *American Political Science Review* 68 (Sept. 1974): 951–1001.

[9] Paul R. Abramson and Ada W. Finifter report from one study that the "data suggest that the basic political trust index has a very substantial component that evaluates political authorities [as opposed to a withdrawal of support for the system]." *American Journal of Political Science* 25 (May 1981): 305.

[10] Many of the findings (and sources) are summarized in two recent volumes. See William J. Crotty and Gary C. Jacobson, *American Parties in Decline* (Boston: Little, Brown, 1980), and David H. Everson, *American Political Parties* (New York: New Viewpoints, 1980), especially Chapters 3 and 6.

[11] V. O. Key, Jr., *Politics, Parties and Pressure Groups*, 4th ed. (New York: Crowell, 1958), Parts 3–5.

[12] For a standard account of organizational decline, see Ruth K. Scott and Ronald J. Hrebenar, *Parties in Crisis: Party Politics in America* (New York: Wiley, 1979), Chapter 4. On the decline of party cohesion in congressional voting, see David W. Brady et al., "The Decline of Party in the U.S. House of Representatives, 1887–1968," *Legislative Studies Quarterly* 4 (Aug. 1979): 381–407.

[13] John S. Saloma III and Frederick H. Sontag, *Parties: The Real Opportunity for Effective Citizen Politics* (New York: Knopf, 1972), p. 345.

[14] See Charles H. Longley, "National Party Renewal," and John F. Bibby,

"Party Renewal in the National Republican Party," both in Gerald M. Pomper, ed., *Party Renewal in America* (New York: Praeger, 1980), pp. 69–86, 102–15.

[15]John Kessel, *Presidential Campaign Politics: Coalition Strategies and Citizen Response* (Homewood, Ill.: Dorsey Press, 1980), p. 246.

[16]Cornelius P. Cotter and John F. Bibby, "Institutional Development of Parties and the Thesis of Party Decline," *Political Science Quarterly* 95 (Spring 1980): 1–27.

[17]David B. Hill and Norman R. Luttbeg, *Trends in American Electoral Behavior* (Itasca, Ill.: F. E. Peacock, 1980), pp. 50–51. This volume takes a skeptical look at a number of the changes mentioned in this chapter.

[18]"The Appearance and Disappearance of the American Voter," in Richard Rose, ed., *Electoral Participation: A Comparative Analysis* (Beverly Hills: Sage, 1980), p. 65.

[19]V. O. Key, Jr., *Southern Politics in State and Nation*, (New York: Random House, 1949), pp. 308–09.

[20]Walter Dean Burnham, "The Changing Shape of the American Political Universe," *American Political Science Review* 59 (1965): 7–28.

[21]Richard McCormick, "Political Development and the Second Party System," in William Nisbet Chambers and Walter Dean Burnham, eds., *The American Party Systems* (New York: Oxford University Press, 1967), p. 95.

[22]Willis, D. Hawley, *Nonpartisan Elections and the Case for Party Politics* (New York: Wiley, 1973), p. 36.

[23]Key, *Southern Politics*, p. 493.

[24]Richard Brody, "The Puzzle of Political Participation in America," in Anthony King, ed., *The New American Political System* (Washington, D.C.: American Enterprise Institute, 1978), p. 296.

[25]Richard W. Boyd estimates that 25 percent of the recent decline in presidential turnout is explained by changing age distributions. See "Decline of U.S. Voter Turnout," *American Politics Quarterly* 9 (Apr. 1981): 133.

[26]See David H. Everson and Joan A. Parker, "Voter Turnout Drops again," *Illinois Issues*, Feb. 1981, pp. 9–10.

[27]Brody, "The Puzzle," p. 293.

[28]Stephen D. Shaffer, "A Multivariate Explanation of Decreasing Turnout in Presidential Elections, 1960–1976," *American Journal of Political Science* 25 (Feb. 1981): 92–93.

[29]See Angus Campbell, "Surge and Decline," in Campbell, et al., *Elections and the Political Order* (New York: Wiley, 1966), pp. 40–62.

[30]Kristi Andersen, "Generation, Partisan Shift and Realignment," in Norman Nie et al., *The Changing American Voter* (Cambridge, Mass.: Harvard Uni-

versity Press, 1976), p. 94. Also see Andersen, *The Creation of a Democratic Majority* (Chicago: University of Chicago Press, 1979), pp. 129–33.

[31] See Thomas William Madron, "Prospects for Political Parties in the Nineteen Eighties," paper prepared for delivery at the 1979 Annual Meeting of the Southwest Political Science Association, Forth Worth, Texas, Mar. 28–31, pp. 5–6.

[32] For representative arguments, see Ronald C. Moe, "Myth of the Non-Voting American," *Wall Street Journal*, Nov. 4, 1980, editorial page; Everett Carll Ladd, "Note to Readers," *Public Opinion*, Apr./May, 1980, p. 32; and Martin Plissner and Warren Mitofsky, "What If They Held an Election and Nobody Came," *Public Opinion*, Feb./Mar. 1981, pp. 50–51.

[33] Everett Carll Ladd, "How to Tame the Special Interest Groups," *Fortune*, Oct. 20, 1980, p. 66.

[34] For a good discussion of single-issue groups and ideological political action committees and their enhanced role in American politics, see William J. Crotty and Gary C. Jacobson, *American Parties in Decline* (Boston: Little, Brown, 1980), pp. 117–55.

[35] M. Ostrogorski, *Democracy and the Organization of Political Parties*, Vol. II (Garden City, N.Y.: Doubleday-Anchor, 1964), p. 658.

[36] *Electoral and Democratic Process*, p. 9.

[37] See *Congressional Quarterly Weekly Report*, Apr. 8, 1978, pp. 849–54.

[38] M. Margaret Conway, "Political Party Nationalization, Campaign Activities, and Local Party Development," paper prepared for delivery at the Midwest Political Science Association Meeting, Cincinnati, Ohio, Apr. 16–18, 1981, p. 11.

[39] *Congressional Quarterly Weekly Report*, Sept. 26, 1980, pp. 2627–2634.

[40] Dennis S. Ippolito and Thomas G. Walker, *Political Parties, Interest Groups, and Public Policy*, (Englewood Cliffs, N.J.: Prentice-Hall, 1980), p. 351. From 1977 to 1978 PACs raised $54 million and "doled out $10.7 to candidates" in the 1978 congressional races; D. M. Alpenn, "The Pressure Cookers," *Newsweek*, Nov. 6, 1978, p. 57.

[41] On the goals and activities of Common Cause, see Andrew J. Glass, "Common Cause," in Judith G. Smith, ed, *Political Brokers* (New York: Liveright, 1972), pp. 261–91. A good account of some personalities in the public-interest movement can be found in David Broder, *Changing of the Guard* (New York: Simon & Schuster, 1980), Chapter 8.

[42] The quotation is from David Cohen, former president of Common Cause. *Springfield Journal Register*, Apr. 20, 1981, p. 15.

[43] Jeffrey M. Berry, *Lobbying for the People* (Princeton, N.J.: Princeton University Press, 1977), p. 6.

⁴⁴Ibid., p. 7. Emphasis deleted.
⁴⁵See description by Crotty and Jacobson, *American Parties in Decline*, pp. 251–52.
⁴⁶T. Mathews, "Single Issue Politics," *Newsweek*, November 6, 1978, p. 49.
⁴⁷Everson, *American Political Parties*, pp. 234–35.

CHAPTER 6

THE MASS MEDIA AND POLITICAL FRAGMENTATION

The previous chapter described the signs of fragmentation, and even hyperpluralism, in American politics. In this chapter we consider the impact of the mass media on contemporary American politics and the extent to which the previously noted changes are a product of media influence.*

A brief review of President Carter's fate in the public opinion polls before and after the Iranian crisis illustrates the substantial effects of significant events, as communicated by the mass media, on American attitudes. It is well known that the public's view of presidential performance tends to grow sour over time.[1] Even so, by comparative standards, President Carter stood exceptionally low in the polls after nearly three years in office.[2] Then, in the space of two months, his popularity rose dramatically in the polls so that by January of 1980 his public support had more than doubled (see Table 6–1). But by March, his ratings had declined to near pre-Iranian crisis levels. No American president had ever been on such a roller coaster ride as far as public opinion was concerned. The crisis played a major role in preserving the renomination for President Carter in his battle with Senator Kennedy.

What caused the swift and dramatic change? The obvious, and no doubt accurate, answer—the Iranian crisis. Critical foreign policy situations frequently generate a "rally round the flag" effect that produces an upsurge in presidential popularity.[3] President Carter's initial restrained response to the crisis gave him a relatively short-lived bonanza in the polls. In that sense, the Iranian crisis caused the sharp rise in the President's popularity.

But the mass media, particularly television, played a crucial role in the roller coaster effect. It was on television that the nation saw the howling anti-American mobs in Tehran, and it was also television that constantly reminded the American people of how long the national humiliation had dragged on. It is arguable that television was the major contributing factor to the intensity and volatility of the response of the American people.

*This chapter was coauthored by Rita Harmony, of the Illinois Legislative Studies Center.

Table 6.1 Carter Job Ratings (October 1979 to March 1980)

	1979 American hostages seized				1980		
	Oct.	Mid Dec.	Late Dec.	Jan.	Feb.	Early March	Late March
% Positive* ratings	25	48	52	54	49	40	31

*Question: "How would you rate the job President Carter is doing as president—excellent, pretty good, only fair or poor?" Positive ratings are a combination of excellent and pretty good.
SOURCE: *Public Opinion*, April/May, 1980, pp. 30–31.

Since 1960, no American President has served out a full two terms. The mass media, television particularly, were significant in the downfall of at least four of these presidents: Lyndon Johnson, Richard Nixon, Gerald Ford, and Jimmy Carter. The question can be (and has been) raised: to what extent is the increased instability and fragmentation of American politics, as evidenced in the rapid ups and downs and electoral vulnerability of incumbent Presidents, a product of the mass media's treatment of politics? David Broder has asserted that "television, as much as any single force, has undercut the role of political parties, eroded the stable alignments of the past and drained politics of its ideological context."[4] If that observation is correct, and if the decline of parties has the central place in the fragmentation of American politics (as argued in Chapter Five), then television has a responsibility for the condition of American politics.

The most frequent assertion about the influence of the mass media is that it defines (or creates) the issue agenda. Stated cautiously by a leftist critic of American politics, the media play an important role in "determining the framework within which decisions are made."[5] Others assert much bolder claims, exclaiming that the media (particularly television) coverage of Vietnam *caused* the loss of the war. But we must be careful not to confuse the message (bad news) with the messenger. However, some would argue vigorously that the media have merely transmitted an accurate view of reality. To a large extent, the downfall of recent Presidents is the result of policy, or other failures, not the result of the manufacture or manipulation of reality by the mass media.

Significance of Mass Media

In a point reiterated many times since, Walter Lippman wrote that "we shall assume that what each man does is based not on direct and certain knowledge, but on pictures made by himself or given to him.... The pictures inside the heads of these human beings... are their public opinions."[6] Most of our knowledge of public affairs is not direct and certain but indirect and fragmentary, and derived from the mass media. The "pictures in our heads" combine personal or direct experience with what we learn indirectly, and thus produce our images of the political world. Even most of the facts that we think we know about public affairs are acquired indirectly.

Moreover, specific events, as portrayed by the mass media, are capable of producing major changes in the pictures in our heads. For example, consider the general switch in public attitudes against building more nuclear power plants in the wake of the accident at Three Mile Island.[7]

It is also important to recognize that the pictures in our heads are always oversimplifications of reality. We cannot even begin to fully comprehend events we experience *directly*. The bits of news we receive, especially over television, are so compressed as to constitute no more than a "headline service."[8] But even long and detailed news accounts in prestigious newspapers or magazines inevitably must be selective as to detail. The media furnish the pictures in our heads, and these pictures are, necessarily, fragmentary.

There are several other reasons to suppose that the mass media have a significant, if not determinative, impact on politics. As mentioned earlier, the media help to define what the political (and policy) agenda is at any given time: "Media...tell people in fairly uniform fashion which individual issues and activities are most significant and deserve to be ranked highly in the public's agenda of concerns."[9] Moreover, the mass media may replace other important societal institutions, such as political parties and families, through the transmission of political values and political information. Whether the media perform these other functions well or poorly is another question.

Overstatement of Media Influence

The foregoing may suggest that media influence is pervasive and all-powerful: media fix the pictures in our heads, tell us what is important in the political world, and determine the nature of our politics. But we should recognize that there are limits on media influence (for example, socialization by the media takes place in a family and social context). In cautioning against overstating media influence, V. O. Key, Jr. presented this vivid analogy: "The flow of the messages of the mass media is rather like dropping a handful of confetti from the rim of the Grand Canyon with the object of striking a man astride a burro on the canyon floor. In some measure chance determines which messages reach which targets."[10] The direct impact of mass media is limited by lack of attention, selective attention, selective perception (and distortion) and, most particularly, by the group affiliations of the receivers of the messages. No one receives the messages of the media unaffected by predispositions that are, in turn, the product of the intervening influence of prior experiences, prior loyalties, and prior values. Consequently, media effects are always mitigated by the characteristics of the audience. Audiences are not a *tabula rosa*.[11]

Mass Media and Presidential Nominations

One of the most dramatic areas of media influence in contemporary American politics is in presidential nominations. Several factors seem to account for the important, perhaps central, role of the media in presidential nominations:

1. the growing prominence of primaries (and caucuses treated like primaries) in the nomination process;[12]
2. the weakening of the state and local political party organizations that used to have an important role in the process.[13]

These changes have altered the process of presidential nomination in ways conducive to media influence. For example, the long sequence of primaries provides a series of "horseraces" for the media to handicap and thus play a critical role in this new nominating process in the following ways:

1. by telling us who is and who is not a serious candidate;
2. by identifying early front-runners and telling us what the "straws in the wind" are;
3. by setting the expectations for candidates in the various primaries;
4. by telling us which primaries are important and which are not;
5. by telling us who "won" or "lost" various primaries (and why);
6. by telling us when the race is over—when a candidate has the nomination locked up.[14]

Of course, media defenders would say, they are just reporting the facts or reporting what the professionals are saying about the campaign, not manufacturing or manipulating reality.

We have selected three examples of media influence in recent presidential nominations to illustrate some of these points: the fall of Edmund Muskie in 1972, the rise of Jimmy Carter in 1976, and the rise and fall of George Bush in 1980.

Media influence in the Muskie campaign (1972)

Edmund Muskie was the front-runner for the Democratic presidential nomination at the beginning of the 1972 primaries. But by March he had slipped significantly in the race and by April it was over. One dramatic event, given heavy media attention, contributed significantly to Muskie's demise as a candidate. The media's tendency to "handicap races" also contributed.

The incident that crippled Muskie's campaign took place in February in New Hampshire. New Hampshire's primary newspaper, the right wing *Manchester Union Leader*, printed an editorial under the title "Sen. Muskie Insults Franco-Americans." The editorial was based on a letter, subsequently discovered to be forged. It told of Muskie laughing at a reference to French Canadians as "Canucks" (an ethnic slur). French-Americans constitute a large portion of the Democratic vote in New Hampshire. The next day the *Union Leader* printed another story about Mrs. Muskie's habits of swearing, smoking, and talking about her hangovers in public.

Muskie was determined to clear the matter during a speech, made in the falling snow in front of the newspaper building, that same day. As he began to defend his wife he choked up and appeared to be crying. David Broder's account of the episode began, "With tears streaming down his face..." The story made the CBS evening news showing Muskie "falling apart" and looking weak while a vigorous Nixon was seen in China. Then on February 29 David Broder wrote of Muskie's erosion as a front-runner. The networks immediately followed suit with the "erosion" theme, an example of "pack" journalism.[15]

Muskie won the New Hampshire preference primary with 48 percent to George McGovern's 37 percent. The outcome, however, was not interpreted by the media as a victory because expectations had been developed that Muskie, a New England native, would (and needed to) do much better and they had originally predicted a two-to-one margin. From that time on, McGovern began picking up the strength that Muskie had lost. Muskie was bitter. The press had made him the front-runner and then helped to destroy that lead.[16]

Jimmy Carter (1976)

It is safe to say that Jimmy Carter's presidency was made possible by the way the mass media treats nomination politics, and that his campaign was planned to take advantage of that. This observation is not to deny that the personal impact of candidate Carter was an important factor in developing a good base of support around the country in the early stages of his campaign—it most definitely was. But the success of the Carter candidacy depended on the mass media's fascination with a new, somewhat Kennedyesque, and unusual candidate. The size of Carter's victories in the Iowa caucuses and New Hampshire (either in terms of magnitude, representativeness, or the number of delegates) did not justify the catapulting of Carter into front-runner status. For example, CBS reported from Iowa that Carter "was the clear winner in this psychologically crucial test" (actually, a plurality of votes had been uncommitted), and after New Hampshire (where he received 28 percent of the vote), NBC declared that Carter was "the man to beat."[17] Doris A. Graber reports that "the media covered Jimmy Carter far more heavily and favorably than other candidates..."[18] Later in the campaign, on the same day he lost in New Jersey and California, the mass media decided that Ohio (which Carter won) was the crucial primary. For example, *Newsweek* reported that "Carter's resounding victory in the Ohio primary last week confirmed that which most Democrats had long suspected: that the Democratic National Convention...would simply gather to anoint the soft-spoken, plain-talking Georgia peanut farmer."[19] Jimmy Carter's success also highlights another media tendency—to pick apart the front-runner. His early success led to charges during the primaries and the general election that he was vague on the issues.

George Bush and the media politics of 1980

Although he had held major positions as a congressman, director of the CIA, envoy to China, and chairman of the Republican National Committee (and his campaign stressed his experience in these posts), George Bush was, like many of the Republican contenders, a relative unknown as the 1980 presidential nomination campaign began. He could be heartened, however, by the successes of George McGovern in 1972 and Jimmy Carter in 1976, who had started their campaigns with similar handicaps. Indeed, Bush seems to have especially copied the Carter campaign plan with his emphasis on attracting media attention by scoring well in the Iowa caucuses (the nation's first contest for delegates) and New Hampshire. The demands of the mass media to get a line on who was leading the horserace had pushed Iowa into the limelight in 1976.[20] Bush's victory in Iowa brought him extensive media attention and he shot ahead of Ronald Reagan in the preference polls for the Republican nomination.

Bush had campaigned and talked extensively with voters in Iowa in order to win there (and he was aided by Reagan's absence). But to carry future primaries and gain the nomination, he needed to build a national constituency via the mass media. Reagan, on the other hand, was well-known throughout the nation and not as dependent on the media for gathering support.

Once again a media event, in this instance a debate, the media's high expectations, and the New Hampshire primary turned the tables. Bush's attempt to get Reagan to debate him and get his messages across to the voters backfired when Reagan, changing the rules at the last moment, insisted that the other GOP candidates be included. "Although there had been no live television coverage of the mayhem,...stories about it spread through the electorate almost instantly. Film of Reagan grabbing the microphone while Bush sat immobile was shown repeatedly on local and network television....It had captured a rare moment in a political campaign—an instant of genuine drama that no media consultant could have plotted."[21] Bush appeared incapable in this "crisis." He lost the primary, his momentum, and was never able to regain the edge that he achieved after Iowa (although he did win some later primaries). This was another instance where the media seemed more interested in the horserace than the issues.[22]

One of the most telling media episodes of the 1980 campaign came in a CBS interview with Senator Ted Kennedy before the primaries actually began. Kennedy's performance was, in the words of one observer, "inarticulate and flustered."[23] The areas where Kennedy seemed to falter were those involving his personal life and his reasons for seeking to unseat the incumbent Democrat.

Two points need to be emphasized with respect to media influence in the presidential nomination process. The first is that the process gives undue weight to early contests that create the front-runners. New Hampshire is the prime example, although Iowa is bidding fair to become an equal media event. In 1976, for example, there were one hundred network television news stories on the New Hampshire primary (2.63 per delegate) as opposed to thirty on the New York primary (.07 per delegate), which was held in early April.[24] The second point is that the nomination process, through the interaction of the primaries and the media, has effectively taken the nomination of the presidential candidate away from the party.[25] The Democratic party (if such an entity existed) would never have chosen Jimmy Carter as its nominee in 1976, but his campaign, geared to the mass media and the sequence of caucuses and primaries, allowed him to capture the nomination. The consequences were felt throughout his administration as he failed to consistently rally the fragmented Democratic party to support his policies,[26] at least on crucial issues.

The Media In General Elections

Early voting studies assumed a significant role for use of the mass media to persuade voters during presidential campaigns. The research that followed did not confirm the assumption. The effects of campaigns via the media were minimal for a variety of reasons:

1. personal influence was more influential than formal mass media communication;
2. media influence was most often indirect, through opinion leaders who were attentive to the media;
3. outcomes were limited by the substantial numbers of voters who had made up their minds even before the campaign (and did not shift);
4. functions of the campaign were less to persuade or to change opinions than to activate previous predispositions and to reinforce them;
5. there was a tendency for those who had partisan leanings to pay attention only to the communications that supported their own point of view;
6. those who were most susceptible to change were least likely to attend to the media.[27]

The findings of the early voting studies on campaign effects have been summarized as follows: "The general conclusion was that persons most exposed to persuasive communication in a campaign were those most likely already to have arrived at a voting decision; those most likely to be influenced by persuasive appeals were precisely those least interested in politics and, hence, least likely to pay attention to campaign communications."[28]

Thus, early study of political campaigns (and other communication studies) resulted in a "law of minimum effects."[29] This law is based on the idea that there are multiple influences in any persuasion situation, that media are only one influence and not likely to be the most significant. The most important factors that limit the direct impact of the media involve the personal characteristics and social context of the voters themselves. In terms of campaigns, the limiting effects of certain characteristics can be readily seen. For example, partisan identification produces selective perception of candidates and issues.[30] And to the extent that partisan identification represented a "standing decision," and that 60 to 75 percent of the voters made up their minds (and did not change) before the campaign began, the effects of media on the decision (if not the intensity of opinion) would be minimal.

Reasons to Expect Increases in Media Effects

There are several reasons to expect that media effects in presidential elections may have increased recently:

1. the studies that produced the "minimal effects" theory were conducted before television became the dominant mode of mass communication (and the most used news source[31]);
2. there has been a decline of partisan identification and an increase in the percentages of undecided voters;
3. group cues for voting behavior have also weakened recently[32];
4. there has been an apparent strengthening of personality influences (of candidates) in voting decisions.[33]

These factors suggest, but do not prove, that media effects should be greater in the contemporary era.

One contemporary work that stresses targeted media effects is *The Ticket-Splitter* by Walter DeVries and Lance Tarrance, political consultants. They insist that communications must be directed at crucial "swing" voters: "The way voters see and use media is becoming one of the most significant factors in the way people make up their minds about candidates. The way to win elections is not through traditional advertising that 'sells' the candidate, but through an overall communications strategy linking the candidate and target groups which constitute the 'crucial minority' that will decide the election."[34] In this more sophisticated view, the communications are shaped to specific groups of voters and their media habits.

One version of media influence in presidential politics can be found in *The Selling of the President 1968* by Joe McGinniss.[35] In this work, McGinniss approvingly quotes Marshall McLuhan to the effect that "the party system has folded like the organization chart. Policies and issues are useless for election purposes.... The shaping of a candidate's integral image has taken the place of discussing conflicting points of view."[36] McGinniss illustrates the attempt to use controlled television for reshaping Richard Nixon's image and winning the presidency in 1968. The McGinniss book is strong on describing what the "image makers" thought they were doing but does not document, except inferentially, that they achieved these effects. It is well to remember that Nixon was running against a stand-in for a very unpopular incumbent and that he almost lost the election anyway.

An empirical study of the 1972 presidential election, by Thomas Patterson and Robert McClure, provides a quite different and in some ways more hopeful picture of the effects of television on political campaigns.[37] There were several provocative findings to this study:

1. In terms of both commercials and television news (*contra* McGinniss), "television image-making power is a myth."[38] This is largely true because of the prior predispositions of voters and selective perception.

2. Television news coverage of campaigns does not increase voter information. Nonwatchers had as much information gain during the campaign as watchers. This is largely true because television news concentrates on the "horserace" aspects of the campaign. Little attention is given to the issue aspects while much attention focuses on the more superficial features.[39]

3. Contrary to most received opinion, candidate commercials

are effective in communicating political information. This is because such information is contained in the ads and because it is repeated.

Media effects in presidential campaigns are neither so dominant that candidates can be merchandised like soap nor so weak that they can be discounted. It is reassuring to find that candidate commercials communicate information, yet disturbing to find that television news transmits so little. Perhaps the major influence of media on presidential elections comes in the winnowing of candidates that takes place in the nomination process, and in the period between campaigns when the media present and interpret political events that alter the public's perceptions[40] of the issues and personalities of presidents and potential candidates. An illustration of the ambiguity of media effects in presidential elections can be found in the conflicting assessments of the consequences of the Carter-Reagan debate late in the campaign in 1980.[41] It was quite likely that despite all the money spent and outpouring of media coverage in the 1980 presidential election, the outcome was determined by the earlier image in the public mind (accurate or not) that President Carter was not very effective in attacking the major problems of the nation.

Mass Media and Public Policy

Beyond presidential elections, media are thought to influence the actual content, and even in some instances the success or failure of public policies. There are two major questions with respect to the mass media and public policy:

1. To what extent do the media determine the public agenda and therefore influence policy by defining what is an issue?[42]
2. To what extent does media treatment of issues determine how they are resolved?

We shall take up the agenda question first. Although it may seem clear that the public agenda reflects or mirrors the media, there are several problems with this simple formulation. Does the media actually reflect public opinion, or vice versa? In social science, straightening out the cause-effect relationships is not always easy. What is the role of political elites in determining the agenda? Do the media perhaps play a subordinate role? And finally, are there issues so obvious and salient that their presence on the agenda is assured and media attention is thus inevitable?

The fundamental hypothesis of "agenda setting" has been expressed in this way by Bernard Cohen: the media "may not be successful most of the time in telling people what to think, but it is stunningly successful in telling its readers what to *think about.*"[43] Several studies have shown a relationship between the content of media and what issues voters said were important in presidential campaigns.[44] A study by Funkhouser went so far as to conclude that "the media, rather than the real world, set the public's agenda."[45] However, subsequent studies have made the following important qualifying points about the agenda-setting functions of the media:

1. The role of political elites in developing the agenda may have been underestimated.[46]
2. The characteristics and predispositions of the audience must be taken into account in assessing media effects in agenda setting: "...media coverage interacts with the audience's preexisting sensitivities to produce changes in issue concerns. Media effects are contingent on issue-specific audience characteristics..."[47] This point, as we have seen, is central to all media influence assessments: audience predispositions shape media effects.
3. Issues vary in the degree to which they are susceptible to "media creation."[48] If there is an earthquake, one does not need television in order to know there is a crisis. Some forms of environmental pollution may be a different matter.
4. Media coverage of certain issues may be mediated through political elites in order to achieve agenda status.[49]

The research on agenda setting is not definitive, but it shows that the matter is more complicated than it may first appear to be. The public agenda is not exclusively defined by the mass media. Other factors that shape the agenda include:

1. actual events (for the most part, the agenda is not "pseudo");
2. the discretion of political elites who choose to stress some issues and ignore others;
3. the predispositions of the audience;
4. the capacity of individuals interested in policy issues to manipulate the media.

But what about media effects on the actual outcomes of policy choices? We now turn to that issue.

To what extent can the media determine the shape and direction of national policy? At one extreme, the claim has been made that the media defeated the United States in Vietnam: "In Vietnam we saw the United States defeated by a fourth-rate country. How could such a thing happen?... A West German who covered the Vietnam War, described it as 'the first war in history that was won by one side essentially via the media of the other side.'... If the news media can be manipulated to bring about America's defeat in a war to which it had dedicated over 50,000 lives and billions of dollars to win, then they can surely be manipulated in other important areas too."[50] Charges such as these, whether from the left or right, usually assume that the mass media are biased politically, thereby giving the American public (and decision-makers) an ideologically distorted view of reality.

Media influence on the Vietnam War policy can hardly be doubted, but that is not the equivalent of saying that the war was lost because of the media. With respect to the war, two examples can be cited that illustrate the sometimes negative impact of the media. The 1968 TET offensive was generally reported as a "defeat for the South Vietnamese and American forces," but it actually was "a defeat for the North Vietnamese."[51] Then, after a visit to the battlefield, Walter Cronkite of CBS declared the war hopeless. Wrote David Halberstam: "It was the first time in American history a war had been declared over by an anchorman."[52] It may be that because the public lacks a reality check on much of foreign affairs, and because the complications of such subjects tend to result in oversimplification, that the media can influence public perceptions and even the direction of foreign policy to a degree that it cannot achieve with bread and butter domestic issues. In addition, crisis events, as communicated by the mass media, may help to tilt public policy in a given direction: "Sensational adverse publicity can also kill programs. For instance, sharp curbs on the production of nuclear energy were made nearly inevitable by the publicity following an accident at a nuclear plant at Three Mile Island...in 1979."[53] But it should be noted that the election of Ronald Reagan in 1980 firmly placed nuclear power back into the energy picture.

Public policy results from a complex interplay of forces. These include history, events, accidents, the actions of political elites, the influences of political institutions, and public opinion as well as media attention and influence. To ascribe to the mass media a determinative (or sinister) role is to ignore the complexity of reality. Yet there is no doubt that media bias and distortion are real problems in specific instances. The policy agenda may be influenced by the media and the quality of political discussion may be enhanced or degraded by the style of the media.

Media and Malaise

One final claim about the media deserves some attention. It is that the media, especially television, are responsible for the decline of confidence in American government, as documented in Chapter Five. The issue is whether "public affairs television fostered cynicism, feelings of inefficacy...?"[54] Of course, as suggested earlier, events such as Watergate could be considered the prime cause of the decline in confidence. Nevertheless, on the basis of experimental and survey research as well as interpretation of the unique status of television, one study concluded that "had all the traumatic events of the last dozen years transpired without television journalism [indeed, *would* they have all transpired without television journalism?] there would have been less change within the American electorate than has, in fact, occurred."[55] The study explains the unique impact of television journalism in terms of the size of the audience, the high credibility of the networks, and the tendencies of television news toward interpretation, negativism, conflict and violence, and anti-institutionalism.[56]

Again our previous cautions seem appropriate. It may be that the decline in confidence is less consequential than many believe. And it is certainly difficult to claim that television journalism (or any other kind) was responsible for the events that triggered the malaise, although the media's interpretation of such events may influence the "pictures in our heads."

Media and Fragmentation

To what extent have the media contributed to the increased fragmentation of American politics? Let us review the most important conclusions of this chapter, in an attempt to answer that question. First, the media have partially supplanted the parties as instruments for securing presidential nominations and as the means of communicating with voters. Second, the media's most important impact on presidential elections, other than in nominations, is to influence our perceptions of political reality, especially what constitutes the significant issues. Third, the media may have contributed to the current level of political cynicism although the overwhelming cause of this has been, in our judgment, events. The crux of the argument, then, is that the mass media are part of a pattern—not the prime cause—of change in American politics, an institution that "fits" into the trends by sometimes reinforcing or accentuating the direction of change. The media, for example, assisted the decline of parties but did not initiate it. Events, political reform, and brute political reality all have had an important role in the changes in American politics.

One of the changes much heralded by the media in the 1970s, capped by the 1980 election, was the move to the right in American politics. To what extent was that an accurate perception? That is the subject of the following chapter.

NOTES
CHAPTER SIX

¹See John E. Mueller, *War, Presidents, and Public Opinion* (New York: Wiley, 1973), Chapter 9.
²In June-July of 1979, President Carter had already racked up the third lowest approval score of all recent Presidents (only Nixon and Truman were ranked lower) and, more significantly, Carter had the lowest approval rating (34 percent) for a President within his own party. *Public Opinion,* Oct./Nov. 1979, p. 21. For a summary of Carter's approval ratings and comparisons with other recent Presidents, see *Public Opinion,* Mar./Apr. 1978, pp. 28–9.
³John E. Mueller, "Presidential Popularity from Truman to Johnson," *American Political Science Review* 64 (March 1970): 27.
⁴David Broder, *Changing of the Guard* (New York: Simon & Schuster, 1980), p. 396.
⁵William Domhoff, *Who Rules America?* (Englewood Cliffs, N.J.: Prentice-Hall, 1967), p. 80.
⁶Walter Lippman, *Public Opinion* (New York: Macmillan, 1961, © 1922), pp. 25, 29.
⁷See *Public Opinion,* June/July 1979, p. 25.
⁸The average 30-minute television news program could be published as the front page of a quality newspaper.
⁹Doris A. Graber, *Mass Media and American Politics* (Washington, D.C.: Congressional Quarterly Press, 1980), pp. 132–3.
¹⁰V. O. Key, Jr., *Public Opinion and American Democracy* (New York: Knopf, 1967), p. 357.
¹¹One clear example of this is that no matter how the media treat a President, he is always regarded more favorably by members of his own party than by the opposition. See source in note 2.
¹²In 1968 there were 17 Democratic and 16 Republican primaries. In 1980, the numbers were 33 and 34 respectively (75 percent of the delegates in both parties were selected in primaries in 1980). William Crotty, "The Presidential Nominating Process in 1980," paper delivered at the 1980 Presidential Election Lecture Series, Legislative Studies Center, Sangamon State University, Oct. 1, 1980, p. 17.
¹³For a useful account of the way the process used to work, see Nelson W. Polsby and Aaron B. Wildavsky, *Presidential Elections* (New York: Scribners, 1964), Chapter 2.
¹⁴On these various points, with varying shades of emphasis, see David S. Broder, "Political Reporters in Presidential Politics," Lanny J. Davis, "The

Primaries: Which Winners Lost and Which Losers Won?" and Donald R. Mathews, "Winnowing: The News Media and the 1976 Presidential Nominations,"—all in James I. Lengle and Bryon E. Shafer, eds., *Presidential Politics* (New York: St. Martin's, 1980), pp. 490–499, 282–297, and 271–281, respectively.

[15] This concept is discussed in Timothy Crouse, *The Boys on the Bus* (New York: Random House, 1973), pp. 7–11.

[16] This abbreviated account of Muskie's demise was pieced together from the following sources: Timothy Crouse, p. 52; James David Barber, *The Pulse of Politics* (New York: Norton, 1980), pp. 97–8; and Theodore H. White, *The Making of the President 1972* (New York: Atheneum, 1973), pp. 82–3.

[17] Quoted by Thomas E. Patterson, *The Mass Media Election* (New York: Praeger, 1980), p. 44.

[18] Graber, op.cit., p. 159. This was at the crucial beginning of the campaign.

[19] *Newsweek*, June 21, 1976, p. 16.

[20] Jules Witcover, *Marathon: The Pursuit of the Presidency 1972–1976* (New York: Viking Press, 1977), pp. 194–215, especially pp. 202–3.

[21] Jack W. Germond and Jules Witcover, *Blue Smoke and Mirrors: How Reagan Won and Why Carter Lost the Election of 1980* (New York: Viking, 1981), p. 129.

[22] See Robert D. McClure, "Media Influence in Presidential Politics," paper delivered at the 1980 Presidential Election Series, Legislative Studies Center, Sangamon State University, Nov. 5, 1980, pp. 14–17.

[23] Germond and Witcover, p. 75.

[24] Mathews, "'Winnowing,'" p. 281. New Hampshire contributes fewer than 1 percent of the delegates to the Democratic convention.

[25] It should be understood that "party" is used here loosely. There never was a tight, disciplined, and centralized organization that controlled nominations.

[26] But see: Jeff Fishel, "Presidential Elections and Presidential Agendas: The Carter Administration in Contemporary Historical Perspective," paper prepared for delivery at the 1980 meeting of the Western Political Science Association, San Francisco, March, 1980.

[27] See Paul Lazarsfeld et al., *The People's Choice* (New York: Columbia University Press, 1968, 3rd edition).

[28] Dan Nimmo, *Political Communication and Public Opinion in America* (Santa Monica, Calif.: Goodyear, 1978), pp. 361–2.

[29] Dan Nimmo, *The Political Persuaders* (Englewood Cliffs, N.J.: Prentice-Hall, 1970), p. 167.

[30] "Identification with a party raises a perceptual screen through which the

individual tends to see what is favorable to his partisan orientation. The stronger the party bond, the more exaggerated the process of selection and perceptual distortion will be." Angus Campbell et al., *The American Voter* (New York: Wiley, 1960), p. 133.

[31] See *Public Opinion*, Aug./Sept. 1979, p. 31.

[32] See Everett Carll Ladd, "The Brittle Mandate: Electoral Realignment and the 1980 Presidential Election," *Political Science Quarterly* 96 (Spring 1981): 14–15.

[33] Dan Nimmo and Robert L. Savage, *Candidates and Their Images* (Santa Monica, Calif.: Goodyear, 1976), pp. 204–5.

[34] Walter DeVries and V. Lance Tarrance, *The Ticket-Splitter: A New Force in American Politics* (Grand Rapids, Mich.: Eerdmans, 1972), p. 92.

[35] Joe McGinniss, *The Selling of the President 1968* (New York: Pocket Books, 1970).

[36] Ibid., quoted on p. 21.

[37] Thomas E. Patterson and Robert D. McClure, *The Unseeing Eye* (New York: Putnam, 1976).

[38] Ibid., p. 73.

[39] For example, in 1972, the networks gave more than twice as much attention to "campaign activity" than to candidate qualifications and issues. Ibid., p. 41.

[40] For a perceptual theory of campaign effects, see Dan Nimmo, *The Political Persuaders*, pp. 179–83. Also see Patterson, *The Mass Media Elections*, pp. 95–96.

[41] See David H. Everson, "The Presidential Campaign of 1980," paper delivered at the 1980 Presidential Election Lecture Series, Legislative Studies Center, Sangamon State University, Oct. 22, 1980, pp. 11–14.

[42] On the general topic of political agendas, see Roger W. Cobb and Charles D. Elder, *Participation in American Politics* (Baltimore: Johns Hopkins University Press, 1972).

[43] Quoted in Laurily Keir Epstein, "Abortion and the Media," paper prepared for Midwest Political Science Association Meeting, April 1978, Chicago, Illinois, p. 2.

[44] See Donald Shaw and Maxwell McCombs, *The Emergence of American Political Issues: The Agenda Setting Function of the Press* (St. Paul: West Publishing, 1977). Also see Patterson, *The Mass Media Election*, pp. 97–100.

[45] Cited in Lutz Ebring et al., "Front Page News and Real World Cues," *American Journal of Political Science* 24 (Feb. 1980): 19.

[46] Jack Walker's research concerning the appearance of safety legislation on the legislative agenda in the 1960s indicates "that in this case the newspaper

[The New York Times] was reacting to events, not stimulating the controversy or providing leadership." "Setting the Agenda in the U.S. Senate," *British Journal of Political Science* 7 (Oct. 1977): 435.

[47] Ebring et al., p. 45.

[48] Ibid., pp. 38–9. They use the example of trust in government: "It is...a genuine media issue—not in the sense that the news media created it, but that it could never have achieved agenda status without them."

[49] Epstein, pp. 11–14.

[50] These quotations are from a letter soliciting subscribers to a conservative "media-watch" publication, *Accuracy in Media*. It is fair to say that the quotations are not unrepresentative of a certain strand of right-wing thinking that sees the national media as a tool of liberalism, if not communism. Similar quotations asserting big business and conservative dominance of the media from the left could doubtless be found.

[51] Graber, p. 60. She is citing Peter Braestrup, *Big Story* (Garden City, N.Y.: Anchor, 1978).

[52] Quoted by Graber, p. 196.

[53] Graber, p. 197.

[54] Michael J. Robinson, "Public Affairs Television and the Growth of Political Malaise," *American Political Science Review* 70 (June 1976): 411.

[55] Robinson, p. 425.

[56] Robinson, p. 426.

CHAPTER 7

A CONSERVATIVE TREND?

In previous chapters, we traced several trends in American politics. These included loss of confidence in government, decline of party, decline of voter turnout, and an upsurge of interest groups. These contribute to a growing fragmentation of American politics: pluralism runs rampant. The effectiveness, in a policy sense, of the political system is threatened.

There are, however, other changes in American politics that seem to have an ideological bent to them. These could represent an effort to recast the dominant public philosophy[1] or, in this case, to revert to a prior public philosophy. Public moods seem to shift. At one time there is great concern over environmental questions. Then an energy crisis looms, and environmental concerns take a back seat. During the 1960s, especially in the presidential elections of 1960 and 1964, there seemed to be a tide running in the direction of political and social liberalism in the United States. More recently, observers profess to see a conservative resurgence; these observations are supported by the results of the presidential election in 1980.

The 1980 elections in the United States brought many surprises and sparked much speculation about change in American politics. For example, "the American electorate on November 4, 1980, rendered a judgment of incompetence on President Carter, on 'liberalism' and on the federal establishment in Washington.... Virtually every prominent Democratic liberal in the Senate who stood for reelection was defeated.... There was likewise a slaughter of liberals from the House of Representatives.... Their defeats followed the defeat in 1978 of five other Senate liberals...."[2] Public opinion, it is claimed, reacted against liberalism and moved in a conservative direction, and that was reflected in the presidential and congressional elections of 1980. But recognizing surface changes and interpreting the meaning of those changes are two different things. It may be that ideology (liberalism versus conservatism) had very little to do with the outcome of the election and that the performance (or perceived performance) of the incumbents was the real issue. The extent of the conservative tide may have been overstated: "many of the liberal Democrats who lost their seats in 1980 had won them only narrowly in 1974"[3] at a time of protest voting against the Republican party. A major purpose of this book is to help untangle such problems of interpretation. In this chapter, we examine some broad trends in issue preferences and ideology in American politics.

Journalists and commentators are fond of assessing public moods and identifying trends. But it is easy to mistake highly visible activity (protests, demonstrations, elections, etc.) for the underlying distribution of opinion. We must be careful not to overgeneralize from the statements and activities of intense minorities or the results of elections to whole populations.

The purpose of this chapter is to examine recent trends in American public opinion to see if it is justifiable to generalize that the United States is becoming more conservative. If there has been such a shift, it would be a partial confirmation of the realignment thesis discussed in Chapter Three.

Policy Dimensions

In order to make assessments of change in public opinion, we are going to employ a simple, threefold division of opinion suggested by Warren E. Miller and Donald E. Stokes: "approval of government action in the social welfare fields...support for American involvement in foreign affairs...and approval of federal action to protect...civil rights."[4] While these three broad dimensions do not exhaust all contemporary policy areas, they do capture a good deal of the ground that has separated liberals from conservatives and Republicans from Democrats. Of course, we know that differences on these policy issues have never been perfectly correlated with ideology or party. The differences between partisans have been clearest on the social welfare dimension, since those issues developed during the New Deal years.

Trends in social welfare

The most critical set of issues from the New Deal era in American politics has been the role of the national government in ensuring the social welfare of its citizens. In the main, these issues have concerned health, education, welfare, and economic security. The objective of government intervention has been to put a floor of minimum security under all citizens to protect them from economic uncertainty. This represented a major shift from a laissez-faire attitude toward the role of the national government prior to the New Deal. As indicated, these issues have consistently divided the mass parties and political party elites.[5] Nevertheless, over the years the Republican party came to accept large parts of the New Deal, and many issues (for example, Social Security) became virtually noncontroversial. We should recognize that there seems to exist a broad and deep public consensus that now (*conservatively*) favors existing government programs such as minimum wage and unemployment compensation.[6]

Let us now consider the trends on a number of social welfare questions consistently asked over several years by the Survey Research Center at the University of Michigan.

One of the broadest social welfare questions asks whether the government should "guarantee a job and a good standard of living." Such a question implies a governmental responsibility for economic welfare that goes beyond the minimum. As Figure 7–1 shows, 57 percent of the population gave assent to this proposition in 1956. By 1978 that proportion had shrunk to 18 percent. The decline was steep from 1960 to 1964 and more gradual thereafter. A portion of the decline can be accounted for by a shift to the "it depends" category.[7] A second item in the social welfare battery has concerned comprehensive national health care. This item has been part of the "unfinished" New Deal agenda for nearly half a century. This particular question has been asked in two forms. In Figure 7–2, the pattern of responses to the item asking whether "the government ought to help people get doctors' and hospital care at low cost" is given.[8] Overall, the proportion favoring national government responsibility for health costs has

123 A Conservative Trend?

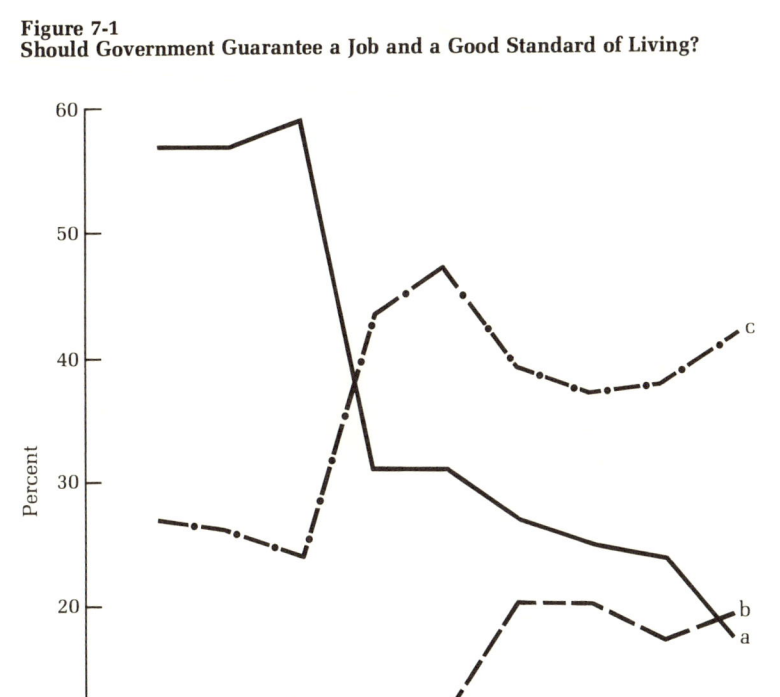

**Figure 7-1
Should Government Guarantee a Job and a Good Standard of Living?**

— a. Gov't. see to jobs
— — b. Depends
—•— c. Each person on his own

No data 1962, 1966, 1970

SOURCE: Warren E. Miller et al., *American National Election Studies Data Sourcebook* (Cambridge: Harvard University Press, 1980), p. 172.

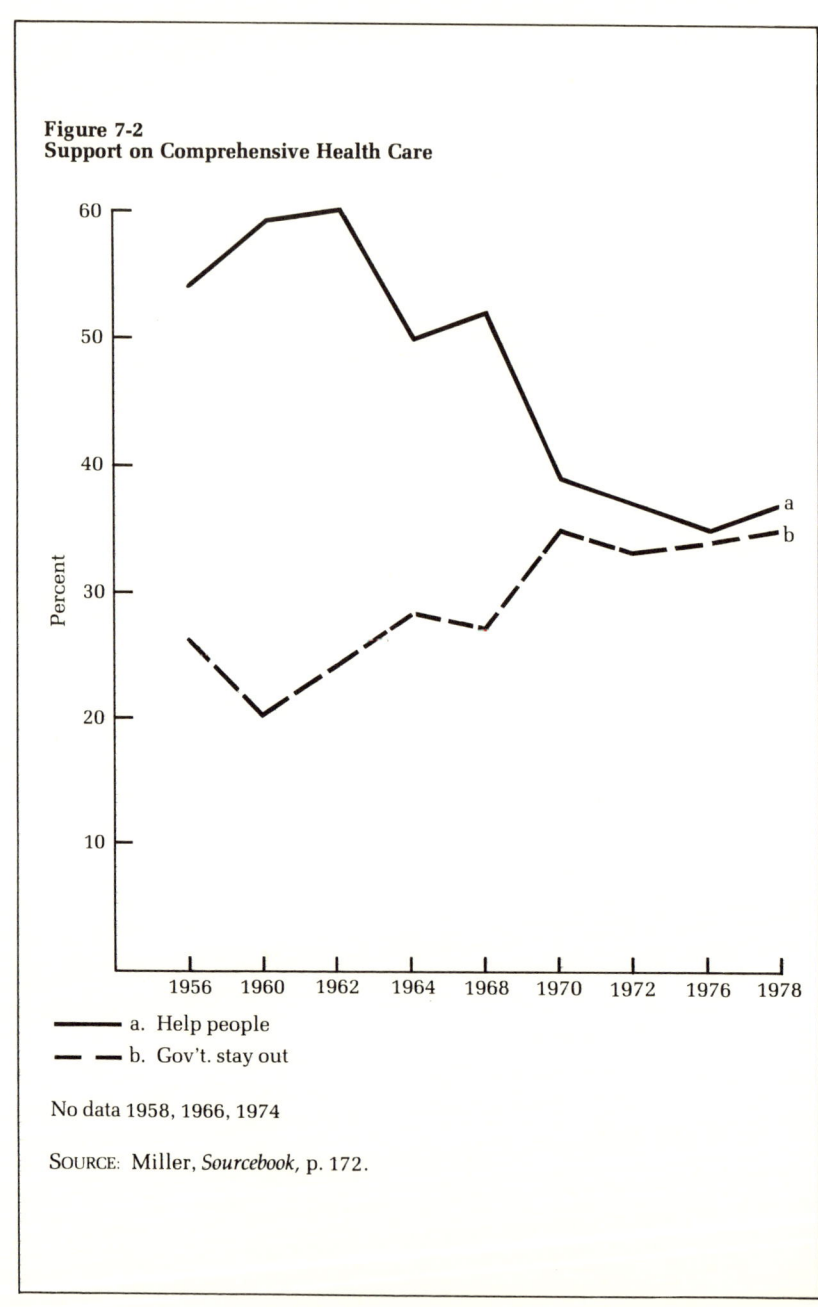

Figure 7-2
Support on Comprehensive Health Care

a. Help people
— — b. Gov't. stay out

No data 1958, 1966, 1974

SOURCE: Miller, *Sourcebook*, p. 172.

declined from 54 to 37. Using a different measure, the percentage favoring a government health plan declined slightly from 40 percent in 1970 to 37 percent in 1978.[9]

A third general welfare issue has been the "power of the federal government." In the 1930s to be for an extension of the powers of the federal government was to be "liberal." In 1964, however, 30 percent of the population (see Figure 7–3) felt that the federal government was "too powerful." By 1978 that figure had grown to 43 percent (the peak was 49 percent in 1976). This item has generated a good deal of comment in the literature because of the evidence that the meaning of the item, in terms of liberalism versus conservatism, has changed—that it no longer distinguishes liberals from conservatives. That is, liberals have become suspicious of big government also.[10] The fact is, however, that conservatives have also accepted the reality of big government, at least in the defense area. Nevertheless, taken in context with other items, the effects on the power of the federal government are consistent with the thesis of a growing conservatism in the mass public.[11]

If we consider these as representative items in the social welfare domain, a trend of increasing conservatism in the past years emerges. Part of that trend may be traced to changed wording or meaning of items. Nevertheless, in 1964 on the three major items an average of nearly 40 percent of the population give social-welfare liberal responses; in 1976, twelve years later, the comparable figure was 26 percent: a trend does exist. It must be kept in mind, however, that this does not mean a preference for "dismantling" existing social programs.[12] Rather, it suggests opposition to further government growth, experimentation, and intervention in the social welfare policy area.

Foreign affairs

A second major policy domain is support for American involvement in international affairs. Historically, "internationalism" has been the more liberal position, and "isolationism" has been con-

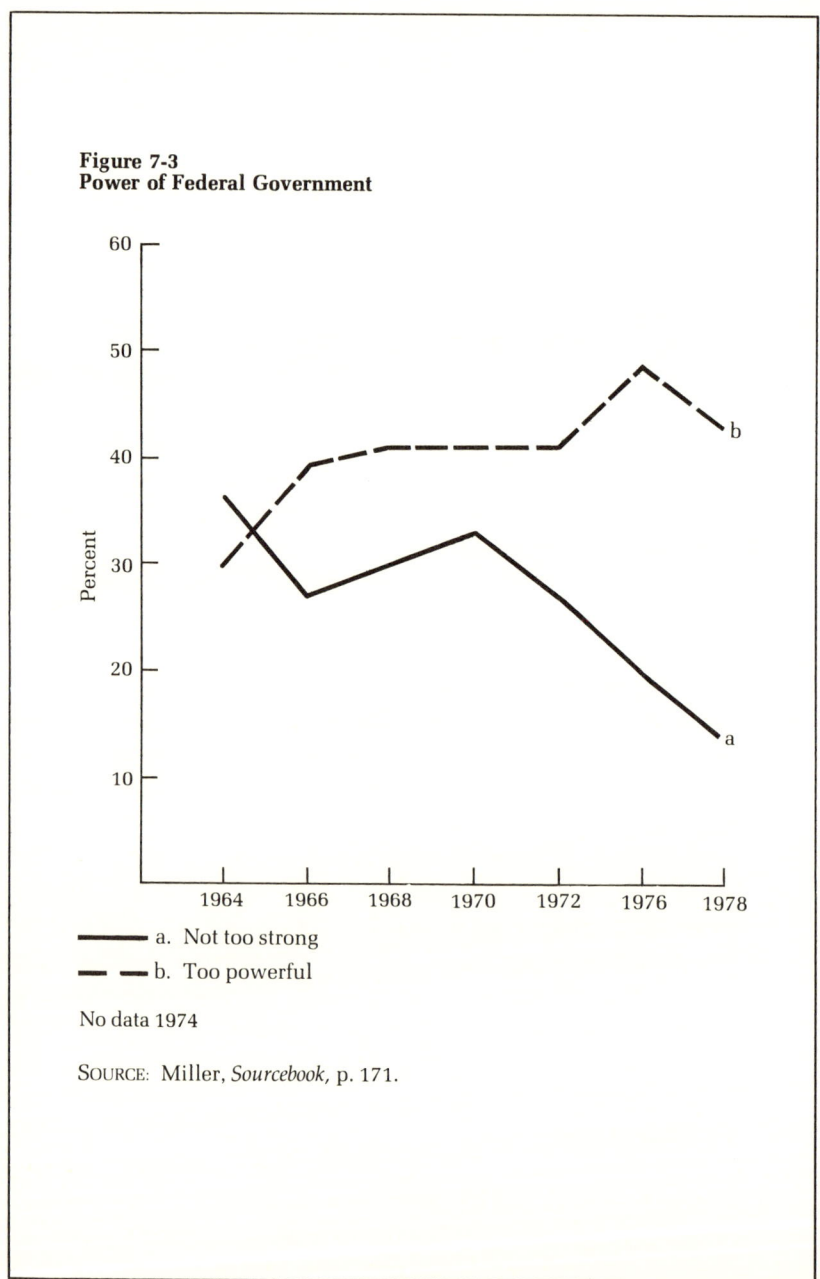

Figure 7-3
Power of Federal Government

a. Not too strong
b. Too powerful

No data 1974

SOURCE: Miller, *Sourcebook*, p. 171.

servative.[13] In its most general terms, support for U. S. participation in international agencies and foreign assistance would still be regarded as liberal. Have American attitudes in this area changed?

Would "this country be better off if we just stayed here and did not concern ourselves with problems in other parts of the world?" This is a classic statement of the internationalist/isolationist division. Figure 7-4 records the pattern of responses. The data make it clear that there has been an increasing acceptance of an international role for the United States in the third quarter of the twentieth century. Only more recently has there been a downturn, although the degree of acceptance of internationalism, broadly defined, is still impressively high. As Dawson noted, "The data indicate the existence of a rather strong and steady consensus in support of the involvement of the U.S. in world affairs."[14] These data are reinforced by findings of Lloyd Free and William Watts that the percentage of "total internationalists" in the American electorate, which had dipped sharply during and just after the Vietnam era, was back to 61 percent in 1980.[15]

In rather sharp contrast to the general internationalism item stand the foreign assistance data in Figure 7-5. This question asks about American willingness to support foreign aid to governments that may not support our foreign policy. Such support has declined sharply since the late 1950s and early 1960s. In the peak year (1964), over half supported foreign assistance, even if other countries "don't stand for the same things we do." By 1976, however, that support had dwindled to 35 percent.

Related to foreign affairs is the question of defense spending. In this realm, an argument could be made that the electorate has become more conservative, if by conservative one meant more likely to support increases in defense spending. For example, in 1974 a clear majority of Americans agreed that the United States "should reduce spending for military and defense purposes."[16] Of course, these figures came from a period when Americans were weary from the Vietnam War experience. Figure 7-6 shows how sharply the public mood on defense spending changed in terms of cutting spending between 1972 and 1976. However, in the

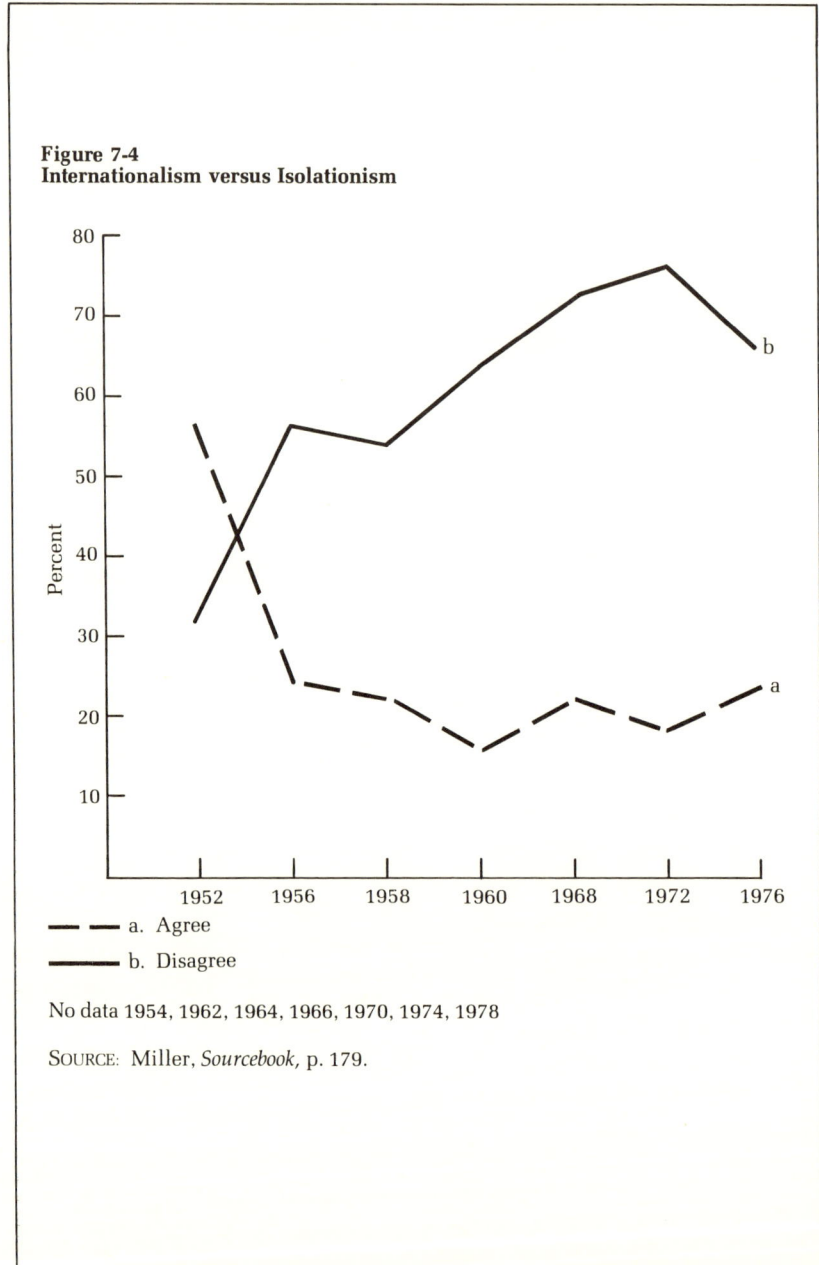

A Conservative Trend?

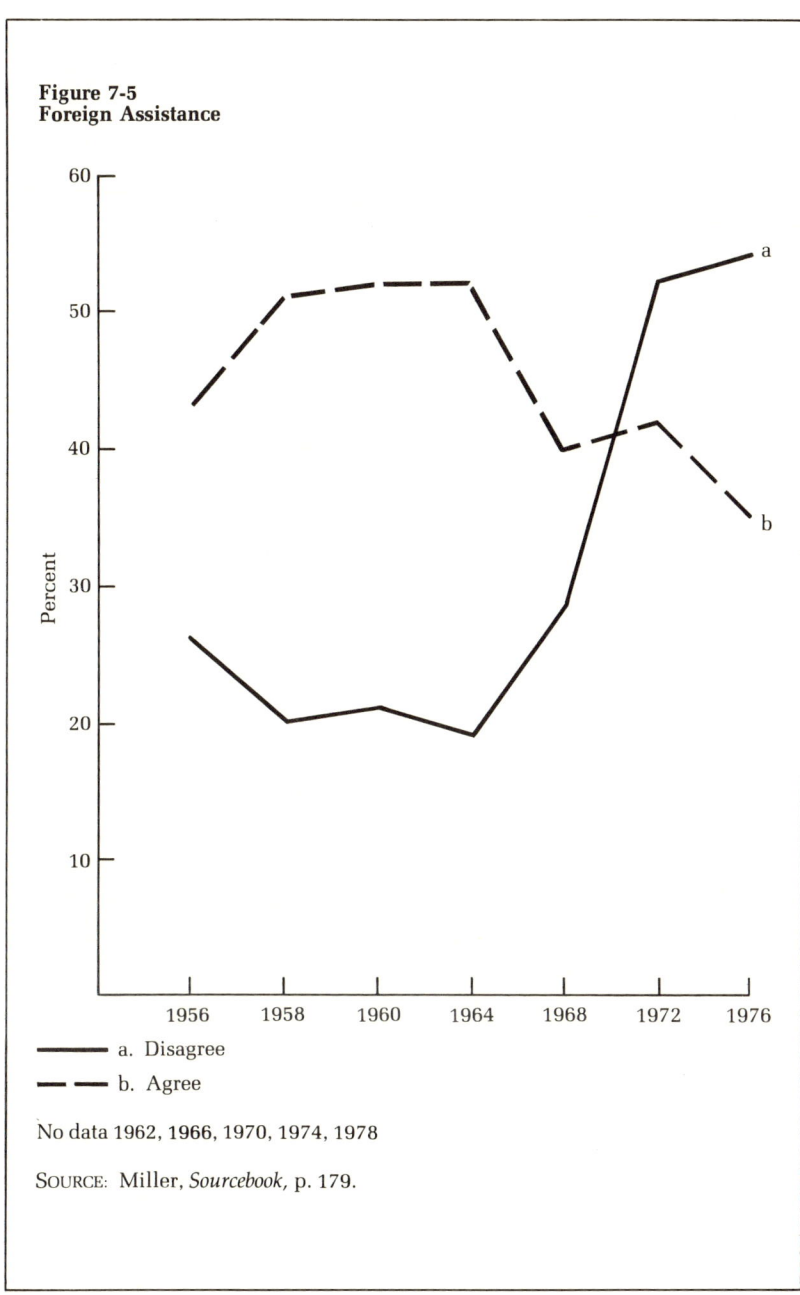

**Figure 7-5
Foreign Assistance**

——— a. Disagree
– – – b. Agree

No data 1962, 1966, 1970, 1974, 1978

SOURCE: Miller, *Sourcebook*, p. 179.

130 Public Opinion and Interest Groups in American Politics

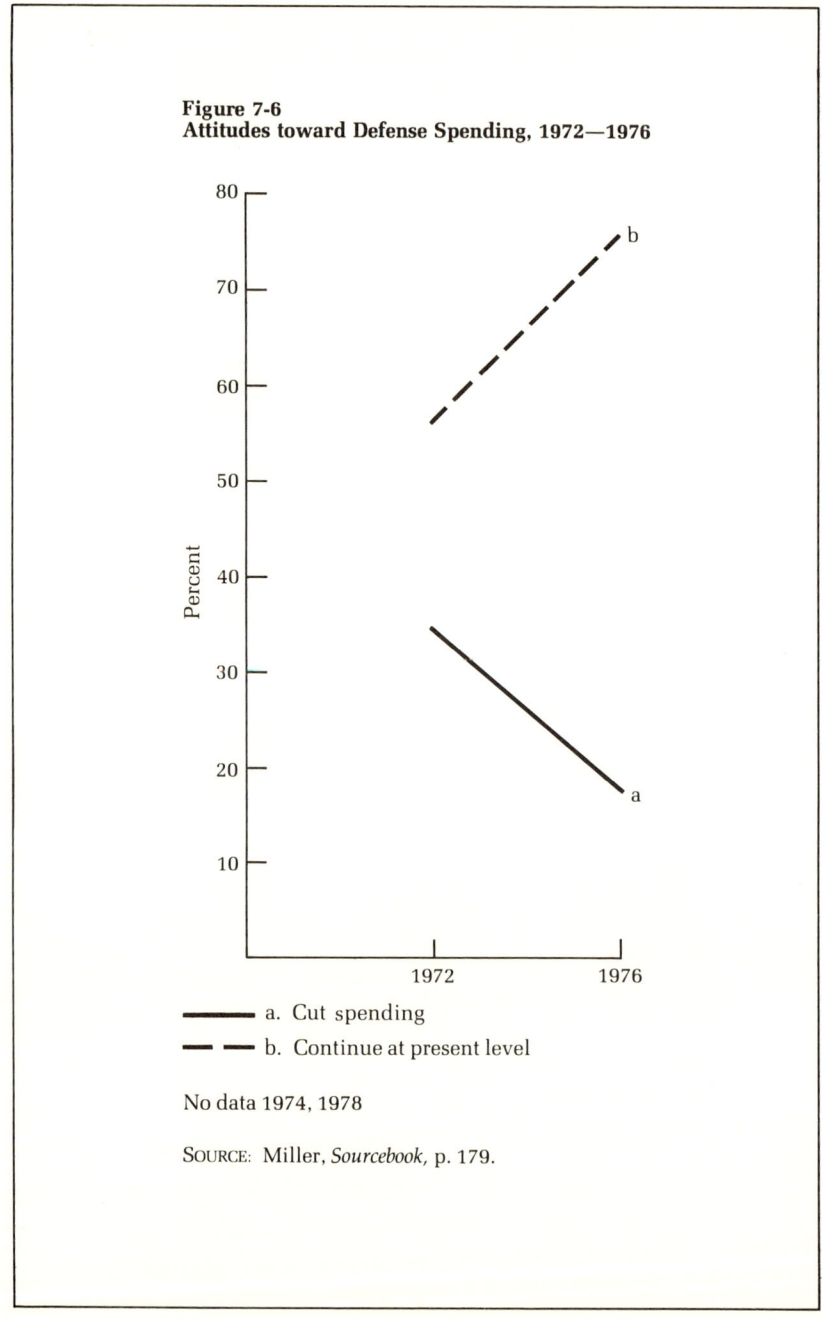

Figure 7-6
Attitudes toward Defense Spending, 1972—1976

a. Cut spending
b. Continue at present level

No data 1974, 1978

SOURCE: Miller, *Sourcebook,* p. 179.

Table 7.1 Defense Spending before and after Iran and Afghanistan Crises (percent)

Defense budget should be:	September 1979	Late January 1980	March 1980
Increased	42	74	55
Decreased	18	5	13
Same	40	20	32

SOURCE: *Public Opinion*, April/May 1980, p. 30.

wake of the Iranian crisis and the Soviet invasion of Afghanistan (1979–80), the public mood altered even more sharply. Table 7–1 gives before and after responses to the defense spending issue recently.

Two points are of interest in Table 7–1. The first is the extraordinary jump between September 1979 and late January 1980, presumably caused by the events mentioned. Yet by March the public had "cooled off" somewhat. Still the level of support for increases was considerably higher than before.

In general, then, we can say that American opinion on foreign affairs is internationalist, but wary of foreign assistance and, after a downturn connected to the Vietnam experience, committed to defense spending at the same or higher levels. Again, a modest shift to the right seems to have taken place.

Civil rights

One area of vast change in public attitudes has been civil rights for minorities, especially black Americans. There is no question that, in the broadest sense, attitudes on civil rights issues have grown more liberal over the past forty years. For example, between

1942 and 1964 the percentage of Americans favoring school integration more than doubled.[17] Since the 1960s, however, the support for a federal government role in this area has slipped.[18]

When one looks at more specific issues, within a more limited period, one sees that the trends are also mixed. On the pro-integration side, from 1972 to 1980 an average of almost 90 percent of white Americans said that "blacks and whites should go to the same schools."[19] In contrast, there was nearly universal opposition to busing as a means of achieving school integration in the 1970s. The percentages expressing support for such a policy have never risen over 10 (see Figure 7–7).

At the same time, support for open housing increased dramatically from 57 percent in 1964 to 85 percent in 1976.[20] Perhaps the most general item that demonstrates the ambivalence of contemporary attitudes on race is one concerning general societal segregation or desegregation. From 1964 to 1978 there has been a consistent decline in the support for an overtly segregated society, from just over 20 to about 5 percent. From 1964 to 1972 there was a consistent increase in the support for a desegregated society (from just over 30 to 45 percent). But support has dropped off since then. In the period from 1964 to 1978 an in-between position was selected by a plurality of the population. The degree of that support, however, has gone from under 50 to over 50 percent (see Figure 7–8).

Hard-line segregationist sentiments are no longer an acceptable public response in the United States. Nevertheless, Americans clearly do not fully and enthusiastically accept the full civil rights/integration agenda. We shall see in the next chapter that there are fairly sharp divisions by race on civil rights and economic issues.

A Note on Social Attitudes

We have examined three standard policy areas: social welfare, foreign policy, and civil rights. But one of the striking aspects of recent political change is the extent to which social attitudes such

A Conservative Trend?

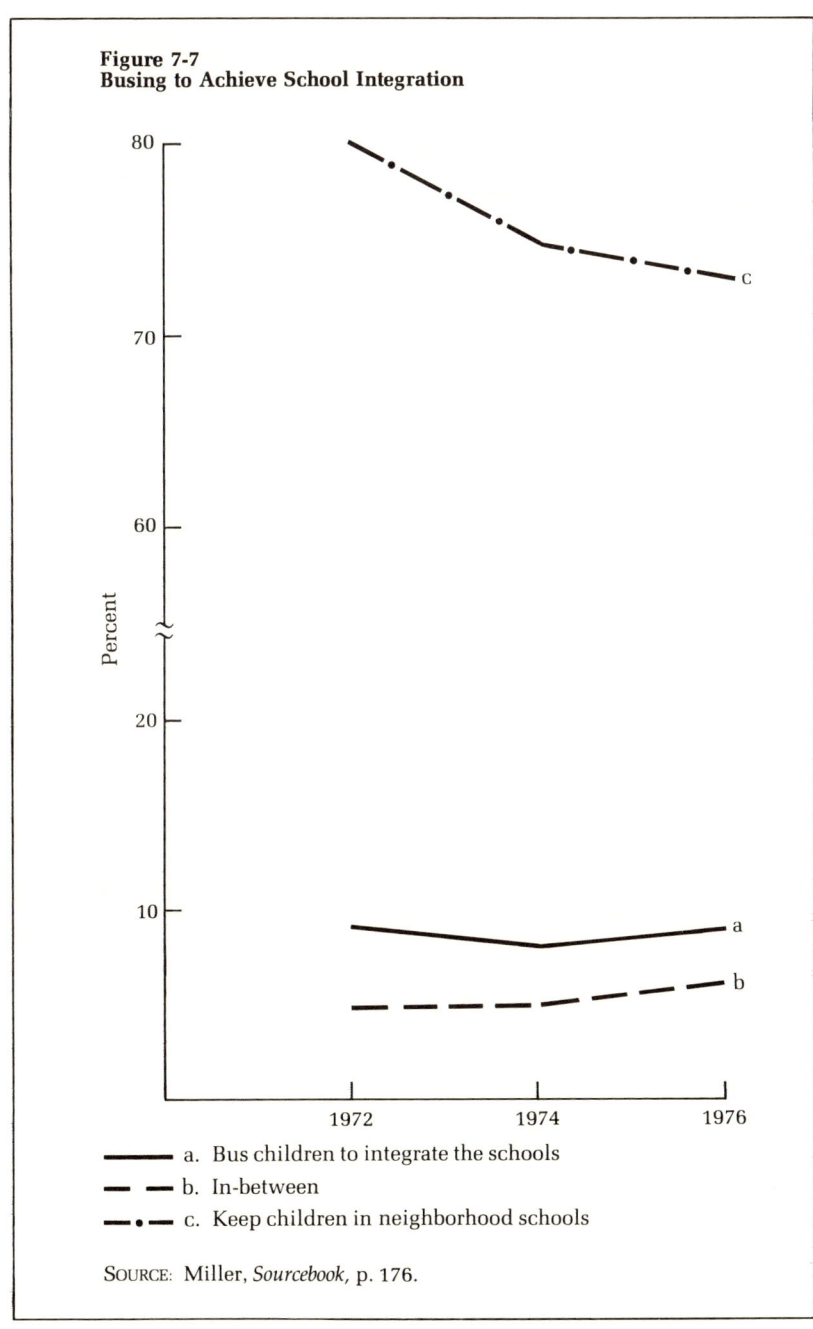

**Figure 7-7
Busing to Achieve School Integration**

a. Bus children to integrate the schools
b. In-between
c. Keep children in neighborhood schools

SOURCE: Miller, *Sourcebook*, p. 176.

134 Public Opinion and Interest Groups in American Politics

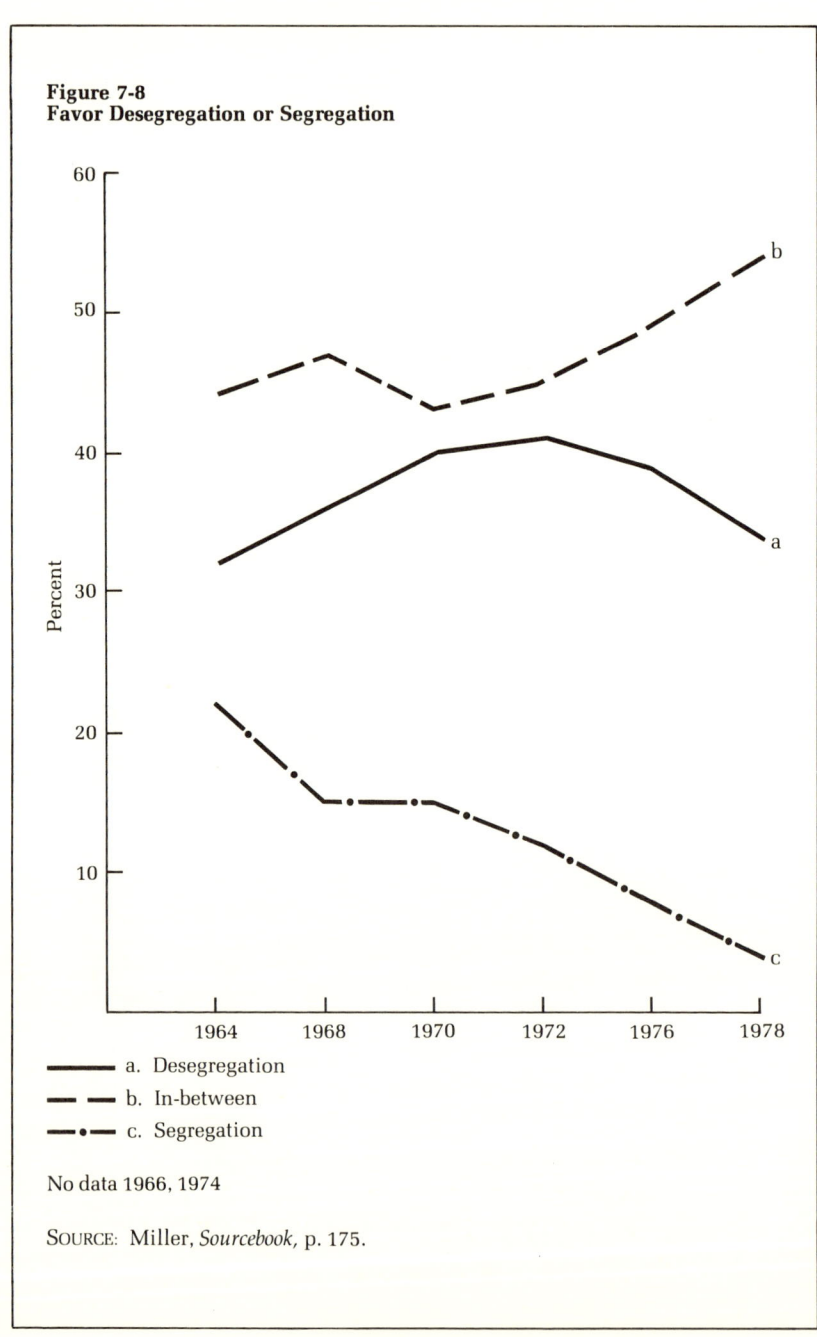

Figure 7-8
Favor Desegregation or Segregation

——— a. Desegregation
— — b. In-between
—•— c. Segregation

No data 1966, 1974

SOURCE: Miller, *Sourcebook*, p. 175.

as those concerning personal values have intruded into the political realm. Again, it is difficult to assess whether these are clear ideological trends. Some brief examples make the point.

In the realm of social attitudes, it could be claimed that there is an increasing trend toward conservatism. For example, from the mid-1950s to the mid-1960s a declining number of Americans favored the death penalty. Since then, those in favor have increased to the point where now two thirds support it. The data are given in Table 7-2.

Table 7.2 Public Sentiment on the Death Penalty, 1953–1981

	1953	1960	1966	1972	1978	1981
Percentage favoring death penalty for murder	68	51	42	57	62	66

SOURCE: Gallup Poll, reported in *Chicago Sun-Times*, March 1, 1981.

It is easy to speculate that the changes recorded in Table 7-2 are rather direct responses to changing perceptions and public attitudes. Until the mid-1960s there was a growing tide of opinion that the death penalty was unfairly applied and inhumane. Then the response to general increases in crime and highly visible and spectacular murders (including assassinations) sparked a reversal of public attitudes. However, whether this means a general shift in the conservative direction is problematic. Opinion seems much more responsive to specific events than to general ideological outlooks.

In other social areas, the trends are not as clear. For example, there is evidence of growing acceptance of premarital sex and use of marijuana.[21] Therefore, while a case could be made for growing conservatism in some specific social policy areas, it would be dangerous to overgeneralize such a conclusion.

Liberalism/Conservatism

We have examined three policy areas: social welfare, foreign policy (internationalism/isolationism), and civil rights, as well as a few social issues. If we turn from issue domains, what have been the general trends in terms of a liberal/conservative ideology? If there has been a clear conservative trend, it ought to show up in Figure 7–9. No such trend can be detected from 1964 to 1976. Although the percentages claiming a liberal position have declined, there was no marked upsurge in conservative support in the 1970s. While the "conservative" category is the largest, it contained less than 40 percent of the population in 1976. The clearest recent trend is the growth of the "neutral" category.

If the conclusion is that there has been no marked upsurge in conservative ideology, how can we explain the Reagan victory in 1980 or the conservative gains in the U. S. Senate in 1978 and 1980? Americans vote less on ideology than on a pragmatic judgment of performance in office. And even where there is a shift in mass attitudes in a conservative direction, the best bet is that this is a direct response to specific events and trends such as inflation. Therefore, the election results do not reflect a clear-cut mandate for conservative ideology but rather a repudiation of the performance of the Carter administration and traditional liberal answers to pressing problems: a rejection but not an affirmation.

A Move to the Right?

The material in this chapter shows how complex making judgments about the general drift of opinion is. Fragments of data can be used to support almost any position—movement to the right, left, or center. Nevertheless, the weight of the evidence would support an interpretation of a modest move to the right.[22] This conclusion, however, must be qualified.

137 A Conservative Trend?

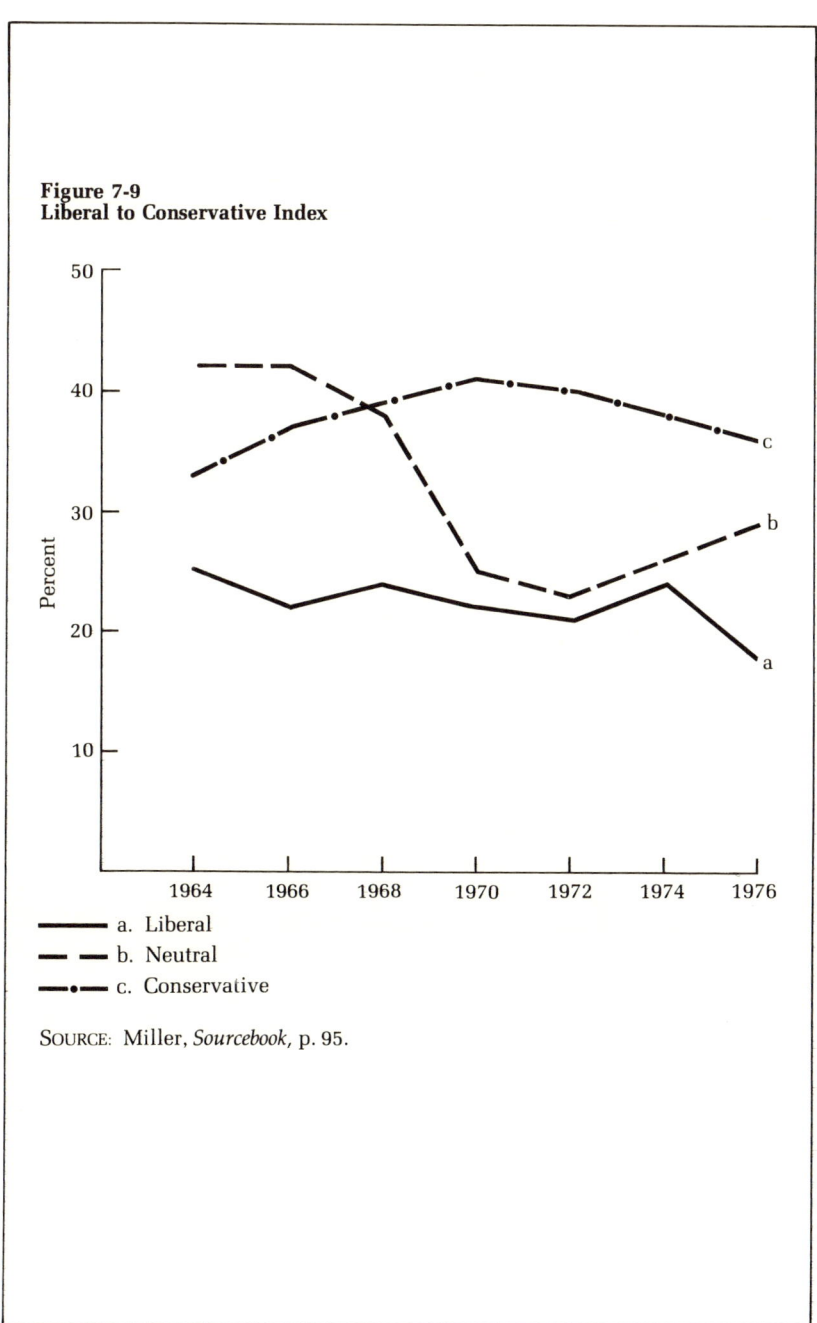

**Figure 7-9
Liberal to Conservative Index**

—— a. Liberal
– – b. Neutral
—•— c. Conservative

SOURCE: Miller, *Sourcebook*, p. 95.

The most important qualification is that each policy area (and the general ideological question) produces a mixed, not crystal clear, trend of responses. One cannot infer a clear, consistent, and unadulterated conservative trend in social welfare, foreign policy, civil rights, or social policy. There are specific questions on which conservative positions dominate and on which the trend has been in the conservative direction. Defense spending is a good example. But in each instance, stubborn contradictory findings stand out. For example, we find strong support for open housing in the civil rights area. Nor can we conclude from the data on liberal/conservative ideology that there has been an unambiguous shift to the right. American opinion seems to reflect events. It drifts to the left when events seem to dictate that response; it becomes more conservative as other events tilt the nation in the other direction.

There is another important point. Even if it appeared that the entire population were moving toward the right, this would not mean that individuals were moving consistently in that direction. If we look at individual patterns of opinion, we find that most people hold mixed opinions—not clearly liberal or conservative.[23]

Suppose we consider the interrelationships of some of the policy domains we have considered. For example, there has consistently been only a modest relationship between positions on social welfare and integration issues, although that relationship increased during the 1960s. There is also some relationship between positions on social welfare and integration issues and the newer social issues. The relationships between the social welfare and foreign policy domains are consistently weak.[24] Such relationships tend to be strikingly modest overall. It is simply dangerous to infer that a shift in mass attitudes is resulting in consistent, across-the-board liberals and conservatives.

A final word of caution. Mass opinion does not automatically translate into policy. The conservative drift does not mean that there will necessarily be a major change in policy. A governing coalition must still be constructed. In Chapter Eleven we will examine the efforts of the Reagan administration to construct such a coalition.

NOTES
CHAPTER SEVEN

[1] See Theodore Lowi, *The End of Liberalism*, 2nd ed., (New York: Norton, 1979), Chapters 1–3.
[2] David Broder et al., *The Pursuit of the Presidency* (New York: Berkley, 1980), p. 326.
[3] *Institute for Social Research Newsletter*, Spring 1981, p. 6.
[4] Warren E. Miller and Donald E. Stokes, "Constituency Influence in Congress," in Angus Campbell et al., *Elections and the Political Order* (New York: Wiley, 1966), p. 356.
[5] On the mass party divisions, see Gerald Pomper, *Voter's Choice* (New York: Dodd, Mead, 1975), p. 168, table 8.1 (items on medical care and job guarantees); on the elite divisions, see Herbert McClosky et al., "Issue Conflict and Consensus among Party Leaders and Followers," *American Political Science Review* 54 (June 1960): 406–27.
[6] Robert S. Erikson et al., *American Public Opinion* (New York: Wiley, 1980), p. 35. The authors have concluded that "most existing social welfare programs receive overwhelming support."
[7] Between 1960 and 1964 the wording on this item changed. This could account for the steep drop, or part thereof, from 1960 to 1964. Of course, it cannot account for the continued decline after 1964. For a discussion, see Norman Nie et al., *The Changing American Voter* (Cambridge, Mass.: Harvard University Press, 1979), pp. 391–92.
[8] Ibid.
[9] See Warren E. Miller et al., *American National Election Studies Data Sourcebook* (Cambridge, Mass.: Harvard University Press, 1980), p. 172.
[10] Nie et al., *Voter*, pp. 125–28.
[11] The point is that when even "liberals" reject big government, a marked change has occurred in the mass public and public philosophy.
[12] When the Reagan administration came to power in 1981 it sought to control federal spending, particularly in the social welfare area. A *New York Times/CBS News Poll* found that Americans favored a balanced budget, "but when asked about specific programs... only one fourth or less of those questioned favored reduced spending levels." *St. Louis Post-Dispatch*, Feb. 8, 1981, p. 6–A.
[13] There is, however, a great potential for confusion here. For example, being liberal on social welfare has not necessarily been an indication of internationalist leanings: many midwestern and western progressives were isolationists, and many domestic liberals opposed the Vietnam intervention.

[14] Richard E. Dawson, *Public Opinion and Contemporary Disarray* (New York: Harper & Row, 1973), pp. 30–31.

[15] Lloyd Free and William Watts, "Internationalism Comes of Age... Again," *Public Opinion*, Apr./May 1980, p. 49. Also see Daniel Yankelovich, "Cautious Internationalism," *Public Opinion*, Mar./Apr. 1978, pp. 12–16

[16] See the *Gallup Opinion Index*, Nov. 1974, p. 10.

[17] Rita James Simon, *Public Opinion in America* (Chicago: Markham, 1974), p. 58.

[18] Miller, *Sourcebook*, p. 176.

[19] *Public Opinion*, Oct./Nov. 1980, p. 28.

[20] Miller, *Sourcebook*, p. 177.

[21] *Public Opinion*, Dec./Jan. 1980, p. 28.

[22] In June of 1981, *Time* concluded (on the basis of a Yankelovich survey) that "a new American consensus is in the making. And, yes, it is conservative.... But it is not the lockstep ideology of the Moral Majority and other far-right zealots, and in many details the consensus differs from the social vision of Ronald Reagan,...a majority of the U.S. public favors the Equal Rights Amendment, opposes making abortions illegal and is strongly in favor of gun control." John F. Stacks, "It's Rightward On," *Time*, June 1, 1981, p. 12.

[23] Erikson, *Opinion*, pp. 65–67. For a comprehensive analysis of the opinions of self-proclaimed conservatives on a wide variety of current issues, which illustrates the heterogeneity of opinion by those who claim the label, see *Public Opinion*, Feb./March 1981, pp. 19–31.

[23] Nie, *Voter*, pp. 124, 135, 136.

CHAPTER 8

THE GROUP BASES OF OPINION

In the previous chapter we scrutinized the assumption that the United States has been moving to the right politically, and we gave a qualified assent to the proposition. But general descriptions of trends in public opinion are always troubling, for they may conceal as well as reveal. For example, if opinion shifts took place in two equal-sized groups but in opposite directions, it would appear from the general data that no change had taken place. This chapter will look at opinion changes within various demographic groups in four areas: social welfare policy, civil rights, foreign policy, and liberalism/conservatism.

Groups and Social Welfare Policy

As we noted in Chapter Seven, the core set of issues generated by the New Deal concerned the role of the national government in ensuring social welfare. In general, we would assume a clear, class-based distinction between less advantaged and more advantaged groups on social welfare policies solely out of self-interest. As Alan D. Monroe has argued, "We suspect that a person's economic position may be a determinant of some of his preferences both because that position determines many other attributes of his life...and because so many issues of public policy seem to involve the allocation of advantages and disadvantages to different economic groups."[1] Indeed, the general finding is that those with lower incomes, less education, and lower occupational status tend to be more liberal on social welfare issues than those with higher income, more education, and higher occupational status.[2]

As an example, let us take the power-of-the-federal-government issue used in Chapter Seven. As an initial illustration, we will examine data from 1964. We will use three polar comparisons: highest versus lowest income, grade school versus college education, and professionals versus blue-collar workers.[3]

Table 8.1 Relationship of Social Status and Response to Power of Federal Government, 1964

		Income	Education	Occupation
Percentage difference index*	High	−22	−9	−17
	Low	15	19	19
Total difference		37	28	36

SOURCE: Miller, Sourcebook, p. 181.
*Percentage saying federal government not too strong minus percentage saying too strong. Negative numbers mean "conservative" responses predominate.

The table needs some interpretation. The percentage difference index (PDI) is the proportion saying the federal government is not too strong minus the proportion saying it is too powerful. Thus a negative number indicates a "conservative" response and a positive number a "liberal" one. Note in each case that the lower-status groups are clearly more liberal. The total difference between the two groups is the absolute sum of the PDI. In this case, the sharpest difference is between the extreme income groups, which include small numbers of the total population (about one quarter). Table 8−1 illustrates two important points. The first is that the predicted relationships do obtain. Lower status is associated with liberalism on social welfare policy. The second is that they are nowhere near their theoretical limits (if 75 percent of each group opposed 75 percent of the other, the total difference would be 100). Status and liberalism were only imperfectly correlated in 1964.

We now raise the issue of whether class-related differences on traditional liberal/conservative social issues have narrowed recently. There are several reasons to expect such a development.

One is the decline in salience of such issues. The generation that directly experienced the depression is fading. A second is the increased income of workers. Finally, if there has been a general trend to the right in American politics, we might expect to find indications in reduced class differences on social welfare issues.

Previous analyses support such expectations. Richard E. Dawson has written that "socio-economic conditions...have become less important in structuring opinion differences on economic welfare."[4] Robert Erikson et al. report that "there is some indication that class differences in social-welfare attitudes are not as great today as they have been in the past."[5] In Table 8-2 we undertake a systematic examination of that proposition. The table

Table 8.2 Class Differences on Social Welfare Issues, 1964–1976

	Total Difference*					
	High vs. low income		High vs. low education		Prof. vs. blue-collar	
	1964	1976	1964	1976	1964	1976
Power of federal government	37	44	28	24	36	2
Medical care (government responsibility)	62	68	61	20	42	21
Job, standard of living (gov't responsibility)	57	69	43	35	39	30

SOURCE: Miller, Sourcebook, pp. 181, 185, 189.

*Constructed from the percentage difference index. If signs are different, total difference equals absolute sum. If signs are same, total difference equals absolute difference.

displays responses by groups to three standard items on social welfare policy used in Chapter Seven. As the reader will recall, each item showed increased conservatism in the whole public.

Table 8–2 is quite revealing. The comparisons support the hypothesis of reduced differences. In each case, the comparisons by education and occupation show a narrowing. In the case of income, it must be remembered that we are using extreme categories. At the income extremes, class differences are as great, or greater, than previously. If we moved in a step at both ends of the income continuum, however, we would find some narrowing of differences.[6] The important point is that the weight of the evidence supports the expectation that differences by class on social welfare issues have become less sharp.

Can we now determine precisely in which groups the observed changes have taken place? Have lower-status Americans become more conservative? Table 8–3 addresses that issue.

The general answer is that, while there has been an overall trend toward conservatism, relatively more change in that direction has taken place among those with less education and lower-status occupations. (In two instances, there was a slight liberal-

Table 8.3 Changes in Social Welfare Attitudes by Education and Occupation, 1964–1976

	Power of Fed. Gov't.			Medical Care			Job		
	1964	1976	Change	1964	1976	Change	1964	1976	Change
High educ.	−9*	−36	−27	−8	−5	+3	−33	−29	+4
Low educ.	19	−12	−31	53	15	−38	10	6	−4
Professional	−17	−33	−16	−4	−9	−5	−35	−35	0
Blue-collar	19	−31	−50	38	12	−26	4	−5	−9

SOURCE: Miller, Sourcebook, pp. 181, 185, 189.
*Figures are PDIs. Negative numbers equal predominance of conservative positions.

ization of opinion among those with higher education.) In all, it seems that a case can be made for the view that the working class has become less liberal on the basic New Deal issues. As Table 8–3 shows, this does not mean that differences on social welfare issues have been wiped out. It does mean that, for example, more blue-collar workers take the conservative side than the liberal side on the question of government responsibility to ensure jobs and a good standard of living. This is a historical shift. The significance of such a change is twofold. First, it means that one of the prime determinants of political conflict has been eroded. To a degree, class, issue position, and party identification were closely aligned as a result of the New Deal. National politics had a certain structure to it. The diminishing of class-related differences on social welfare may be seen as an index of the decline of the New Deal party system and ought to be paralleled by declines in the relationship of class to voting behavior and partisan identification (see Chapter Nine). As Dawson has written, "The waning influence of social-economic position in structuring political divisions and agreements represents the demise of a major ordering component and of significant political reference points."[7]

The other significant aspect of the change is the opportunity for the Republican party to make inroads into the core support of the Democratic party by conservative appeals. This is a delicate task because these groups, and the population in general, still support existing government programs such as Social Security. What they oppose is dramatic expansion of government activity in this field.

The most obvious possible exception to these observations is the response of black Americans to social welfare issues. Blacks are clearly more liberal than the rest of the population on these issues,[8] probably for class-related reasons. Blacks, as a group, have the most to gain from an expansion of national government responsibility in social welfare. Let us consider the response of blacks (as opposed to whites) to these same social welfare issues.

The results of Table 8–4 are most surprising. Blacks are no exception to the trend of (relatively) increased conservatism in American politics. Although there remain sharp black/white dif-

Table 8.4 Change in Social Welfare Attitudes
of Black versus White Americans, 1964–1976

	Blacks			Whites		
	1964	1976	Change	1964	1976	Change
Power of federal government	52*	4	−48	0	−34	−34
Medical care (government responsibility)	77	32	−45	24	−4	−28
Job, standard of living (gov't responsibility)	80	38	−42	25	−21	−46

SOURCE: Miller, *Sourcebook*, pp. 181, 185, 189.   *Figures are PDIs.

ferences on these issues, both groups have moved in the same direction, and black change has been greater.[9] And nonetheless, black support for Democratic presidential candidates, as we shall see in Chapter Nine, remains extraordinarily high.

Foreign Policy

How does status relate to liberalism on foreign policy issues? Our general expectation is that higher status should correlate with liberalism on this noneconomic issue. For example, Lipset tells us that "when liberalism is defined in non-economic terms—as support of civil liberties, internationalism, etc.—...The more well-to-do are more liberal, the poorer are more intolerant."[10] Higher levels of education are often cited as the explanation for these differences. It is asserted that education leads to greater tolerance of differences and a longer-range view of politics and self-interest. More recent data tend to continue to support these contentions: "For example, people of higher status and education are most in favor of such internationalist policies as foreign aid, trading with Communist nations, and admitting Red China to the United Nations."[11] This expectation is confirmed by data from Miller's *American National Election Studies Data Sourcebook*. Let us consider the general internationalism/isolationism item. The item asks if the United States "would be better off if we just stayed home and did not concern ourselves with problems in other parts of the world?" Table 8–5 gives the responses by education, race, and occupation for 1960 and 1976.

Table 8.5 Internationalism by Race, Education, and Occupation, 1960, 1976

	Race		Education		Occupation	
	Black	White	College	Grade School	Prof.	Blue Collar
1960 PDI*	34	49	78	20	80	54
1976 PDI	−3	46	70	−15	66	34

SOURCE: Miller et al., *Sourcebook*, p. 235.

*Percentage who disagree minus percentage who agree. Positive numbers equal internationalist position.

Table 8–5 reveals two points clearly. The first is that status is indeed correlated with internationalism in the expected direction. The second is that, whatever decrease in overall internationalism has taken place, the bulk of the change is due to the increased isolationist sentiments of blacks, blue-collar workers, and those with a grade school education. These changes may reflect rather directly disenchantment with American interventionism, particularly in Vietnam. It has been found, for example, that people of lower status were more inclined to oppose American involvement in Vietnam than were those of higher status.[12]

Civil Rights

As with foreign policy, the primary expectation about the relationship of status to civil rights attitudes is that those with higher status will be more in favor (the obvious exception is that we expect blacks to be more in favor than whites): "Regarding white attitudes toward civil rights for Negroes, liberalism or prointegration sentiment increases somewhat with status."[13] In this section, we will examine both status differences on civil rights issues and changes. We will begin with two items: general desegregation versus segregation, and school integration.

Table 8.6 Attitudes toward Desegegation by Status, 1964, 1976

	College	Grade sch.	Professional	Blue-collar	Race White	Black
1964 PDI*	29	−8	22	9	2	66
1976 PDI	47	13	45	22	24	69
Change	+18	+21	+23	+13	+22	+3

SOURCE: Miller et al., Sourcebook, p. 209.
*PDI equals percentage of "desegregation" minus percentage of "segregation."

Table 8–6 would certainly seem to suggest that support for integration has increased among all status groups and especially among whites. While status differences continue to exist on civil rights, the table suggests a liberalization of attitudes on race among those of lower education and occupation.[14]

Table 8–7 looks at the school integration issue in a similar manner.

Table 8.7 Attitudes toward School Desegregation by Status, 1964, 1976

	College	Grade sch.	Professional	Blue-collar	Race	
					White	Black
1964 PDI*	11	−7	1	11	−4	56
1976 PDI	−12	−8	−12	−16	−23	52
Change	−23	−1	−13	−27	−19	−4

SOURCE: Miller et al., Sourcebook, p. 217.
*PDI equals percentage "desegregation" minus percentage "segregation."

School integration is quite another matter. In 1964 the higher-status/more liberal relationship held up for both education and occupation. It was not as clear in 1976, however. Among those with a college education, a considerable "illiberal" trend had taken place so that those with higher education were actually less liberal. In occupation, a decrease in liberalism had taken place among both professionals and blue-collar workers. The data on race show clearly a growing polarization on school desegregation caused by the decreased white support of a national government role in school desegregation.

What about the most controversial of the recent civil rights issues, school busing? The data on that issue by education, occupation, and race for 1972 and 1976 show some decrease in opposition to busing among those with low education and among blue-collar workers, no change among those with high education or among professional workers, and increased black/white polarization on that issue. Except for black Americans (in 1976), all other groups remained steadfastly opposed to busing.[15]

The trends in black/white differences on civil rights seem to depend on the nature of the issues. Where the issues are remote and general, some convergence in opinion has taken place. Where the issues are more immediate and specific, as well as controversial, decreased liberalization among whites has brought divergence.

Status and Conservatism

In Chapter Seven, we discussed the inconclusive trends with respect to the general self-identification measures of liberalism/conservatism. Now we will examine trends within status groups. The general expectation would be that higher status would be associated with greater conservatism. This expectation is clearly based on the assumption that liberalism is primarily thought of in social welfare terms. Two recent changes, however, could upset that expectation. One is the growing liberalism of the new, affluent, and highly educated middle class. This group embraces a "new liberalism"—largely rooted in noneconomic (or style) issues as opposed to the old social welfare–based liberalism of the New Deal.[16] Such a change could actually result in an inversion of the old class structure or, as some have put it, "Marxism turned upside down."[17] The second change is the growing conservatism of lower-status groups on social welfare issues. In combination, these trends could reduce the expected relationship between status and self-identified ideology.

Table 8–8 examines the self-placement of liberal and conservative by status groups for 1972 and 1976.

Table 8.8 Self-placement on Liberal/Conservative Scale by Status Groups, 1972, 1976

	College	Grade sch.	Professional	Blue-collar	Black	White
1972 PDI*	−2	−6	−11	−4	23	−12
1976 PDI	−11	−7	−19	−7	22	−13
Change	−9	−1	−8	−3	−1	−1

SOURCE: Miller et al., Sourcebook, p. 100.
*PDI equals percentage liberal minus percentage conservative. A minus score means a predominance of conservative opinion.

In terms of education and occupation, the only instance of inversion (that is, of higher status being more liberal) is in 1972 (education). Moreover, the trend has been for higher-status groups to become more conservative. But what is striking about the data is that status makes so little difference in terms of self-identification as a liberal or conservative.

Race is a different matter, however. Two points stand out there. The first is that there was almost no change from 1964 to 1976. The second is that blacks clearly adopt the liberal designation much more frequently than whites.

One explanation of these findings is that (except for blacks) the meaning of liberalism/conservatism has changed sufficiently so that it is no longer exclusively, or even primarily, identified with the social welfare dimension. And "in most [noneconomic] policy areas, whites in the higher socioeconomic status categories have become decisively more liberal than the middle and lower cohorts."[18] This does not mean they adopt the designation "liberal." It does mean they are more likely to favor change as opposed to the status quo, especially on noneconomic and life-style issues.

Noneconomic Liberalism

Suppose we take one of the newer issues that is primarily noneconomic and examine attitudes of status groups. If the basic thesis is correct, higher-status groups should (as in the civil rights and foreign relations areas) turn out to be more liberal. The women's rights issue is a good example. The following table explores the attitudes of social groups toward an equal role for women.

Table 8.9 Equal Role for Women by Social Groups, 1978

	College	Grade sch.	Professional	Blue-collar	White	Black
PDI*	59	−5	59	24	34	41

SOURCE: Miller et al., *Sourcebook*, p. 227.
*PDI equals percentage equal role minus percentage role interest. Positive numbers mean "liberal."

In terms of education and occupation, the table clearly supports the expectation. Interestingly, blacks are more liberal than whites on the role of women.

The fact is that on a broad range of social and noneconomic questions, higher-status individuals are more liberal. In a burst of enthusiasm, Louis Harris noted in the mid-1970s that "the thrust for change—with the exception of the blacks and Chicanos—was coming from the most privileged.... The old economic, class divisions had been blurred and were almost extinct."[19] From this, Harris drew the conclusion that change-oriented candidates would be successful in the future. To a degree, he was correct for 1976 but badly wrong for 1980. He failed to recognize that inflation, resentment of big government, and the impact of international events would make the conservative perspective attractive on economic and foreign-policy grounds. Timing and issue salience are everything in politics.

Conclusions

Several major findings and conclusions drawn in this chapter need to be highlighted:

1. There is evidence that class differences on social welfare issues have narrowed (even among blacks).
2. Isolationist sentiments have increased among lower-status groups.
3. On civil rights, evidence points to black/white polarization on issues such as busing.
4. There are no marked differences between status groups on self-identification as liberal or conservative.
5. Higher-status groups are more liberal on noneconomic issues.

These findings lead to two important conclusions. The first is that the attitudinal base for liberalism, defined in terms of social welfare, has withered in its natural constituency: lower-status groups. As the party that has traditionally been identified with that type of liberalism, this is bad news for the Democrats. We should be able to detect erosion in group support for the party on that basis. This is the subject of the next chapter.

The second conclusion is that liberalism is not dead: it has changed its face. New issues—women's rights, social issues, environmental and consumer issues, abortion rights, and so forth—have developed. These issues are particularly attractive to the young, the well-educated, and the affluent. There is a new "crosscutting" in American politics in which liberalism on the newer issues may be crosscut by conservatism on the older ones or vice versa. Thus a young, well-educated voter might favor a conservative candidate on economic grounds and a liberal one on lifestyle issues. The effect on political behavior—voting, for instance—will depend on which set of issues is predominant at a given time.

NOTES
CHAPTER EIGHT

[1] Alan D. Monroe, *Public Opinion in America* (New York: Dodd, Mead, 1975), p. 84.
[2] Robert S. Erikson et al., *American Public Opinion* (New York: Wiley, 1980), p. 164.
[3] In the case of income, the comparison is between these in the 0–16th percentile versus those in the 95–100th percentile. All comparisons ignore middle categories. See Warren E. Miller et al., *American National Election Studies Data Sourcebook 1952–1978* (Cambridge, Mass.: Harvard University Press, 1980), p. 181. All of these are "objective" measures of status or class. For a good discussion of the merits of objective versus subjective measures, see V. O. Key, Jr., *Public Opinion and American Democracy* (New York: Knopf, 1967), pp. 132–42.
[4] Richard E. Dawson, *Public Opinion and Contemporary Disarray* (New York: Harper & Row, 1973), p. 90.
[5] Erikson, p. 157.
[6] Miller et al., pp. 181, 185, 189.
[7] Dawson, p. 188.
[8] "On all of the social welfare...issues the blacks are decidedly more liberal than whites," Dawson, p. 117.
[9] As we pointed out in Chapter Six, some argue that the meaning of the "power of the federal government" item has changed. Although that could account for the findings with respect to that item, it does not explain the changes on the medical care and job and standard of living items.
[10] Seymour Martin Lipset, *Political Man* (Garden City, N.Y.: Doubleday-Anchor, 1963), p. 92.
[11] Erikson et al., p. 161.
[12] Ibid., p. 162.
[13] Robert S. Erikson and Norman R. Luttbeg, *American Public Opinion* (New York: Wiley, 1973), p. 173. They go on to say, "The relationship is far from strong, however." With respect to education and pro-integration sentiments, Mary R. Jackman has challenged the contention; see her "General and Applied Tolerance: Does Education Increase Commitment to Racial Integration?" *American Journal of Political Science* 22 (May 1978): 307–24.
[14] The data, however, may be somewhat misleading because the PDI does not include the "it depends" category, which has been growing (see Chapter Six).

[15]Miller et al., p. 221. Gallup poll data also support this finding. In 1970 the black/white split on busing was 32 percent; in 1980, it was 49 percent; *Public Opinion*, Apr./May 1980, p. 38.
[16]Everett Carll Ladd, Jr., with Charles D. Hadley, *Transformation of the American Party System*, 2nd ed. (New York: Norton, 1978), pp. 212–17.
[17]Louis Harris, *The Anguish of Change* (New York: Norton, 1973), pp. 35–52.
[18]Ladd and Hadley, p. 213.
[19]Harris, p. 51.

CHAPTER 9

GROUP VOTING PATTERNS

Politicians and students of American elections pay careful attention to group patterns of voting. As John Petrocik has noted, "the supporters of America's political parties have been distinguished by social, economic, demographic, and religious differences. This distinctness is so strong that it is the working politician's guide to what he must do to win votes."[1] And changes in group patterns of voting may herald those durable shifts in electoral patterns and outcomes called "critical realignments."

The 1980 presidential election again raised questions about whether such a realignment was in process. As noted previously, primary speculation now focuses on a conservative/Republican realignment.[2] Should such a realignment be in the making, it would show up in changes of group affiliation with party and group voting patterns. In this chapter we will explore the relationship of groups to partisan identification and to presidential voting. In addition, we will make some observations about group influence in elections and about the effect of the turnout of groups.

Group Basis of Partisan Identification

Because partisan identification has been so closely related to voting behavior (even in the era of party decline), it seems reasonable to begin the discussion of changes in group voting with a consideration of "partisan identification"—a long-term sense of identification with, and loyalty to, a given party. It structures not only voting but also one's view of the whole political world.[3]

In *The American Voter* Angus Campbell and coauthors introduced a model of group influence that is quite useful for talking about groups and partisan identification. The model connects the individual, the group, and the political world. As the authors noted, "At the simplest level, there is a triangle of elements involved in the situation: (1) the individual, (2) the group, and (3) the world of political objects. This triangle suggests three different relationships... (a) the relationship of the individual to the group; (b) the relationship of the group to the political world; and (c) the relationship of the individual to the political world. These three relationships determine the types of variables that we take into account" (p. 299). The triangular relationships are illustrated in Figure 9.1.

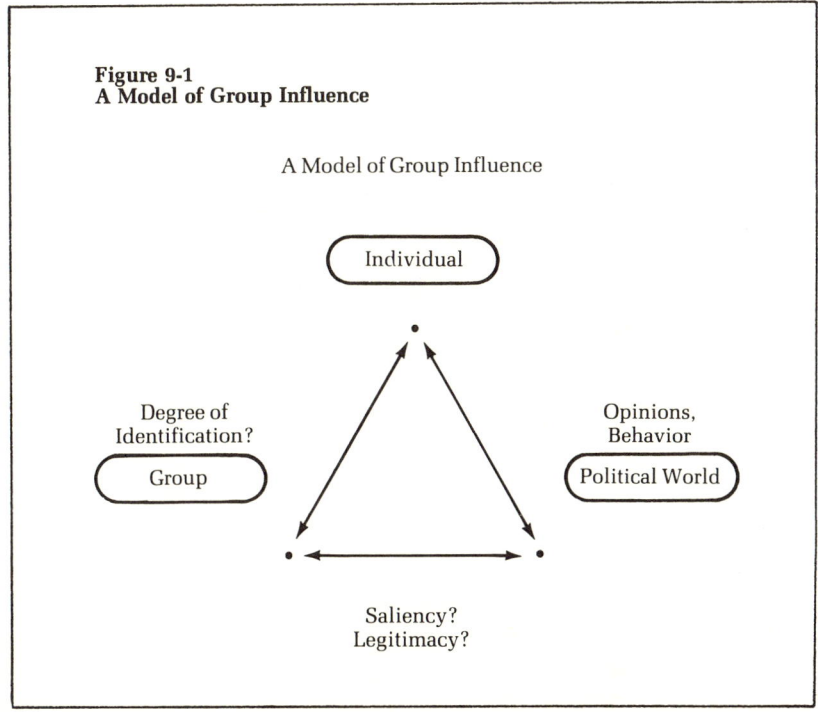

Figure 9-1
A Model of Group Influence

The model suggests that the more closely an individual identifies with a group, and the more salient and legitimate the group is perceived to be with reference to the world of politics, the more the opinions and behavior of the individual will mirror those of the group. There is a social-psychological underpinning for distinctive group behavior.

Partisan identification is a good example of the assumptions of the model: "In all major elections, its salience is absolutely high: one candidate is always a group member.... The legitimacy of its activity in politics goes without question."[4] To the degree that group membership gets tied in with partisan identification, a long-standing commitment to party is reinforced by group norms and pressures. In other words, part of the meaning of being a member of the group is to be a Democrat or Republican.

In an era of party decline, we must also consider not only group shifts in partisan identification but also movement toward independence. That is, realignment may become dealignment.

As a result of the New Deal and its aftermath, there developed (or continued) a pattern of group identification with party that included the following Democratic party coalition for presidential voting: residents of central cities, low-income groups, blacks, members of union households, Catholics, and southerners. For the most part, these disparate groups were bound together by support for the social welfare liberalism of the New Deal.[5] Table 9–1 examines changes in partisan identification of the above groups.

The starting point for the comparisons, the year 1964, is appropriate for two reasons. First, it represents the high tide of Democratic identification in recent years (along with a Democratic landslide election victory). Second, the sharp drop in overall partisan identification began after the 1964 election.[6] The national figures in Table 9–1 do show a near doubling of the percentages of independents in the population from 1964 to 1976 and a substantial loss of identification with the Democratic party. The Republicans were not, therefore, the prime beneficiaries of the change, except perhaps in the actual voting behavior of independents. The changes in the New Deal coalition groups can then be compared with the national changes.

Blacks have remained most loyal to the Democratic party and have shown little movement toward independence or to the Republican party. Prior to the New Deal, blacks supported the Republican party and were relatively slow to move to identification with the Democratic party. The 1964 election cemented black loyalty to the Democratic party, probably because of the espousal of civil rights by President Johnson and the perceived opposition of Republican candidate Goldwater.[7] The groups that have moved farthest away from the Democratic party are members of union

Table 9.1 Changes in Party Identification of
New Deal Coalition Groups,
1964 and 1976 (in percentages)

	National			Central City			Low Income			Black		
	'64	'76	Ch	'64	'76	Ch	'64	'76	Ch	'64	'76	Ch
Dem.*	61	52	−9	67	61	−6	65	60	−5	82	85	+3
Ind.	8	15	+7	9	10	+1	9	14	+5	6	8	+2
Rep.*	31	33	+2	23	29	+6	23	26	+3	8	6	−2

	Union			Catholic			Southern		
	'64	'76	Ch	'64	'76	Ch	'64	'76	Ch
Dem.*	77	62	−15	69	64	−5	71	60	−11
Ind.	6	15	9	9	11	+2	7	13	+6
Rep.*	17	22	+5	21	25	+4	21	25	+4

SOURCE: Miller et al., *Sourcebook*, p. 85.
*Includes strong and weak partisans as well as "independent leaners."

households and southerners. It is easier to explain the latter development as a consequence of the growing disenchantment of the white South with the civil rights and social welfare policies of the national Democratic party. A good proportion of this change did benefit the Republican party.[8] The threat to Democratic hegemony represented by these changes was substantial because union support and the solid South were at the core of the Democratic majority coalition (as can be seen in Table 9–2, nearly 60 percent of the Democratic vote in 1952).

In all, each of the groups remained overwhelmingly Democratic in sentiments in 1976. Nevertheless, there had been significant ebbing of the extent of identification with the Democratic party. Not a great deal of that had, as yet, translated into support for the Republican party.[9] But there could be little question that the intensity of support for the Democratic party among its traditional constituency had withered significantly.[10]

To assess the impact of changes in partisan identification, it is necessary to look at group voting in elections. First, let us consider the impact of groups.

A Note on Group Influence in Elections

In order to win American elections, parties must build coalitions. The most readily identifiable building blocks of those coalitions are demographic groups. The influence of a group in an election might be thought of as its "contribution" to a winning coalition.

That contribution can be measured in terms of the size of the group, its turnout, and its degree of loyalty to one party or the other.[11] The greatest contribution will naturally be made by an extremely large group that turns out in great numbers and is exceptionally loyal. Deficiencies in one area of contribution can, of course, be made up in others. For example, let us consider the demographics of the Democratic presidential vote in 1952 and 1972:

Table 9.2 Contribution of Groups to Democratic Vote, 1952, 1972

	Year	Poor	Black	Union	Catholic	South	Central Cities
% Contribution	1952	28	7	38	41	20	21
to Dem. Coalition	1972	10	22	32	34	25	14

SOURCE: Robert Axelrod, "Communications," *American Political Science Review*, (June 1974): 718.

It is clear that the black contribution to the Democratic coalition increased enormously in the twenty-year period. This change was due to both increased turnout and increased loyalty to the Democratic party. It is correspondingly true that the contribution of other traditional Democratic groups such as labor, white southerners, and Catholics has declined. Most notable is the decline in the contribution of the poor.

It is commonly asserted that a given group's contribution to a winning coalition is central or pivotal to the outcome of an election. In American presidential politics, the argument often takes this form:

1. Presidential elections are won in states by capturing the electoral votes of a state as a unit.
2. In close presidential races, in large states, the votes of a given minority are crucial (take those votes away and the election is lost).
3. Therefore, candidates owe their victories to such groups, and candidates should be particularly responsive to such groups.

This argument has been used frequently. For example, it was applied to the black vote for Carter in 1976 and the vote of the "moral majority" for Reagan in 1980.

There are several fundamental logical flaws in this argument, however. As E. E. Schattschneider has noted: "Finally something ought to be said about the logical fallacy of the straw that broke the camel's back.... In a concrete instance the argument runs as follows: Iowa corn growers... elected Mr. Truman President of the United States.... It is true that Mr. Truman carried Iowa by 28,000 votes and that Iowa corn growers might conceivably have provided that many votes in the election. However, Mr. Truman polled 522,000 votes in Iowa in the 1948 election, and obviously each... contributed equally to his victory.... This would have been true even if Mr. Truman had carried the state by a single vote."[12] For votes to be truly pivotal, they must be the ones that put the candidate over the top (as at a convention). In an election, however, *all* votes that contribute to a winning margin are, as

Schattschneider points out, equal in value. Nevertheless, political judgments do not necessarily depend on detecting logical fallacies.

A second point is that for group power to be effective it must be perceived that groups can withhold or transfer votes from one party or candidate to another. For years, no Democratic candidate for President would waste time campaigning in Georgia. But flexibility in group support is the exception; group loyalties to party are relatively fixed in the short run: there is a lot of inertia to group voting patterns. Nevertheless, the case for group decisiveness is strengthened when a group *switches* its vote from one election to the next.[13]

A Note on the Turnout of Groups

There is a persistent feeling that high turnout favors the Democratic party in American elections. This feeling was particularly expressed in the 1980 presidential election as President Carter sought to motivate higher turnout among traditional Democratic groups. The feeling is based on the following reasoning:

1. Lower-status groups tend to be Democratic (true).
2. Lower-status groups tend to have lower turnout (true).
3. Therefore, increases in turnout will differentially benefit the Democratic party (not necessarily true).

This argument is inherently appealing and may, in some circumstances, be accurate. Nevertheless, it is not invariably true, especially in an era when partisan loyalties are weakening. First, an illustration: the surge in turnout from 1948 to 1952 (documented in Chapter Five) did *not* benefit the Democratic party. The surge in voting went disproportionally to the Republican candidate, Eisenhower.[14] Philip Converse has shown that the effects of turnout increases on the expected Democratic share of the vote are not major.[15] James De Nardo has also shown that the presumed relationship "ain't necessarily so." As he points out, when "the association between the vote and the partisan alignment of the electorate disappears,"[16] then the peripheral voters who had previously voted Democratic will go where the forces of personality and the issues take them. Thus, upsurges in turnout, as in 1952, will not necessarily benefit the Democrats. Despite that, many still attributed Jimmy Carter's margin of defeat in 1980 to low turnout.

Myths persist about the group vote. Nevertheless, group influence is widely perceived to exist, and shifts in group patterns of voting do occur. Since the New Deal, the Republican party has made repeated efforts to cut into the old New Deal coalition and reestablish itself as the majority party. The events of 1980 represented the latest, and perhaps the most successful, of these efforts. Did the Reagan victory amount to a critical change in group voting patterns in the United States?

Group Voting Patterns

At this point, we will consider group voting in the United States, especially that of status groups, and we will see how these groups have changed over the past twenty years. It is important to remember that here we are defining "group" in the broadest possible way—people who share similar demographic characteristics. We are not considering "group" as a psychological reality, as discussed earlier.

Historically, the main line of conflict in modern democracies has been between classes based on socioeconomic inequalities. Class divisions in voting behavior have never been overwhelmingly strong in the United States, but the New Deal did create an imperfect class structure of voting.[17] More recently, there is some evidence that class divisions in political behavior in the United States have diminished or even become "inverted."[18] Some of the attitudinal changes discussed in Chapter Eight underlie these

Table 9.3 Percent Democratic among Status Groups, 1940 Presidential Election

	High Status	Med. Status	Low Status	Difference (low minus high)
% voting Dem.	29	44	65	36

SOURCE: Paul Lazarsfeld et al., The People's Choice, p. 19, chart 3.

developments. Early voting research, done shortly after the development of the New Deal coalition, highlighted the class basis of voting (see Table 9-3).

Findings such as these, which are consistent with a class interpretation of voting, led the authors to generalize that "social characteristics determine political preference."[19] Note, however, that the relationship between class and voting was far from perfect. Later elections showed even less class basis to voting in the United States.[20]

It is possible to produce data that would call into question the notion of major change. Table 9-4 compares the results of the 1960 and 1976 presidential elections, both close Democratic victories, in terms of group support for the Democratic party.

If one looked only at these data, comparing 2 recent close Democratic victories, the thesis of a decline in class-related, New Deal-based voting would not be sustained. But the point is that the Democrats have won only three of the last eight presidential elections. Of course, 1960 and 1976 may be special cases. What happens if we look at the last eight presidential elections?

The reliability of the New Deal coalition in producing presidential election victories has been suspect in recent elections, especially those in 1972 and 1980. Table 9-5 summarizes some of the voting patterns for selected groups from 1952 to 1980. The table shows clearly that there were group differences in the pat-

Table 9.4 The New Deal Coalition and
Democratic Presidential Voting, 1964, 1976

	% for Democratic Party		
	1960	1976	Difference
National	49	51	+2
Strong Democrats	91	92	+1
Weak Democrats	72	75	+3
Central cities	60	57	−3
Low income	46	67	+21
Blacks	71	95	+24
Union households	64	64	0
South	51	54	+3
Blue-collar workers	63	66	+3
Catholics	83	58	−15

SOURCE: Miller et al., Sourcebook, pp. 334–44.

terns of voting in the 1952 to 1980 presidential elections by status, race, religion, and class.

Marked changes in patterns have been generally consistent with diminished class differences on voting. For example, in 1952 there was a 19 percent gap between professionals and manual workers in voting; in 1980 that gap was 8 percent. Similar findings are apparent for education and religion. In contrast, racial divisions have sharpened (36 to 51 percent). Except for race, the data would indicate a decline in traditional group bases of Democratic party support. The elections of 1972 and 1980 are particularly suggestive that the old New Deal bases of politics have diminished sharply in the 1980s.

In 1980 Ronald Reagan cut heavily into traditional areas of Democratic group support. According to *New York Times/CBS*

Table 9.5 Group Voting Patterns, 1952–1980*

	1952	1956	1960	1964	1968	1972	1976	1980	Change
College ed. vs. Grade school ed.	18	19	16	14	21	12	14	9	−9
White vs. Nonwhite	36	20	19	35	35	55	37	51	+15
Catholic vs. Protestant	19	14	40	21	16	18	11	6	−13
Professional vs. manual laborer	19	18	18	17	21	12	15	8	−11

SOURCE: *Public Opinion*, December/January 1981, pp. 38–39.

*Numbers are the percent above national vote for Republicans for one group *plus* the percent below the national average for the other. The larger the total, the greater the difference between the two groups.

News surveys, President Carter received less than majority support from Catholics (40 percent), low-income voters (50 percent), blue-collar workers (46 percent), voters with a grade school education (50 percent), members of labor union households (47 percent), and southerners (44 percent). The only traditional Democratic groups to give more than majority support were residents of central cities (54 percent) and blacks (82 percent). Fully one third of Democrats defected to vote for Reagan (26 percent) or Anderson (6 percent).[21] These figures are convincing evidence that the New Deal coalition folded its tent in 1980.

Party Decline or Realignment

The evidence is compelling that the New Deal coalition faded during the 1960s and 1970s and collapsed in 1980. But what does this mean? One interpretation is that this is an end product of a dealignment—a weakening of the party-in-the-electorate in which presidential voting has become increasingly detached from previous group and partisan loyalties. The shell of the old system remains, but it has "the qualities of a hibernating mammal; not quite dead, not even moribund, but not very lively either, neither exerting much influence on its immediate environment, nor being very affected by it."[22] Presidential elections are determined by short-term forces. At times, these favor the reemergence of the Democratic coalition as a majority. But often, they do not. One element of such a system is a diminished class basis to voting. Under such conditions, the political leverage of lower-status groups may be significantly reduced.

An alternate interpretation is that the 1980 election marked one step in the emergence of a conservative/Republican majority similar to the Roosevelt majority of the New Deal. It could be argued that the Nixon victories of 1968 and 1972 were part of this transition. An important aspect of such a new majority is the conversion of traditional Democratic groups to Republican loyalties. The data in Chapter Eight, concerning the social welfare and civil liberties of lower-status groups, support such an interpretation.

The standard response to these two alternatives is "It depends." Indeed, it does—on the performance of the Reagan administration, particularly with respect to the economy. Can the effects of a "hyperpluralistic" system be overcome to produce nonincremental change? We will address this question in the next two chapters.

NOTES
CHAPTER NINE

[1]John Petrocik, *Party Coalitions* (Chicago: University of Chicago Press, 1981), p. 19. For a critique of the group approach, see Warren E. Miller and Teresa E. Levitin, *Leadership and Change: Presidential Elections from 1952 to 1976* (Cambridge, Mass.: Winthrop, 1976), pp. 21–30.
[2]See Kevin Phillips, *The Emerging Republican Majority* (Garden City, N.Y.: Arden Books, 1970), for an early statement of this thesis.
[3]Angus Campbell et al., *The American Voter* (New York: Wiley, 1960), Chapter 6.
[4]Ibid., p. 327. Of course, these claims must be modified in light of independent candidacies for the presidency and the loss of salience of party identification.
[5]Of course, some identification with the Democratic party existed before the New Deal, and some developed later. White southerners are an example of the former, and blacks of the latter. See Everett Carll Ladd, Jr., with Charles D. Hadley, *Transformations of the American Party System*, 2nd edition (New York: Norton, 1978), Chapters 1 and 2.
[6]See Philip E. Converse, *The Dynamics of Party Support* (Beverly Hills: Sage, 1976), p. 32.
[7]Petrocik points out that these changes were different in the North (a shift to the Democratic party) and the South (a mobilization of a previously inactive electorate), *Coalitions*, pp. 104–06.
[8]Ibid., p. 103.
[9]In the wake of the 1980 election, numerous polls showed a significant upsurge in Republican identification. It remained to be seen whether this was a temporary response to the Reagan victory. See *Public Opinion*, Apr./May 1981, pp. 29–31.
[10]If one looks only at intensity, the picture is clearer:

Percent of Strong Democrats

	1964	1976	Change
Central cities	32	22	−10
Low income	34	23	−11
Blacks	52	35	−17
Union	38	20	−18
Catholics	31	18	−13
South	36	18	−18

The decline of strong Democrats in the coalition is striking. This is significant because strong partisans are more likely to vote on party lines. The data are from Warren E. Miller et al., *American National Election Studies Data Sourcebook* (Cambridge, Mass.: Harvard University Press), pp. 85–94.

[11] Robert Axelrod, "Where the Vote Comes From," *American Political Science Review* 66 (Mar. 1972): 11–20.

[12] E. E. Schattscheider, *The Semi-sovereign People* (New York: Holt, Rinehart & Winston, 1960), pp. 55–56.

[13] See the arguments of Richard M. Scammon and Ben J. Wattenberg, "Jimmy Carter's Problem," *Public Opinion* Mar./Apr. 1978, pp. 4–5.

[14] See Angus Campbell, "Surge and Decline," in Campbell et al., eds., *Elections and the Political Order* (New York: Wiley, 1966), pp. 45–51.

[15] Philip E. Converse, "The Concept of a Normal Vote," in Campbell et al., *Elections*, pp. 28–30.

[16] James De Nardo, "Turnout and the Vote," *American Political Science Review* 74 (June 1980): p. 417. Also see John R. Petrocik, "Voter Turnout and Electoral Oscillation," *American Politics Quarterly* 9 (Apr. 1981): 161–80.

[17] Ladd with Hadley, pp. 67–68.

[18] Ibid., pp. 227–28.

[19] Paul Lazarsfeld et al., *The People's Choice* (New York: Columbia University Press, 1944), p. 27.

[20] See Robert S. Erikson et al., *American Public Opinion* (New York: Wiley, 1980), pp. 166–67.

[21] Gerald M. Pomper, "The Presidential Election," in Pomper et al., *The Election of 1980* (Chatham, N.J.: Chatham House, 1981), pp. 71–72.

[22] Petrocik, *Coalitions*, p. 162.

CHAPTER 10

NORMAL POLICYMAKING

The purpose of this chapter is to provide a general overview of how public policy normally gets made in the United States, primarily at the national level. The view presented here is a standard one: that the policymaking process in the United States should be characterized as multistage, decentralized, pluralistic, and complex (if not chaotic). The process shapes American public policy in an incremental direction. Major changes in policy direction are rare and difficult.

The purposes of sketching this general description of the policymaking process are two. The first is to have a standard against which to judge particular cases, especially the case of the Reagan economic program (Chapter Eleven). The second is to specify the role of public opinion, interest groups, political parties, and other political actors in the process. The place to begin is with governmental structure.

Fragmentation of Formal Structure

The chief formal characteristic of American government is fragmentation. By deliberate design, American government is decentralized and divided. The American political tradition is, as we have seen, suspicious of the concentration of political power and in favor of dispersing formal authority. A classic account of the result is Edward C. Banfield's description of the governments of the Chicago area: "The Chicago area from a purely formal standpoint, can hardly be said to have a government at all. There are hundreds, perhaps thousands, of bodies each of which has a measure of legal authority and none of which has enough of it to carry out a course of action which other bodies oppose."[1] This description, while derived from urban government, could as easily have been made about the whole of American politics.

American national government is divided, both horizontally and vertically. Horizontally, within the national government, the Constitution has "separated institutions sharing powers."[2] For example, the President shares legislative power with Congress via the executive veto. The system of checks and balances was deliberately conceived to ensure that "ambition would check ambition." The three branches of government, while sharing powers, are indeed separate and do act to restrain one another. Those who doubt this need only recall the experiences of recent Presidents with Congress. In a vertical sense, the federalism of the Constitution divides real power between the states and the national government. Even in an era of national government power, the authority of states is real.[3]

The significance of the formal dispersion of power lies in two areas. First, there are multiple points of entry (or access) to the government. Groups and individuals seeking to influence public policy have to decide where to attempt to gain access. In *The Governmental Process*, David Truman noted the advantages and disadvantages for interst groups given the peculiar structure of American governments. He argued that "the existence of the federal system itself is a source of unequal advantage in access."[4] Some groups may find ready access at all levels of government. Others may have resort only to particular institutions. The courts have been a traditional access point for groups and individuals who lacked political resources to influence policy in other areas. Second, policy must move through many stages or barriers in the process from conception to implementation. Vetoes, both formal and informal, can occur at many points. The formal decentralization deliberately makes the creation of majorities in favor of policies difficult to achieve and sustain. The bias in the American system favors the status quo. This is true whether one is trying to make liberal or conservative (return to status quo ante) change.

Multiple Stages of Decision

As noted, the formal structure, while not describing perfectly how decisions proceed, virtually determines that policy decisions must pass through a series of barriers to action. We may oversimplify the total process by noting that policies must first move from raw, unarticulated interests to appearance on the political agenda, then to the formulation of feasible political alternatives, on to legislative enactment, and finally to implementation of the policy. There is no guarantee, of course, that any given policy will complete this treacherous journey.[5] The dispersed formal structure, along with the pluralistic character of American society, means that no central authority controls all the key decisions in the process.[6]

In addition, each major stage breaks down into a series of substages. For example, in the legislative process, bills in Congress (and state legislatures) must move through a complicated "dance of legislation."[7] Circumscribing the legislative process are rules of the game that help to determine the shape of outcomes. Some of these rules are defined by the formal structure (the President's veto, for example). Other rules of the game are informal and understood by the participants in the process. One is reciprocity: do a favor for another legislator where possible.[8] These rules give the advantage to some interests in the policy struggle and pose a disadvantage to others. Therefore, there will always be a degree of conflict over the rules and their interpretation. The Supreme Court has often played an important role in the interpretation of the rules of the game in American politics. The reapportionment decisions of the 1960s are an example.[9]

Role of Major Actors in the Policy Process

We shall briefly mention several sets of actors in the policymaking process at the national level. The chief actor is the President. In the "textbook" view, the President is the initiator and head legislator in the system as well as the executor of policy.[10] This view of the presidency evolved in the twentieth century. It seems clear that the President bears major responsibility for policy failure in the American system. It is not surprising that presidential elections often seem to be referenda on presidential performance. (It may be somewhat surprising that presidential performance also seems to influence the outcome of congressional elections.[11])

Substantial resources are available for presidential influence on the policymaking process. The President can effectively set and dominate the policy agenda, especially with adroit manipulation of the mass media. The President can command the attention of the media in a way that no other actor can and can use symbols to dramatize an issue. President Carter, for example, made a major energy address wearing a sweater to demonstrate commitment to conservation. Moreover, the presidency carries with it the moral authority and legitimacy that are consequences of election from a national constituency and the aura of the office. The President can claim to represent a national majority in a way no other actor can. Also, Presidents can offer specific and concrete inducements to those who are cooperative. Presidential support for public works projects in a constituency may, for example, be a powerful source of influence with a congressman. Finally, there are the formal powers of the presidency, which include the powers of appointment and the veto.

But, although the President is the single most powerful political actor on the national stage, several important constraints on presidential power must be noted, along with some important qualifications to the notion of the President as the foremost actor in the political system. First, one should note that major initiatives can come from outside the executive branch of government, and one must distinguish the origin of ideas from the successful promotion of them. While the President may appear to be the source of policy ideas, the reality is that he must choose which of a series of alternatives to support. For example, President Reagan's tax-cut plan had its clear intellectual origins outside and prior to his administration. He adopted the Kemp-Roth plan,[12] an application of "supply-side" economics, in his race for the presidential nomination. It should also be noted that Congress has reasserted its role vis-à-vis the President in a number of areas including budget and national security. The constraints on presidential power have been well spelled out by Richard Neustadt. In essence, he argues that the power of the presidency is the power to persuade other actors that it is in their interest to act cooperatively with the President.[13] To move policy through the American system requires the consent or acquiescence of numerous other actors.

Other major actors include Congress, the bureaucracy, the federal courts, interest groups, political parties, and the mass media. These actors all have influence on the policy process in varying degrees, depending on the issue. Congress is the decentralized, fragmented institution par excellence. The basic units of decision are the many committees and subcommittees of the Congress. Legislation must move through a complex, multistage process. There are numerous opportunities for delay, obstruction, and even veto. The Congress has, in the past decade, become a more individualistic institution; it is therefore more difficult for parties or legislative leadership to impose order on the outcomes.[14] In addition, congressional committees or subcommittees in particular policy areas may act in concert with government bureaus or departments and affected interest groups to form an alliance (often called an "iron triangle," or a subgovernment) to dominate a given policy area.[15] Congress is a force to be reckoned with in national policymaking, as President Carter (and all recent Presidents) discovered.

As we argued earlier, American political parties traditionally play a secondary role in the policy arena. The parties are more interested in elections than in public policy. Nevertheless, the parties are significant in several senses. One is that the national party platforms do help to establish and define the national political agenda.[16] Moreover, party affiliation is crucial in organizing the Congress and is the most important factor structuring voting in the Congress.[17] Nonetheless, parties are not a dominant force in centralizing policy formulation and enactment, even when the same party controls the presidency and Congress.

Interest groups are influential throughout the policymaking process and the implementation-of-policy stage in the United States. The conventional view is that policy moves through a pattern of mutual adjustment and compromise—that policies generate support and opposition depending on the self-interest of the organizations and that such groups operate within a broadly understood framework of rules of the game. The results of any given conflict may not be totally satisfactory to any of the affected interests. In this view, public opinion in general has only the broadest, most indirect influence on policy. Public opinion, *as represented by organized interest-group activity*, is a prime determinant of policy. General public opinion has a more uncertain status.

It is increasingly clear that the mass media are also major actors on the policy stage.[18] As we saw in Chapter Six, the media heavily influence the political agenda: if the media do not treat a problem as a political issue, then that problem is not a political issue. Recent concern with issues such as child abuse, spouse abuse, and elderly abuse illustrates the point. These issues have only recently received media attention. This does not mean, of course, that such problems did not exist before their "discovery." Moreover, there are those who are convinced that the media are responsible for the decline of confidence in American government or that they are biased (and influential) in a liberal or conservative direction.[19] Some claim that the media have replaced the political parties as prime determinants of presidential nominations and as the major intermediaries between voters and candidates in presidential elections. In any case, the capacity of the media to shape political perceptions and hence indirectly shape political outcomes seems substantial.

The most direct efforts to use the media to influence political attitudes and perceptions take place during political campaigns. As previously discussed, for a considerable period of time, political scientists were skeptical of "media effects" in political campaigns.[20] Recently, there has been a reevaluation of that conclusion. A central aspect of that reevaluation has been weakening partisanship. Campaign effects were minimized when partisanship was strong; most voters made up their minds how to vote before the campaigns began and did not waiver. With weakened partisanship, one strong and enduring cue for voting has been reduced, leaving more room for campaign effects. Indeed, in 1976 and 1980 voters increasingly made up their minds later in the campaign. Television has become the preeminent instrument of the presidential campaign. Thomas E. Patterson has noted that "today's presidential campaign is essentially a mass media campaign...it is no exaggeration to say that, for the large majority of voters, the campaign has little reality apart from its media version."[21] Nevertheless, it is important to remember that the media are only one of a host of influences on American politics.

Courts have always played a substantial political and policy role in the United States. Nevertheless, in recent years the activism of the U. S. Supreme Court has pushed the courts into more and more areas of public policy. As Martin Shapiro has noted: "In the past twenty-five years the Supreme Court has been a major domestic policy-maker in the United States. It has initiated at least five major policies."[22] There is, and always has been, enormous controversy over the policy role of the courts. Nevertheless, the reality of American politics is that the courts, and especially the Supreme Court, are destined to play a significant policy role.

Finally, the federal bureaucracy is an important actor in the national policymaking process. Policies must be interpreted and implemented to be effective. There can be many a slip between legislative intent (which is often not clear anyway) and administrative execution. There are many reasons for this. One is that government agencies develop interests (which they defend) that may be at odds with changes in policy. A second reason is that agencies may be asked to accomplish unclear or unrealistic goals, or they may not be provided with enough resources to do what is asked. Third, bureaucratic rigidity is a real phenomenon. In any case, Presidents (and Congress) often agree with former President Truman: "In the early summer of 1952, before the heat of the campaign, President Truman used to contemplate the problems of the General-become-President should Eisenhower win the forthcoming election. 'He'll sit here...and he'll say, "Do this! Do that" And *nothing will happen*'."[23] The existence of a federal bureaucracy geared to large-scale social programs may prove to be a special problem for an administration attempting to cut back the size and role of the national government.

So the policy process involves a complex interplay of actors, many of whom must act in concert if policy changes are to be achieved.

Incremental Outcomes

When one puts the fragmented structure, the number of influential actors, the multiple points of access, and the multiple stages of decision together (in short, a pluralist process), the policy outcomes are likely to be *incremental*.[24] Incremental outcomes are modest departures from the status quo. Results are likely to be incremental for several basic reasons. The first is the weight of existing policy: much of what is done in the policymaking process is the correction or elaboration of existing policy and therefore the actors must operate within the constraints of existing policy. Policymakers must (for the sake of sanity) assume that the general direction of policy is largely fixed. Trying to alter the course of existing policy is a little like trying to redirect the path of an avalanche. Second, there are limitations of time, resources, and intelligence on the ability of policymakers to conceptualize major alterations in existing policy or to think up entirely new policies. Third, major departures from existing policy are politically risky because of the high costs of failure.

Specifically, it has been forcefully argued that budgetary politics is basically, perhaps inherently, incremental. Aaron Wildavsky has shown that budgeting involves such complex decisions that officials must simplify the process. They do this by assuming the budgetary base[25] and then making only incremental changes from year to year: "Budgeting is incremental, not comprehensive."[26] Since budgets determine the direction government can go, incrementalism in the budgetary process means that major shifts in direction are rare.

Policy Typologies

To this point, we have described the presumed effects of structure and process on policy outcomes. One of the important insights from the study of the policymaking process is that policy influences process—that is, the type of policy at stake reflects the way in which policy moves or fails to move through the governmental process. Specifically, the type of policy at issue influences the nature of the interest-group conflict.

Theodore Lowi's threefold typology of policy (distributive, redistributive, and regulatory) is useful for considering the relationship of policy to process.[27] The following are definitions of each of the types:

Distributive: "governmental actions that convey tangible benefits to individuals, groups, or corporations. Distributive policy is synonymous with governmental subsidy."

Regulatory: "governmental actions that extend government control over particular behavior of private individuals or businesses."

Redistributive: "involves a conscious attempt by the government to manipulate the allocation of wealth, property rights, or some other value among broad classes or groups in society."[28]

Lowi's hypothesis is that each policy arena engenders its own characteristic process. Therefore, the American political process is not invariably pluralist and incremental: some policies cause a pattern of conflict at odds with the norm. For example, a redistributive issue is likely to generate broader, and more class-based, conflict. The participants define the conflict in ideological terms, and the perception is that "zero-sum" stakes are at issue. It should be noted that redistributive issues must be rare; otherwise, the nature of American politics would be fundamentally different. The great bulk of the issues generates conflict that is less visible, less clear-cut, and more susceptible to the bargaining climate of pluralist politics.

What conditions produce a marked departure from the normal process? At times, nonincremental change takes place within a specific policy area. Enactment of severe restrictions on auto-emissions pollution in 1970 is an example. This drastic change seems to have been stimulated by a perception of a massive public demand that major government action be taken. Charles O. Jones shows that between 1965 and 1970 there was a dramatic increase in the percentage of those saying that pollution was a major problem. And in April 1970 a "massive student-organized environmental 'teach-in' occurred in major cities throughout the nation."[29] Literally, the Congress enacted standards which, at that point, were not technologically feasible. The subsequent history of amendments to the legislation shows that a more pluralist/incrementalist pattern reasserted itself.[30]

At other times, broad-scale shifts in the policy agenda seem to take place allowing for nonincremental changes. These may be associated with critical realignments, as we have mentioned. The following conditions seem to be associated with such nonincremental changes:

1. a widespread perception of crisis or fundamental policy problems;
2. leadership that is willing to be experimental with respect to policy change (risk-taking leadership);
3. a sufficient degree of bipartisan support or an overwhelming majority for one party;
4. a newly elected President with what appears to be an electoral mandate;
5. events that dramatize the "necessity" of action.

In an extreme case, a new political agenda may be created and a political realignment stimulated—the emergence of a new political era.

The normal policy process in the United States has now been described. It is complex, multistage, decentralized, pluralist, and incremental. This system is a mess to those who believe in swift, efficient, positive governmental responses to economic and other similar problems. As shown in Chapter Three, advocates of responsible parties have sought a means to overcome the fragmentation of the American system without success. As noted in Chapter Five, it is possible to argue that fragmentation of the process moved near its theoretical limits in the late 1970s. A paralysis of the national government on major issues seemed imminent. Hyperpluralism seemed a distinct possibility.

Yet we know the system does not always function "normally." The election of Ronald Reagan in 1980 may be an indication of the capacity of the system to respond to the need for major change. There was a widespread perception of economic crisis. The election could be interpreted as a mandate for a major change in the direction of policy. Certainly, the new administration interpreted the results in that way. In the next chapter, we will examine the Reagan economic policy as a case study of nonincremental change in the United States.

NOTES
CHAPTER TEN

[1]Edward C. Banfield, *Political Influence: A New Theory of Urban Politics* (New York: Free Press, 1961), p. 235.
[2]Richard E. Neustadt, *Presidential Power: The Politics of Leadership from FDR to Carter* (New York: Wiley, 1980), p. 26.
[3]See Daniel Elazar, *American Federalism* (New York: Crowell, 1966).
[4]David B. Truman, *The Governmental Process: Political Interests and Public Opinion* (New York: Knopf, 1951), p. 323.
[5]For a good discussion, see George C. Edwards III and Ira Sharkansky, *The Policy Predicament: Making and Implementing Public Policy* (San Francisco: Freeman, 1978).
[6]This conclusion is, of course, disputed by some elitist theorists and numerous conspiracy advocates. It should be obvious that this book does not accept such premises—that the Trilateral Commission selects U.S. Presidents, for example. It would, however, take quite a different book to attempt to refute such fantasies, and in the end the effort would be futile.
[7]The phrase was Woodrow Wilson's. It is the title of an excellent account of the legislative process: Eric Redman, *The Dance of Legislation* (New York: Simon & Schuster, 1973).
[8]One of the best discussions of the legislative rules is Donald Mathews, *U. S. Senators and Their World* (New York: Vintage Books, 1960), pp. 92–102.
[9]The initial case was *Baker v. Carr*, 369 U.S. 196 (1962).
[10]For an important critique of the textbook presidency, see Thomas Cronin, "The Textbook Presidency and Political Science," in Stanley Bach and George T. Sulzner, eds., *Perspectives on the Presidency* (Lexington, Mass.: D. C. Heath, 1974), pp. 54–74.
[11]See, for example, Samuel Kernell, "Presidential Popularity and Negative Voting," *American Political Science Review* 71 (Feb. 1977): 44–66.
[12]This plan was, of course, an initiative of two Republican congressmen who were in turn influenced by the economist Arthur Laffer, and so on.
[13]Neustadt, Chapter 3.
[14]See James L. Sundquist, "Congress, the President, and the Crisis of Competence in Government," in Lawrence C. Dodd and Bruce I. Oppenheimer, eds., *Congress Reconsidered* (Washington, D.C.: Congressional Quarterly Press, 1981), p. 357.
[15]For a good discussion, see Randall B. Ripley and Grace A. Franklin, *Con-

gress, the Bureaucracy and Public Policy (Homewood, Ill.: Dorsey Press, 1976), pp. 5–7.

[16]The evidence on the significance of party platforms is clear and compelling. See Gerald M. Pomper with Susan S. Lederman, *Elections in America: Control and Influence in Democratic Politics*, 2nd ed., (New York: Longman, 1980), Chapters 7–8.

[17]Robert L. Peabody, "House Party Leadership in the 1970s," in Dodd and Oppenheimer, eds., pp. 138–39.

[18]There is growing literature on the role of the mass media. For a representative example replete with good illustrations from British politics, see Colin Seymour-Ure, *The Political Impact of Mass Media* (Beverly Hills: Sage, 1974).

[19]On the alleged liberal bias of the media, see Edith Efron, *The News Twisters* (Los Angeles: Nash, 1971). The classic statement of the role of the mass media in perpetuating the existing structure of power in society is that of C. Wright Mills, *The Power Elite* (New York: Oxford University Press, 1959), pp. 311–16. On the effects of the media on the political malaise, see Michael I. Robinson, "Public Affairs Television and the Growth of Political Malaise," *American Political Science Review* 70 (June 1976): 409–32.

[20]Paul Lazarsfeld et al., *The People's Choice*, 3rd ed., (New York: Columbia University Press, 1968), Chapters 8–11.

[21]Thomas E. Patterson, *The Mass Media Election* (New York: Praeger, 1980), p. 3.

[22]Martin Shapiro, "The Supreme Court: From Warren to Burger," in Anthony King, ed., *The New American Political System* (Washington, D.C.: American Enterprise Institute, 1978), p. 179. Shapiro mentions school desegregation, reapportionment, criminal rights, obscenity, and abortion.

[23]Neustadt, p. 3.

[24]For a good discussion of incremental policymaking, see Edwards and Sharkansky, pp. 265–75. The locus classicus is, of course, Charles E. Lindblom, "The Science of 'Muddling Through,'" *Public Administration Review* 29 (Spring 1959): 79–88. While Lindblom's classic is about administration, it applies to all of the policy process, in my judgment.

[25]Aaron Wildavsky, *The Politics of the Budgetary Process* (Boston: Little, Brown, 1974), p. 13.

[26]Ibid., p. 15.

[27]Theodore Lowi, "American Business, Public Policy, Case Studies, and Political Theory," *World Politics* 16 (1964): 677–715.

[28] Definitions are from Randall B. Ripley and Grace A. Franklin, *Congress, the Bureaucracy and Public Policy* (Homewood, Ill.: Dorsey Press, 1976), pp. 16–18.

[29] Charles O. Jones, "Speculative Augmentation in Federal Air Pollution Policy-making," in James E. Anderson, ed., *Cases in Public Policy-Making* (New York: Praeger, 1976), p. 65.

[30] See Bernard Asbell, *The Senate Nobody Knows* (New York: Doubleday, 1978).

CHAPTER
11

REAGANOMICS: NONINCREMENTAL CHANGE?

The first hundred days of the Ronald Reagan administration produced anything but normal policymaking. Radical changes in the overall budget, major increases in defense spending, and significant tax cuts were proposed, and considerable success was achieved in moving toward these ambitious goals—success that went beyond the normal "honeymoon" given any new administration. This chapter examines the fate of the Reagan economic proposals in their initial tests in Congress. The comparison the reader should keep in mind is with the pluralist/incrementalist model developed in Chapter Ten. But before turning to the story of the conflict over the President's proposals, let us first consider the Reagan election victory and its significance.

What Type of Mandate?

It would be difficult to overstate the extent of the Reagan/Republican/conservative victory in the 1980 elections. As Gerald Pomper has noted: "The Reagan victory was undoubted. He won 44 of the 50 states..., amassing 489 electoral votes....He led in every area of the country including liberal Massachusetts, economically depressed Michigan, booming Texas, traditionalist Utah, and contemporary California. Of the 86 million Americans who cast their ballots, the Republican candidate won a clear majority, and he gained an even larger share of the vote for the two major parties, 55.3 percent."[1] The first three states mentioned could be considered normal Democratic territory these days (liberal Massachusetts, labor-oriented Michigan, and conservative Democratic Texas respectively). Moreover, Ronald Reagan campaigned as a genuine conservative with a specific program for increases in defense spending, decreases in domestic spending and federal regulation, and tax cuts.[2]

If the results in the presidential race were decisive (President Carter conceded before the polls closed on the West Coast), the Senate elections were shocking: "Of 25 incumbents who stood for reelection, only 16 survived....Every one of the 9 incumbents who lost was a Democrat; the Republicans experienced a net gain of 12 seats, the largest for either party since the days of Herbert Hoover...of the 18 new freshmen senators, 16 are Republicans...."[3] Not only did the Republicans wrest control of the Senate (53 to 47) for the first time since 1953–54 but the Democrats who lost were among the most liberal senators. Consider the liberal Democratic incumbents who lost: Frank Church of Idaho, Birch Bayh of Indiana, John Culver of Iowa, George McGovern of South Dakota, Warren Magnuson of Washington, and Gaylord Nelson of Wisconsin—liberals all, with a total of twenty terms (120 years) in the Senate. For the most part, these liberals were replaced by conservatives. Moreover, key committee chairmanships passed into the hands of conservative Republicans as a result of the upsets and the change in partisan control of the Senate.[4]

The House results were not as decisive as those in the Senate, but they did shift the balance of power in the Republican and conservative direction. "The results were that the Republicans gained a net of 33 seats...the new House...would have 243 Democrats and 192 Republicans. It was still under Democratic control, but would have a strikingly conservative tilt."[5] Among the major Democratic casualties were John Brademas of Indiana and Al Ullman of Oregon. One observer concluded that on "an important issue freighted with ideological implications, the possibility for a working conservative majority in the House is at hand."[6] This observation would prove to be accurate.

It is almost overwhelmingly tempting to read into these results a mandate for President Reagan and the Republican party, along with some conservative allies in the Democratic party, to enact the Reagan program, especially his economic plan for cutting both government spending and taxes. Clearly, the President and his spokesmen made great use of this argument in their campaign to induce Congress to act on the program. But it is appropriate to be skeptical of such sweeping claims despite the striking election results.

There are, in fact, two types of election mandates—one positive and one negative. In the positive one, voters are rational. Activists who select from alternative programs and affirmatively indicate their choice from alternative programs. In the negative form, voters simply say that it is time for a change but do not specify the content of change. The evidence is substantial that 1980 produced that kind of a negative mandate. As Kathleen A. Frankovic interprets the public opinion data, "there is no evidence that indicates a turn to the right of the nation. Reagan was not elected because of increasing conservatism of the country."[7] She argues that there was *not* a major shift in public attitudes between 1976 and 1980. Earlier, we presented evidence that a modest shift had taken place between 1964 and 1976. But the evidence is clear that the public, even the portion that voted for Reagan, was not uniformly conservative. Some 10 percent of the Reagan voters even called themselves "liberals."[8] The most convincing evidence that a positive mandate was *not* given in 1980 comes from a paper by Paul T. David: "When asked a...question on what their main reason was for voting as they did, 38 percent of the Reagan voters simply said that 'it's time for a change.' This was almost twice the number who gave any other reason, and far more than the 11 percent who said they voted for Reagan because 'he's a real conservative.'"[9] As James Q. Wilson noted, "the 1980 election was an opportunity, not a mandate."[10] As is typical, Americans voted negatively and retrospectively, not positively.

In general, the notion of an affirmative mandate in American politics is obscure. But that does not mean that the idea has no political effect. If politicians believe a mandate has been given, regardless of whether it has or not, they will act on that basis. In that sense, the "mandate" is real. In any case, the degree of sympathy for the mandate claim would be strengthened by the election of numerous Reagan sympathizers to the Congress.

Conditions for Nonincremental Change?

The 1980 elections seemed to create, or reflect, some of the classic conditions for nonincremental change in the United States: a landslide election, the perception of a mandate, the possible creation of a (conservative) majority in Congress, the widespread perception of an economic crisis, the massive desire for change, and the presence of innovative and risk-taking leadership.

The Reagan win was a landslide[11] in the opinion of the media and public, largely because it was so pervasive (the actual margin of victory was not nearly as stunning as Nixon's rout of McGovern in 1972). The perception of a landslide, plus the relative clarity of the choices offered in the election, contributed to the sense that a mandate had been given. And while the Republicans did not seize partisan control of both houses, they could certainly claim an ideological majority in Congress. No one could doubt, either, that—at least among those who voted for Reagan—there was a widespread sense that the economy was not working and that major change was needed. But what turned out to be most surprising in the situation was that President Reagan was willing to gamble on economic proposals, especially those on tax cuts, which were widely regarded as untested and risky in the extreme.

But the forces arrayed against large-scale change in American politics are formidable. The Reagan economic program would face challenges from entrenched minorities in the Congress, in the bureaucracy, and in the ranks of the multitude of organized special interests. These "iron triangles" could be expected to fight hard against the proposed budget cuts.

Reaganomics

The landslide election of Ronald Reagan in November 1980 signaled a historic effort to change the direction of the nation by reducing the role of the federal government. Contrasts with the New Deal effort to use government for positive purposes were inevitable. As the *Washington Post* observed, "the new Director of the office of Management and Budget [David Stockman] is working feverishly to produce a plan for revolution in American government—'a more far-reaching set of proposals for changing the federal government than anything since the New Deal.' "[12] The major tool in the effort was the budget. Early in his administration

(February 1981) President Reagan unveiled a plan of record budget cuts. This extraordinary effort should provide insight into incremental versus nonincremental models of public policymaking in the United States. The budget defines the priorities of the national government. Although in theory nearly everyone is in favor of a balanced budget or budget reductions, it is usually the case that groups feel their slice is legitimate and that others should bear the burden. Moreover, at the level of cuts the administration was proposing, this was a *redistributive* issue.[13] It would be highly visible, emotional issue, likely to generate class-based and partisan divisions. A second aspect of the Reagan program was equally controversial and equally redistributive in its implications: large-scale, across-the-board tax cuts for individuals.

Formation of Reagan Economic Policy

The 1980 presidential election was considered by the winners to be a referendum on the future direction of American public policy. Although, as we have seen, it is dangerous to read mandates into American election results, this may have been the clearest choice of policy direction since 1964 (with the opposite result). The 1980 choice was between a moderate Democrat and a conservative who proposed to change dramatically the pattern of growth in spending of the national government. The Reagan alternative—to do something radically different—was awarded landslide support. And the new administration, to the surprise of some, proceeded to implement its "mandate."

One of the first important acts of the new administration was the appointment of David Stockman as director of the Office of Management and Budget (OMB). Stockman was to become both the chief architect and the point man for the Reagan program. Stockman, a thirty-four-year-old "whiz kid," had been a two-term member of the House from Michigan and a staunch fiscal conservative and supporter of the Kemp-Roth tax-cut proposal. *Time* described Stockman in these terms: "Of all the administration's senior officials, Stockman is clearly the boldest and the most ideological. He often uses sweeping, strident language as when he called the federal budget an 'automatic coast-to-coast soup line.'"[14] Indeed, it was suggested that Stockman was "following a detailed personal blueprint he has carried in his head for half a dozen years."[15] He was also quickly to become one of the strongest members of Reagan's new team.[16]

The details of the Reagan economic blockbuster were developed in OMB and were closely guarded until Stockman was ready to make his announcements: "The budget-reduction proposals are being kept secret in part to discourage special interest groups from mounting pre-emptive protests."[17] The various agencies involved and key congressional figures were brought into the process at a second stage of reaction. The evident purpose of the procedure was to resist the tugging and pulling by the clientele interests that the particular agencies represent. Too broad a participation in the formation of policy is inconsistent with an integrated, comprehensive program. While compromise might later be necessary, at least the program can be intact at the beginning.

Nevertheless, leaks developed, and at some point agencies (and Congress) had to be informed. The immediate response of the State Department to proposed foreign aid cuts illustrates the dilemma faced by budget cutters. Although foreign aid has no large domestic constituency, secretary Alexander M. Haig was able to orchestrate a strong negative response to the cuts: "Foreign aid has become the focal point for a dispute within the Reagan administration over the president's promise to slash federal spending. The battle was joined when an Office of Management and Budget (OMB) memo proposing drastic cuts in U. S. foreign aid was leaked to the press. The memo...provoked sharp protests from members of Congress and from foreign governments—as the leak presumably was intended to insure it would do....Haig was said to have received cables protesting the OMB plan from dozens of U. S. allies."[18]

The cuts were not made across the board. Anticipating negative reactions to some cuts, which were theoretically possible, the

Reagan proposal "spared from the massive OMB spending scaleback...seven popular government programs...basic Social Security retirement benefits; medicare; veterans' disability programs, supplementary benefits for the blind, disabled, and elderly poor; school lunch and breakfast programs; the Headstart preschool program; and the summer youth jobs program."[19] The administration consistently referred to these exemptions as a "safety net" for the truly needy.

Even before the specifics of the Reagan/Stockman plans became known, interest-group opposition began building: "The giant AFL-CIO is organizing a nationwide letter-writing campaign to put pressure on lawmakers to save such programs as trade adjustment assistance and unemployment benefits from the OMB's budget-cutting ax."[20] Nevertheless, throughout the budget fight, the opposition seemed fragmented, disorganized, and demoralized.

The actual program was two-pronged: spending reductions and tax cuts. The first focus on the spending side was to reduce President Carter's fiscal 1982 budget (October 1981 to October 1982). Many of these cuts were definitely nonincremental. For example, the funding for the National Endowment for the Arts and Humanities "would be cut in half, for a savings in fiscal 1982 of $85 million."[21] In addition, severe cuts were proposed in government support for the sciences. The National Science Foundation was hit particularly hard: "The targets in NSF are considered particularly dramatic. The cuts would include $47 million from the science education budget, bringing it down 42 percent; $30 million from the social and economic research budget, a 75 percent reduction; the entire $98 million budget of 'cross-directive' programs including new instruments for universities, and programs for women and minorities in science."[22] These proposals made deep slashes in the budgetary bases of these programs. The *Washington Post* (among others) predicted an "epic political struggle" over the proposed cuts.[23]

To grasp the totality of what was proposed, it is necessary to review the programs that received substantial cuts: (1) a cap on medicaid grants to the states; (2) cuts in health planning; (3) consolidation of categorical grants for social, community, and health programs into a single block grant (at 80 percent levels); (4) reduction of spending for the food stamp program; (5) cuts in welfare; (6) cuts in the energy budget that "are nearly revolutionary"; (7) cuts in the Department of Housing and Urban Development that "signal a dramatic shift away from economic and community development as the mainstay of federal urban policy"; (8) some tightening up of Social Security benefits; (9) eliminating "the controversial public jobs program"; (10) reductions in jobless benefits; (11) gutting "the trade adjustment assistance program"; (12) cutting federal assistance for construction of municipal waste treatment plants; (13) reducing support for the export-import bank; (14) cuts in aid to education; (15) cuts in aid for transportation; and (16) shlashing farm credit by 25 percent.[24] In addition, the administration proposed to defer or cancel NASA projects and subsidies for the arts, to reduce support for the Postal Service and Amtrak, and to cut dairy price supports.[25]

The list of affected groups and potential opponents is indeed impressive. In order to circumvent the opposition, "Reagan's objective is...to keep the coming battle out of the trenches, where the lobbyists and the logrollers can coalesce and trade votes in a program-by-program defense of their interests."[26] The bottom line of the budget was that the administration was advocating a budget slash of 40 to 50 billion dollars for fiscal 1982.

The tax side of the equation called for an "income tax cut of 10 percent a year for three years and a stepped-up schedule of write-offs for capital investment by business—a total revenue loss of $53.9 billion in fiscal 1982 alone."[27] Normally, more political support could be generated for tax cuts than for budget cuts, but this time that rule did not apply: "A crowning irony of the new age now dawning in Washington is that it has become safer politically to come out against the biggest tax cut in history than to oppose cutting the budget."[28] The reason offered was that the public had accepted the need for a balanced budget even at the expense of a tax cut.[29]

General public opinion on the Reagan budget cut proposals was not enthusiastic. A *New York Times/CBS News Poll* showed that "there was little backing for specific cuts, other than in food stamps."[30] For example, only one quarter of the population favored reduced spending on unemployment compensation, whereas more than 70 percent favored the same or increased benefits.

President Reagan moved quickly to try to arouse public support for his economic proposals: "The White House timed the address to reach voters just as Congress prepares to head home on its Lincoln Day recess, hoping that Mr. Reagan could stimulate public pressure on members of Congress."[31] This address was general and concentrated on the perilous state of the economy. He pointed out the corrosive effects of inflation, the growth of the national debt and asserted that "we now know that inflation results from that deficit spending." He argued that the United States had reached "a turning point" and that the way to check inflation was to bring "government spending back within government revenues." He also asserted that "excessive taxation of individuals has robbed us of incentive." He called for the Congress to cooperate "in a bipartisan manner." He left the details of his proposal deliberately obscure, preferring to make the general arguments for the budget and tax cuts.[32]

On February 18, 1981, President Reagan made an address to a joint session of Congress during which he spelled out some of the specifics of his proposals. In his speech, he defended his plan against accusations that it was constructed on the "backs of the poor." He pledged that "those who through no fault of their own must depend on the rest of us...can rest assured that the social safety [nets] of programs they depend on are exempt from any cuts."[33] This assertion would, of course, become a focal point of the conflict over the proposed cuts: do they protect the truly needy?

Reagan versus The "Iron Triangles"

The specific issues involved in the Reagan program would be fought out in Congress in decisions involving organized interest groups, government bureaus, and congressional committees and subcommittees: "If President Reagan's plan to cut the federal budget and reduce government regulation is to pass muster in Congress, it will first have to run the gantlet of the 'iron triangles,' interlocking government and private interests that work to protect and expand their favorite federal programs." These "iron triangles" are made up of "middle-level bureaucrats, members of highly specialized congressional panels and lobbyists for the beneficiaries of government programs."[34] They are sometimes called "subgovernments,"[35] for they make and sustain policy largely out of the view of the public.

The subgovernments dominate routine decision-making in a given policy area. Because a substantial portion of policymaking is routine, it can be said that subgovernments control a major share of national policymaking. The reasons for this are numerous: the growth of federal government activity and the complexity of policy areas it gets into; the weakening of central executive authority; and the fragmentation of Congress, particularly the explosion of subcommittees dealing with particular policy areas.[36] The major advantages of the subgovernments are information (in complex policy areas) and coordination. Interest groups support committee and subcommittee members with substantial campaign contributions. Movement of individuals from one leg of the triangle to another is not infrequent.[37]

An example may help to make the subgovernment phenomenon clear. There is a Soil Conservation Service (SCS) in the Department of Agriculture whose mission is the "development of a national soil and water conservation program." The policies include "building small dams to help conserve soil, prevent floods, and increase recreational opportunities in rural areas." Requests go from local districts to the SCS to Congress: "The subgovernment that emerges from this process includes SCS watershed bureau officials, members of the House and Senate Agriculture committees..., and members of the House Appropriations Subcommittee on Agriculture. Relevant nongovernmental participants underlie representatives of the National Association of Soil Conservation Districts and the Izaak Walton League of Americans. The decisions of this subgovernment are quiet and continuous."[38]

Reagan's task was to convert hundreds of these "invisible" and "routine" decision-making processes into visible and nonroutine budget reductions.

This task was aided by the conservative Republican victories in the 1980 elections, which helped to break one of the legs of some of the iron triangles. For example, in the public health area, former Senator Magnuson, "a staunch defender," lost, and the Democratic chairman of one of the committees in the House, which had jurisdiction over public health service hospitals, a target for Reagan budget cuts, "was defeated in November."[39] The fact is that the results of the election reached below the surface to disturb long-held patterns of behavior. One quick indication that the power of some of the clientele interests was diminished was that the Senate defeated efforts to restore $300 million to the "politically popular veterans' health programs," and the House killed a proposal to increase milk price supports, "a total victory over the dairy lobby, traditionally one of the most effective in Washington."[40]

The Reagan Program in Congress

The President had no sooner introduced his budget than its assumptions and projections were assaulted by the Congressional Budget Office (CBO), "which concluded that the large range administrative projections for the fiscal 1984 budget would be off by $50 billion dollars. To put it mildly, the CBO was essentially assuming less rosy results than the administration."[41]

The tool the administration was to use to force the budget reductions in Congress was "reconciliation." As described by Congressional Quarterly, "Reagan and Republican congressional leaders have decided that many spending cutbacks...can be achieved through enactment of an omnibus reconciliation bill making legislative changes in current program-tightening eligibility for disability insurance benefits, for example."[42] Reconciliation would force committee actions in line with general spending limitations. It became intensely controversial as the budget process unwound because it "could set off an enormous shift of power in the government, transferring influence from the traditional congressional committees [and subcommittees]...to the relatively new House and Senate Budget committees and the Office of Management and Budget in the White House."[43] Senior Democrats were particularly worried that this process would endanger their favorite programs. In the Senate, a reconciliation order was introduced on February 24 calling for "$125.9 billion in savings through fiscal 1983...the Senate Budget Committee will determine how much each authorizing committee must cut in fiscal 1982 in order to meet its budget-slashing goals."[44]

Members of Congress were openly skeptical that the reconciliation bill could be moved through Congress according to the administration's timetable (which was the end of June): "A Democrat on the House Budget Committee noted that last year...it took Congress more than six months to act on the bill. The House-Senate conference committee alone had more than 100 members, and it debated the bill for more than two months."[45]

In the Senate, the Budget Committee ultimately approved a reconciliation resolution that gave the President virtually everything he wanted by a unanimous vote: "In preparing its package of far-reaching cuts, the Budget panel virtually rubber-stamped Reagan's savings proposals. Only a few of the 100-plus recommended reductions were altered." The unanimity on the final vote was not indicative of committee consensus on the details. Although "many of the reductions had been opposed by Democrats...they joined their GOP colleagues in voting to report the resolution to the Senate floor."[46] We must remember that the Republicans were now the majority on the committee and in the Senate. There was a temporary setback on the budget resolution, but that problem was quickly redressed.[47] On April 2, 1981, the Senate approved the budget cuts by an 88–10 vote.[48]

The matter would not be so simple in the House Budget Committee. There the Democrats, led by Chairman James Jones, organized to submit an alternative budget.[49] The vote in the House Budget Committee was 17–13 in favor of the Democratic alternative. The party division on the committee was 18–12 (in favor of the Democrats), and the vote was party-line with one exception, Democrat Phil Gramm of Texas. The vote meant "that the House Democrats—unlike their counterparts in the Republican-dominated Senate... didn't splinter apart in their first budget test."[50] But the success in committee did not hold on the floor, where the Democrats did splinter.

The Disorganized Democrats

The Democratic majority in the House faced severe dilemmas with respect to the President's proposals. First of all, their party was split at least three ways: the liberals, whose instincts would be to fight the President all the way; the conservatives, who might be expected to support him; and the moderates, who recognized the need for some budget trimming but who were looking for other alternatives. The Democrats were described in these terms by Martin Tolchin: "a party whose urban liberals, suburban moderates and rural conservatives often have irreconcilable differences."[51] In general, opposition to the President could be risky individually and in terms of control of the House in 1982. If the Democratic majority were able to thwart the President, that would make a good campaign issue in 1982.[52] We assume that concern for reelection dominated the floor responses of many Democrats.[53]

The conservative Democrats were a particular target of the Reagan lobbying effort. Dubbed "Boll Weevils" and coming largely from the South and West, they numbered forty-seven (the Democratic margin over the Republicans in the House was fifty-one). House Speaker Thomas P. (Tip) O'Neill named several to key positions after the 1980 elections, in recognition of their pivotal power in the House: "Many of the Boll Weevils are plainly sympathetic to Reagan's views on the budget."[54] In the end, they deserted the party anyway.

The Democrats' dilemma was personalized in the troubles of Speaker Tip O'Neill: "O'Neill is criticized by Democratic conservatives for his liberal outlook and his reluctance to go along with the Reagan administration budget-cutting fervor. At the same time, liberals say he has not been fighting hard enough to save the endangered social spending programs for which the party is best known."[55] O'Neill's impotence was merely a reflection of a divided, confused, and demoralized majority party unable to agree on an approach to the Reagan juggernaut.

The Assassination Attempt

At the time of the attempted assassination of President Reagan (March 30, 1981), the fate of his budget cuts was up in the air. House Democrats had passed an alternative in committee. The final decision would be made on the floor. The attempt itself, and the graceful manner in which he handled it, buoyed the President's personal popularity.[56] In something of a gamble, the recently wounded President addressed the Congress on April 28: "In an address to a joint session of Congress that was interrupted by applause twelve times, never more warm than when he challenged the legislators to agree...that old ways of doing business are no longer acceptable, Reagan mixed conciliatory overtures toward Congress with a warning that people are on his side."[57] These near-tragic events seemed to put the President in position to score a convincing victory in the House.

Victory in the House

In his address, the President endorsed a "bipartisan" budget plan sponsored by Representatives Delbert Latta (Republican, Ohio) and Phil Gramm (Democrat, Texas—one of the Boll Weevils), which was substantively similar to his own. On May 7 that budget was approved by a whopping 253–176. The vote "provided cold, hard proof that the fragmentation among the Democrats...is extremely serious. Sixty-three Democrats joined all of the House Republicans to overwhelmingly endorse the Reagan budget plan."[58]

The vote on the various amendments to the budget showed the deep divisions in the Democratic party: "...69 of the most liberal Democrats voted for a proposal endorsed by the Congressional Black Caucus that would have balanced the budget with less money for defense and more taxes; 118 voted for a similar, though not as dramatic, version...; 176 voted against the Reagan backed package...."[59] Among the sixty-three Democrats who voted with the Republicans were twenty from northern or western states.[60] These included erstwhile Democratic moderates such as Albosta of Michigan, Evans and Jacobs of Indiana, Hall and Luken of Ohio, and Patterson of California.[61]

This was just a first step in a long process but it was an important one, for it was "viewed as a vote of confidence in President Reagan's economic recovery program...and because [in the House] the reconciliation instructions required 16 authorizing committees to come up with $36.6 billion in cuts by June 15."[62] On May 14 "House and Senate budget conferees agreed...on a fiscal 1982 spending blueprint made to order for President Reagan."[63] This would not be the end of the fight, because the standing committees would still have to make the specific cuts, but it was an important first step.

"It's not supposed to be that way"

It is difficult to overstate President Reagan's achievement in getting the budget cuts through the first stage in Congress virtually unscathed. In doing so, he had to overcome the weight of bureaucratic opposition, an opposition majority in the House, and the image of someone dedicated to robbing the poor in favor of the rich. He worked a revolution in the federal budget.

The fight was, of course, not over. *Congressional Quarterly* asked three questions about the program: "Will the American public continue to support Reagan's economic plan when it realizes precisely what the spending cuts he is seeking mean in terms of slashing social programs? Will lobbying by special interest groups be more effective at the committee level in saving pet projects than it was in the budget resolution and reconciliation instructions? Will economic conditions deteriorate to such a degree that it will be impossible, socially and politically, to make such deep spending cuts?"[64] In addition, would he have as much support for his three-year, 10 percent, across-the-board tax cuts as he had for the spending cuts?[65]

But despite these qualifiers, the achievement was enormous. In a special section on January 26, 1981, *Newsweek* asked (about the presidency): "Can anyone do the job?"[66] The article made many of the points cited in Chapter Ten about the difficulties of achieving large-scale change: "The concern most frequently pressed today is not whether the Presidency is imperial but whether it is impotent.... He [Reagan] comes with a rough mandate to cool inflation, cut back Big Government and stand up to the Russians, with no clear consensus as to how. The Congress awaiting him is atomized, undisciplined and, after Vietnam and Watergate, resistant to Presidential leadership. The bureaucracy nominally under his control is huge and probably unmanageable.... The media watching and judging him have grown suspicious of presidents to the point, some say, of cynicism."[67] Add to these difficulties the iron triangles discussed above, and the outlook for major presidential initiatives seemed bleak.

In addition, the Reagan proposals amounted to raising a redistributive issue. The proposed cuts were extremely threatening to a variety of interests dependent on extensive federal government activism in the fields of health, welfare, and employment. An analysis by David E. Rosenbaum showed that the cuts "would bite deeply into a variety of social programs in which the beneficiaries are disproportionately black."[68] The proposals should have raised opposition to a fever pitch. Instead, lobbyists for the poor were relatively ineffective: "Owing to the breadth and magnitude of Reagan's proposals and their apparent momentum on Capitol Hill, many defenders of the poor have found themselves spread thin in the job of defense."[69] Only rarely are redistributive issues raised in American politics, much less pressed to the point of success. Moreover, it is exceptionally difficult to argue for redistributive policies that seem to threaten the poor. Nevertheless, that is exactly what happened in this case.

So how was President Reagan able to succeed in this first round? An interest-group/pluralist/incremental model is simply not capable of accounting for what happened. We are clearly in the area of "abnormal" politics. Five points seem central to understanding the Reagan success.

First, some elections are decisive with respect to public policy change even if objectively no mandate as such exists. The election of 1932 was one such instance; that of 1980 was another. The sheer scope of what happened in November of 1980 seems to have sent an electric shock through the political system. The effects were felt most clearly in the upheaval in the Senate—the change in partisan control. But the election effects were just as important in the House, with the 1982 elections just around the corner. Second, the results of the election created a perception of a massive change in public opinion in the conservative direction (actually, as noted in Chapter Seven, the change was more mixed and modest). Evidently, leaders do respond to their perceptions of what the public wants. Third, the newly elected President displayed extraordinary communication skills (and timing) in pressing his program through a series of appeals to the public and Congress. Reagan adroitly mixed "personal diplomacy" with persistent, but gentle, reminders of the potential citizen reaction to the failure of Congress to respond. Fourth, the disorder of the Democrats, particularly in the House, opened the door for a cohesive Republican party, united behind the President's program, to work its will. Party discipline among Republicans, with the exception of a brief wavering on the budget resolution, was exceptionally strong, whereas Democratic cohesion was rent by the defection of many moderate and conservative Democrats. Finally, events worked in the President's direction. The assassination attempt, and the graceful recovery of the President, aided Reagan's personal popularity and undoubtedly helped to recover the momentum of the program. In other words, conditions were ripe for one of those unique moments in American politics—a period of genuine nonincremental (and redistributive) policy change.

Postscript

At the next step in the process, the committees would have to reconcile the specific budget cuts with the overall blueprint adopted by the Congress. This process was painful, and many Democrats in particular charged that it amounted to giving up the prerogatives of Congress. Some early signs indicated that the process would not be as smooth as the reconciliation fight had been in the House.[70] In a story titled "The Honeymoon Is Over," *Newsweek* noted that the emboldened Democrats were no longer submissive and would try to force a series of votes on key amendments on the floor, thereby holding the President's supporters' feet to the fire and forcing them to vote against popular programs: "O'Neill and his colleagues began to like the idea of letting amendments come to a vote one by one, less because it would be fair than because they thought they could win." Definitely, the honeymoon was over. It was unlikely that the President would be able to win this fight as decisively as he had the reconciliation battle (in the House): "But the dimming glow on the honeymoon and the faint scent of blood in the air did not alter the fact that the President has already won 85 to 90 percent of the budget cuts he wanted."[71] Any President winning 85 to 90 percent of a redistributive issue in an era of fragmented politics must be considered, on that issue, an extraordinary politician.

But when the crucial procedural vote was taken in the House on June 25, the President won again, although more narrowly than before: "The House first voted, 217 to 210, to reject an attempt by the Democrats to split into six separate votes the President's request for $5.2 billion in additional budget cuts in the next fiscal year. The House then voted, 214 to 208, to allow the President's package to be voted on as an entity." In these votes, the President received the support of "a core of 29 conservative Democrats who voted with the Republicans, on an alliance that threatens to undermine the control of the House Democratic leadership."[72] The de facto conservative majority in the House held, causing consternation among the majority Democrats who had been optimistic about winning the vote. Some Democrats talked of punishing the party-bolters.

The President's men exulted over the victory: "Top aides to President Reagan...hailed the administration's budget victory as a historic development...it means the federal budget now will be balanced in fiscal 1984; that inflation, interest and unemployment rates will progressively decline, and that Reagan now has a working philosophical majority...in the Democratic-controlled House."[73]

The final act of Reagan's triumph came in early August. After a presidential address to the nation, many tax concessions to possible supporters of a Democratic alternative, and assiduous personal lobbying, the Senate approved his tax cut plan 89–11 and, in a major surprise, a nearly identical plan "cleared the Democratic House in a stunning 238–to–195 upset."[74] The Reagan economic package, almost intact, had sailed through Congress in less than six months. The Democratic party in the House was riddled by defections. The only consolation the Democrats had was that there could be no shirking of presidential and Republican party responsibility for the economy in 1982 and 1984.

The Reagan victory had serious implications for the whole functioning of normal politics in the U. S. Congress. Among other things, it called into question the power of committees and committee chairmen, "upset the tradition that programs...created by legislation...must be terminated the same way," and "showed the emerging power of the Sun Belt states."[75] In all, a revolution as dramatic as Roosevelt's in 1933 had been engineered by an aging ex–movie actor and a new conservative coalition in Congress.

NOTES
CHAPTER ELEVEN

[1] Gerald M. Pomper, "The Presidential Election," in Pomper et al., *The Election of 1980* (Chatham, N.J.: Chatham House, 1981), pp. 65, 67.

[2] Henry A. Plotkin, "Issues in the Presidential Campaign," in Pomper et al., pp. 49–51, 59.

[3] Charles E. Jacob, "The Congressional Elections," in Pomper et al., p. 122.

[4] Some Republicans who gained such chairmanships are Helms of North Carolina (Agriculture, Nutrition, and Forestry), Tower of Texas (Armed Services), Garn of Utah (Banking, Housing, and Urban Affairs), Domenici of New Mexico (Budget), McClure of Idaho (Energy and National Resources), Dole of Kansas (Finance), Thurmond of South Carolina (Judiciary), and Hatch of Utah (Labor and Human Resources). See Charles O. Jones, "The New, New Senate," in Ellis Sandoz and Cecil V. Crabb, eds., *A Tide of Discontent* (Washington, D.C.: Congressional Quarterly Press, 1981), p. 106, table 5–7.

[5] Neil MacNeil, "The Struggle for the House of Representatives," in Sandoz and Crabb, eds., p. 80.

[6] Jacob, p. 132.

[7] Frankovic is referring to change from 1976 to 1980; Kathleen A. Frankovic, "Public Opinion Trends," in Pomper et al., p. 113.

[8] Pomper, "The Presidential Election," in Pomper et al., p. 87.

[9] Paul T. David, "The Election of 1980 and Its Consequences," paper delivered at the 1980 Presidential Election Lecture Series, Legislative Studies Center, Sangamon State University, Springfield, Illinois.

[10] James Q. Wilson, "Does Reagan Have a Mandate?" *New York Times Book Review*, June 7, 1981, p. 3.

[11] The notion of a landslide in 1980 must be qualified in at least two senses. First, it was more a landslide in electoral-college terms than in the popular vote (see Table 12.1). Second, with the turnout rate being around 50 percent, Reagan received the vote of about one quarter of the potential electorate.

[12] Robert G. Kaiser, "High Visibility and Higher Stakes," *Washington Post*, Feb. 5, 1981, p. 1.

[13] For example, they were proposing a 25 percent slash in the food stamp program. See *Washington Post*, June 28, 1981, p. A–2.

[14] *Time*, Feb. 16, 1981, p. 11.

[15] Robert G. Kaiser, "High Visibility and Higher Stakes," *Washington Post*, Feb. 5, 1981, p. 1.

[16] See "Meet David Stockman," Newsweek, Feb. 16, 1981, p. 24.
[17] Time, Feb. 9, 1981, p. 70.
[18] Congressional Quarterly Weekly Report, Feb. 7, 1981, p. 262. Also see John M. Goshko and Hobart Rowan, "Haig and U. S. Allies Thwart Stockman's Planned Aid Slash," Washington Post, Jan. 31, 1981, pp. A–1, A–3.
[19] Congressional Quarterly Weekly Report, Feb. 14, 1981, p. 312. Also see Lee Lescaze, "Ax Spares Seven Popular Programs," Washington Post, Feb. 11, 1981, pp. 1, 4.
[20] Congressional Report, Feb. 14, 1981, p. 311. One writer opined that organized labor, state and local governments, the elderly, and exporters would be upset by the cuts: Timothy B. Clark, "Want to Know Where the Ax Will Fall?" National Journal, Feb. 14, 1981, p. 274.
[21] Congressional Quarterly Weekly Report, Feb. 14, 1981, p. 312.
[22] Washington Post, Feb. 11, 1981, p. 2.
[23] The cuts promise "to produce a year of epic political struggle unlike anything seen before in modern Washington." Washington Post, Feb. 8, 1981, p. 1.
[24] This summary is from Clark, "Want to Know," pp. 274–81.
[25] Newsweek, Feb. 16, 1981, pp. 22–23; Mar. 2, 1981, p. 27.
[26] Newsweek, Mar. 2, 1981, p. 24.
[27] Ibid., p. 22.
[28] Ibid., p. 24.
[29] "Balancing the Federal budget is much more important to the American public than a large tax cut, but there is little enthusiasm for the cuts in Federal spending President Reagan is likely to propose to reach that goal." Adam Clymer, "Public Prefers a Balanced Budget..." New York Times, Feb. 3, 1981, p. 1.
[30] Ibid., p. B–9.
[31] Hedrick Smith, "Reagan's '81 Campaign: To Sell Line on Economy," New York Times, Feb. 5, 1981, p. 20.
[32] The quotations are from the transcript of the President's speech printed in the New York Times, Feb. 6, 1981, p. 12.
[33] Quotation from the text of a speech reported in Congressional Quarterly Weekly Report, Feb. 21, 1981, p. 361.
[34] Timothy B. Clark, "The President Takes on the 'Iron Triangles,'" National Journal, Mar. 3, 1981, p. 516.
[35] "Subgovernments are clusters of individuals that effectively make most of the routine decisions in a given substantive area of policy....A typical

subgovernment is composed of members of the House and/or Senate, members of congressional staffs, a few bureaucrats, and representatives of private groups or organizations interested in the policy area. Usually the members of Congress and staff members are from the committees or subcommittees that have principal or perhaps exclusive jurisdiction over the policy area dominated by the subgovernment": Randall B. Ripley and Grace A. Franklin, *Congress, the Bureaucracy and Public Policy,* rev. ed. (Homewood, Ill.: Dorsey Press, 1980), pp. 8–9.

[36] Clark notes that the number of subcommittees in the House grew from 83 in 1955 to 149 in 1980: "The President Takes on the 'Iron Triangles,'" p. 517.

[37] Ibid., p. 516.

[38] Ripley and Franklin, p. 98.

[39] Linda E. Demkovich, "Hospital System Backers Lose Influential Allies," *National Journal,* Mar. 28, 1981, p. 522.

[40] *Washington Post,* Mar. 27, 1981, pp. 3–4.

[41] *Washington Post,* Mar. 24, 1981, p. A–4.

[42] "Reconciliation Emerges as Key Budget Tool," *Congressional Quarterly Weekly Report,* Feb. 28, 1981, p. 378.

[43] Robert G. Kaiser, "Budget Reconciliation," *Washington Post,* June 14, 1981, p. A–9.

[44] "Congress Shapes Strategy for Reagan Economic Plan," *Congressional Quarterly Weekly Report,* Feb. 28, 1981, p. 376.

[45] David E. Rosenbaum, "Congress to Have Key Role in Effort to Curb Spending," *New York Times,* Feb. 7, 1981, p. 7.

[46] "Reagan Plan Clears First Hurdle," *Congressional Quarterly Weekly Report,* Mar. 21, 1981, p. 499.

[47] Three conservative Republicans opposed the budget resolution because it projected budget deficits for 1981–84. The Democrats on the Budget Committee also opposed the budget and were able to chide the Republicans. Senator Moynihan of New York said, "You promised miracles and you are now encountering reality." *Congressional Quarterly Weekly Report,* Apr. 11, 1981, p. 621. Also see Martin Tolchin, "Senate Panel...Rejects Plan for Budget," *New York Times,* Apr. 10, 1981, pp. A–1, A–14. The Republicans soon reversed their action after nudging from Budget Director Stockman, *Newsweek,* May 11, 1981, p.24.

[48] *Congressional Quarterly Weekly Report,* Apr. 11, 1981, p. 619.

[49] For a useful account of the attempt, which focuses on Chairman Jim Jones

and the Democratic "gang of four" (Congressmen Mineta and Panetta of California, Gephardt of Missouri, and Wirth of Colorado) and their efforts to construct an appealing alternate package, see "Reagan's Budget Sails On," Newsweek, Apr. 13, 1981, pp. 72–75.

[50] Washington Post, Apr. 8, 1981, p. A–5.

[51] "Democrats in House Press Attacks on President's Economic Proposals," New York Times, Apr. 9, 1981, p. A–1.

[52] A simplified game-theory analysis of the Democrats' dilemma by Leonard Silk noted: "A nation sympathetic to the President, especially after the assassination attempt, would doubtless be angered with the Democrats and punish them in the 1982 Congressional elections." "Economic Scene," New York Times, Apr. 10, 1981, p. D–2.

[53] See David Mayhew, Congress: The Electoral Connection (New Haven: Yale University Press, 1974).

[54] Newsweek, Aug. 11, 1981, p. 24.

[55] Irwin B. Arieff, "Budget Fight Shows O'Neill's Fragile Grasp," Congressional Quarterly Weekly Report, May 9, 1981, p. 786.

[56] Los Angeles Times Poll, Apr. 26, 1981.

[57] Lee Lescaze, "Says People Are Losing Patience," Washington Post, Apr. 29, 1981, p. A–1.

[58] Congressional Quarterly Weekly Report, May 9, 1981, p. 783.

[59] Richard Cohen, "The 'Fun and Games' are Over," National Journal, May 16, 1981, p. 888.

[60] Ibid., p. 890.

[61] A cursory check in the Almanac of American Politics, 1980, shows that each of these congressmen had district-related reasons to support the President. For example, Jacobs represents conservative Marion County, Indiana.

[62] Congressional Quarterly Weekly Report, May 9, 1981, p. 783.

[63] Congressional Quarterly Weekly Report, May 16, 1981, p. 839.

[64] Congressional Quarterly Weekly Report, May 23, 1981, p. 887.

[65] In early June, the Reagan administration compromised on a three-year tax plan with cuts of 5, 10, and 10 percent. Whether this plan would pass Congress remained to be seen, although prospects seemed bright: "The new plan scales back individual cuts as well as business depreciation, and adds a potpourri of tax bonuses for individuals that were selected to lure conservative Democrats." Congressional Quarterly Weekly Report, June 6, 1981, p. 979. Later, in response to business protests, some of those cuts were restored.

[66] Newsweek, Jan. 26, 1981, pp. 35–51.

[67] Ibid., p. 36.
[68] David E. Rosenbaum, "Blacks Would Feel Extra Impact," *New York Times*, June 2, 1981, p. 1.
[69] *Congressional Quarterly Weekly Report*, Apr. 18, 1981, p. 660.
[70] As the committees began to work on the specifics of the Reagan proposals in June, Congress showed signs of recalcitrance. For example, the House Education and Labor Committee rejected the President's "block grant proposals completely": *New York Times*, June 10, 1981, p. 1. In addition, as noted above, the President's tax cut plan was still up in the air.
[71] Peter Goldman et al., "The Honeymoon Is Over," *Newsweek*, June 29, 1981, pp. 36–37. For the Democratic and Republican maneuvering in the House, see Martin Tolchin, "Opposition of Democrats to Specific Benefit Cuts Expected to be Strong," *New York Times*, June 15, 1981, pp. 1, 14, and Tolchin, "Republicans Press Criticism of House Version of Budget," *New York Times*, June 16, 1981, p. 9.
[72] Martin Tolchin, "Reagan's Plan Wins," *New York Times*, June 26, 1981, p. 1.
[73] Jerome R. Watson, "Reagan's Top Aides," *Chicago Sun-Times*, June 28, 1981, p. 4.
[74] "Rest In Peace, New Deal," *Newsweek*, August 10, 1981, p. 16.
[75] Jay Perkins, "Dems Say Reagan Usurped Congress Powers," *Chicago Sun-Times*, June 28, 1981, p. 42.

CHAPTER
12

THE FUTURE OF AMERICAN POLITICS

This book began with sketches of three versions of democratic theory: pluralist, majoritarian, and classical. Pluralism, with its emphasis on diversity, multiple centers of power, and competition, seems best to describe what happens in American politics most of the time. But pluralism, in form and outcome, is not democratic enough for many critics. Pressure for reform in American politics comes from two sources. The majoritarians seek "responsible parties" that would allow for the institutionalization of majority rule. Classical or participatory democrats seek to maximize individual participation in political decision-making. Given the reality of nation-state politics in the United States, this has meant advocacy of initiatives, referenda, direct primaries, regulation of interest groups, and so forth. In recent years, this strand of reform has concentrated on making political parties more open, accessible, and democratic.

The policymaking process in the United States has typically reflected the pluralist biases of the system. The process was strongly influenced by the fragmented formal structure, the pluralist political parties, and the relatively strong influence of organized interest groups on the process. Except for infrequent bouts of "abnormal" politics, the results have been incremental policies.

Change in American Politics

Two sets of changes have influenced the course of American politics in recent years. One set involved increased fragmentation of the system to the point of hyperpluralism. These changes included growing mistrust of government, the decline of political parties, the fall in voter turnout, and the increased activity and influence of organized interest groups. These changes amounted to a deinstitutionalization of American politics to the point that it became increasingly difficult to move some policies through the process.[1] The second set of changes involved the direction of public opinion on public policy: the widely discussed shift to the right in the American public. As indicated in Chapter Seven, this shift was neither so sharp nor so unambiguous as some might have indicated, but it was real. The presidential election of 1980 seemed to be a logical consequence of the increased conservatism of the American public. But the tantalizing question that remained was whether the two trends, fragmentation and increased conservatism, were somehow connected.

Realignment—What Again?

The political events of 1980–81 seemed to show that the American political system could respond in rough conformity with the broadest concept of democratic theory: that public opinion should determine elections, which in turn should define public policy. In this instance, a shift in public opinion to the right was followed by a decisive election victory for the conservative (Republican) party and its standard-bearer (Ronald Reagan), and that in turn was followed by a nonincremental shift in public policy to the right. Of course, the qualifications to the broad thesis are also important. The election results probably overstated the degree of shift to the right, and in turn the budget slashing of the Reagan administration probably overstated the election "mandate." Nevertheless, contrary to all expectations, the early days of the Reagan administration were remarkable for the congressional acceptance of dramatic shifts in spending priorities: "Even though it has cut corners and could falter in the final stretch, the 97th Congress already has made history with a wrenching departure from a half-century of trying to advance social welfare through ever more government spending."[2]

As with other similar instances in American political history, presidential leadership was a key variable in translating crude public opinion into public policy. Reagan's performance in the early days of his administration was frequently compared to that of FDR. The comparison was ironic in that he was attempting to reverse Roosevelt's revolution. The chief weapons President Reagan had in his arsenal were the perception of his mandate, his personal charm and popularity, and his ability to communicate a vision of a vital, strong, and productive United States. It did not matter that the public philosophy he espoused of a major reduction in the role of government was one that had been judged by some as irrelevant to the reality of modern government.[3] There remained enough resonance with the American public, for Reagan's public philosophy was essentially liberal enough, in the Lockean sense,[4] for it to seem fresh and appealing to a significant portion of the electorate.

Repeatedly we have raised the question of realignment (and contrasted it with a thesis of party decline). A coherent argument can be made that the 1980 elections continued a realigning era in American politics (stretching back to 1968) and that the major policy agenda shifts begun in 1981 are the fruits of that change. After all, the Republicans captured the presidency in 1968, 1972, and 1980. President Carter's 1976 victory could have been an after-shock of Watergate. What remains to complete the realignment may be the enactment of the rest of the Reagan program, a widespread public perception of the success of that program, and a subsequent shift in the balance of partisan identification of the population. In that case, the Reagan agenda could dominate the politics of the 1980s as the Roosevelt agenda dominated the 1930s.

In the near term, the 1982 congressional elections will provide some clues as to whether such a great transformation is taking place. Normally, the President's party loses ground in the House; the last time this did not happen was 1934. If the Republicans should overcome this tradition—perhaps even to take partisan control of the House—and if the Republicans should continue or strengthen their gains in the Senate, and if readings of partisan identification continue to show gains for Republicans, all these will be hard evidence of a realignment.[5] In early 1981 Republican confidence was running high: "...the Republican National Committee announced that...'the Republican party is on the verge of majority-party status for the first time in generations.'"[6] But that assumes incapacity or passivity on the Democratic side.

Because of the nature of the issues raised by the Reagan administration, as well as their apparent success, a reaction may be expected among Democrats and those groups adversely affected by the redistributive budget cuts. But the Democratic party faces two internal problems. The more serious one is the absence of a consensus on what to propose as an alternative to the Republicans. As illustrated in the fight over the Reagan budget, the policy and philosophical divisions in the Democratic party are deep and serious. The liberal wing of the party is temporarily on the defensive, but it is also the driving force of the party. The second problem is organizational. The Republicans have stolen a march on the Democrats in terms of the techniques of modern campaigning. The GOP had successfully linked Democratic control of the Congress with economic misery in the minds of the voters in 1980 and had urged voting "Republican for a change." This was a departure from an exclusive focus on presidential responsibility for the economy. The success of this appeal in 1980 is obvious. Perhaps the Democrats will relearn the lesson of linking policy and control of Congress in the 1982 elections.

Groups that traditionally support the Democratic party were either divided or imperfectly mobilized in 1980. As we have seen, part of the explanation is the decline in the New Deal/social welfare/Democratic party connection that defined American politics for thirty years or more. Big government is no longer regarded as automatically good. The narrowing of the electorate (turnout decline), along with the weakening of partisan identification, also has hurt the Democratic party. The policies of the Reagan administration, and their concrete effects, should do much to energize the Democratic coalition. But whether it would be a majority coalition at present is uncertain. Party polarization on the issues affecting lower-status people and minorities should result in some clearer distinction between the parties, but the presence of other issues such as energy will prevent clear-cut divisions. It may be that two minority parties will face each other over the barricades with the majority of the public participating sporadically.

Cycles in American Politics

It has frequently been suggested that American politics is cyclical in nature. There seems to be a good deal of truth to these observations. One such cyclical view was presented on pages 49–50, a view that postulated a cycle of movement from normal politics to disturbance to critical elections to abnormal politics and realignment to a gradual return to normal politics. Normal politics creates the conditions for disturbance, critical elections, and partisan realignment because the pluralist/incrementalist system of politics is incapable of dealing with new issues created by shifts in the nonpolitical realm: "It can be taken as a necessary consequence of the realities of incremental bargaining politics in the United States that they will tend to produce crises which lead to nonincremental change."[7] Abnormal politics results in relatively brief, intense bursts of government activity. The new majority is allowed to govern without much effective opposition. After the agenda is transformed and certain fundamental changes are achieved, the pluralist/incrementalist system reasserts itself. Political opposition recovers and is able to use the fragmented structure to delay, modify, or thwart the putative majority. Partisanship defines the main lines of political conflict around the issues generated out of the realignment, but partisan polarization recedes.

Another product of the disturbances leading to realignment may be a push for political reform resulting from a sense that the policy process is not working. Certainly such reform movements can be detected during the realignment of the 1890s and in the late 1960s and early 1970s. As William Crotty has observed, "The reforms...tend to cluster in highly concentrated and usually quite brief periods of time. These reform periods run in cycles."[8]

In the recent period, there was a focus on reforming the presidential nomination process,[9] although there have also been efforts at campaign finance reform. For the most part, these reforms were justified by the rhetoric of classical democracy in that they were touted to enhance participation and equality.

Given the apparent cyclical nature of American politics, the 1980 election might be seen as "critical," leading to an emerging conservative Republican majority. There is, however, another possibility. The distinction between normal and abnormal politics may no longer be valid, resting as it does so heavily on the assumption of durable partisanship in the electorate, interrupted by realignment and then reestablished with different parameters. The shape of normal politics is determined by the relationship of partisanship to issues. Politics is defined, structured, comprehensible. The decline of party weakens the structure of politics. What if the trends toward party decline were not checked? Politics would then be defined by the relationship of political personalities, which are transient, and salient issues. The abnormal would become normal: that is, each election would be decided de novo. Reagan's 1980 triumph could be followed by a liberal Democratic presidency in 1984.

If we look at the current situation (1980–81) in light of the potential for increased fragmentation in American politics, we might conjecture that the policies of the Reagan administration could spur a decline in confidence in the national government among disadvantaged groups. Efficacy and turnout among these groups could fall even further. It can be asserted that the Reagan election victory resulted from massive partisan defections based on a repudiation of the competence and effectiveness of the Carter administration and not from an endorsement of the Reagan prescriptions for change. In general, it can be argued that the decline of party favors conservative presidential candidacies because it weakens the mobilization of lower-status groups. It should be recalled that the 1980 election saw voter turnout decline again for the fifth consecutive presidential election and that interest groups committed to conservative causes, such as the National Conservative Political Action Committee, were very active and successful in the 1980 elections. All these trends are consistent with a continued decline of party and increased fragmentation of American politics.

In the short run, then, the decline of party plus the drop in voter turnout seems to favor conservative political interests. This may be due not so much to a shift to the right in the whole public, although that has taken place to a degree, as it is to the shrinking of the electorate and the influence of well-organized and active conservative interests. It is a telling point that early in 1981 even the Democratic party had adopted the business perspective on tax cuts.[10] It is somewhat ironic that the *effects* of party decline versus the effects of realignment in the near future may be virtually indistinguishable. The telling differences would be observed in partisan identification, especially of young voters.

Even if the decline of party did not bias the political system ideologically, it would still have negative effects on the politics of American democracy. The removal of party loyalties as a major force in presidential voting fundamentally changes the character and significance of the election process: "the 1980 presidential contest...has all the makings of a primary."[11] The presidential electorate has become increasingly volatile in the general election.[12] The mass media have become prime determinants of the selection of the nominees and the outcome of the election. Last-minute events may significantly affect the outcome of the election. And intense issues, which are not anchored to party, may move large numbers of voters. The product of such confusion is not likely to be a coherent system of governance.

It simply cannot be determined which of these interpretations, realignment or dealignment, is correct at the moment.

The Effects of Reform

Political reform in the United States has been fueled by both majoritarian and participatory sentiments. It has tended to be cyclical. Recent reform concentrated on increasing participation and openness in the nomination process in the Democratic party. In the wake of the 1968 Democratic National Convention, which was filled with bitter intraparty strife, the Democratic party created a Commission on Party Structure and Delegate Selection (popularly called the McGovern-Fraser Commission), which "recommended eighteen specific guidelines under which delegates to the 1972 convention should be selected."[13] The guidelines were concerned with opening up the delegate-selection process to greater participation and with increasing the representation of blacks, women, and young people in delegations. Although some deny the causality, the expansion of presidential primaries followed on the heels of reform.[14] Regardless, the fundamental basis for reform was the drive to democratize the party and increase participation, and this has been characteristic of American political reform: "There is a line of progression to the process—and this is its most encouraging feature—toward an ever increasing democratization of political power."[15]

But reform movements generate counterreformations. By 1980 concern for the state of political parties and for the health of the presidential nomination process was widespread, particularly in the Democratic party. Various suggestions were made—for example, to reintroduce the influence of officeholders into the nomination process. Although it seemed likely that some retrenchment of reform would take place in the 1980s, the clock could not be turned back to the era of the brokering of the nomination by state party "bosses," big city machines, and congressional "whales."

The proposition to be examined here is that party reform may have hastened party decline. The call for more participatory democracy in parties and for curbs on interest-group activity have broad appeal but unintended consequences. For example, public financing of presidential elections seems to have stimulated the movement of special interests into congressional elections and the creation of PACs, thereby strengthening even more the position of special interests in the policymaking process—surely not the intended result.[16]

It is at least provocative to consider whether, in fact, reform has contributed to both a decline of party and a withdrawal from electoral politics. In turn, it can be argued that the destructuring of partisan politics has blurred the traditional, class-based distinctions between the parties. If "partyless" politics and low turnout benefit Republicans and conservatives, then unintentionally reform in the Democratic party has played a role in the shift to the right in American politics (and also led to less, not more, participation). This is an uncomfortable and controversial conclusion. Can it be sustained?

Did party reform lead to party decline? Jeane J. Kirkpatrick has argued that "reform, along with its intended and unintended consequences, is...the most important cause of...party decline."[17] The most specific consequence of party reform has been the party's loss of control of presidential nominations. The primaries, and the media's interpretation of them, decide the nominations. In particular, this has seemed to weaken the Democratic party both in contesting the election and, when successful, in constructing a governing coalition. The surface results of the last three presidential elections help to make the point. The Democrats have not fared well. (It should be noted that they have lost three of the last four presidential elections). Table 12–1 includes the turnout figures for the past three presidential elections. The most striking observation is that the Democratic percentage of the

Table 12.1 Democratic Performance in
Presidential Elections versus Turnout, 1972–1980

	Dem. % 2-party vote	Dem. % Electoral College	Turnout	Turnout decline
1972	37.5	3	55.5	−5.4
1976	51.1	55	54.3	−1.2
1980	44.7	9	53.8	−.5
Average =	44.4	22.3	54.5	−2.4

electoral vote in the last three elections has been just over one fifth. In addition, the Democrats have won less than 45 percent of the two-party popular vote, and turnout has declined in each succeeding election. One reading, of course, is that the Democratic weakness is a result of Republican strength. For a variety of reasons, such an hypothesis seems unlikely.

Until just recently, Republican party identification has hovered around 20 percent. The Democrats have controlled both houses of Congress and most state governorships and state legislatures. As recently as 1974–75 the Republican party was considered to be in perilous shape. As shown in Chapter Nine, however, the underlying Democratic coalition has withered in attachment, psychologically and behaviorally, to the party at the presidential level. And turnout has declined correspondingly.

Democratic presidential nominations from 1972 on have not resulted in votes commensurate with majority party status. Can that be traced to reform? The case here is more tenuous. Clearly, decline began before reform, so reform cannot be the sole cause. The election of 1972 may be the best case for the anti-reform position: the reforms were just in effect, the convention delegates were unrepresentative of the Democratic party as a whole[18] and the result was a massive defeat for the party. Nevertheless, the results of the 1972 election cannot be attributed solely to the McGovern candidacy, which in turn cannot be traced solely to reform. The incumbency of Richard Nixon had something to do with the McGovern defeat, as did the sharp divisions within the Democratic party. In 1976 the Democratic nominee was able to paste together the New Deal coalition for the election but not for governing. The nominating process allowed the nomination of a candidate not bound to party. At the same time, President Carter was never able to construct an effective governing coalition. This led to the Democratic disaster of 1980.

It would be unfair to claim that reform is the sole cause of Democratic weakness. Internal conflict in the party (as in 1968, 1972, and 1980) is as important and is likely to remain troublesome. Reform hastened, but did not cause, party decline. But the paradox is that reform was intended to expand participation and to create opportunities for the disadvantaged. But participation in the general election has dropped since reform.[19] And by weakening the Democratic party, reform weakened the capacity of the party to govern or to oppose effectively, thereby weakening the liberal side of the political equation.

Projecting the 1980s

Political projections are, at best, uncertain. Who would have predicted the resurgence of the Republican party in the light of the 1974–1976 national elections? The safest course may be to swim somewhat against the current.

These projections are rooted in three assumptions. The first is that the preponderance of evidence suggests that "decline of party" rather than "dawn of a new era" is the better interpretation of the 1980 election. Everett Carll Ladd has asserted the point even more confidently than I would: "By now it is wholly evident that the dealignment interpretation of contemporary American electoral politics is correct.... The progress of dealignment gives its distinctive cast to the 1980 presidential election. And the 1980 mandate is brittle, not because some liberals and Democrats want it thus, but because it cannot be otherwise with a dealigned electorate."[20] Ladd cites various features of the 1980 election that argue for the dealignment thesis, including: the familiar survey evidence (of detachment from parties), the volatility of the electorate, the postponement of the vote decision, and the disappearance of stable electoral alignments. A major part of Ladd's argument is that the public has not turned decisively to the right. Rather it is ambivalent about the role of government: "Had Americans turned decisively against government and adopted a generally conservative response on matters involving public spending for social programs, the 1980 presidential election might well have evidenced a realignment ushering in long-term Republican ascendancy. This has not occurred because the public's antigovernment mood remains balanced by its progovernment mood."[21] The second is that the Reagan economic proposals, even if enacted, will fail to work the miracle of balancing the budget, checking inflation, and reducing the tax burden on individuals and businesses. (If this assumption is wrong, all bets are off.) The third assumption is that there will not develop a clear line of political conflict between the parties centered on a cluster of similar issues: multiple dimensions of political conflict will prevail. The first and third assumptions are heavily drawn from material presented earlier in this book.

If these assumptions hold, then the prospects for the politics of the 1980s in the United States are bleak. Among the likely consequences are a dwindling electorate, frequent swings in partisan control of the presidency, and policy stalemate. Hyperpluralism will reassert itself. And, if the arguments of this chapter are correct, conservative ideology will hold the upper hand. The answer to these difficulties, if there is one, does not lie in efforts to "democratize" the political system in a classical sense. The best remedy for the malaise of the American political system is to work to strengthen the two political parties. Whether it is too late to do that remains to be seen.

NOTES
CHAPTER TWELVE

[1] Perhaps the leading illustration would be the problems in moving HEW's budget, because of fights over limitations on the funding of abortion. For the perspective of the secretary, Joseph Califano, see his *Governing America* (New York: Simon & Schuster, 1981).

[2] Helen Dewar, "Spending Cuts Make 97th Congress Unique," *Washington Post*, June 14, 1981, p. A–6.

[3] See Theodore J. Lowi, *The End of Liberalism* 2nd ed., (New York: Norton, 1979), pp. 42–49.

[4] Louis Hartz has argued that Lockean liberalism is the American consensual value system. A prime element in this form of liberalism is "limited government." See Hartz, *The Liberal Tradition in America* (New York: Harcourt, Brace and World, 1955).

[5] Such a realignment could be enhanced by population shifts to the South and West and by reapportionment decisions in some states, which would benefit Republican congressional candidates.

[6] David S. Broder, "Puzzle for Democratic Leaders: Seek Shelter or Shout Defiance," *Washington Post*, June 7, 1981, p. A–2. In May of 1981, for the first time in at least thirty years, a survey found as many self-identified Republicans as Democrats. The survey was conducted by Ronald Reagan's pollster Richard Wirthlin. Nevertheless, other poll results pointed in the same direction (see Chapter Nine, n. 10); reported in *National Journal*, June 13, 1981, p. 1081. That same survey also found that "the biggest Republican gains are coming among young people... under 35." That is very good news for the Republicans. See David S. Broder. "Big Switch to GOP May Be for Real," *Chicago Sun-Times*, June 28, 1981.

[7] Walter Dean Burnham, *Critical Elections and the Mainsprings of American Politics* (New York: Norton, 1970), p. 137.

[8] William J. Crotty, *Political Reform and the American Experiment* (New York: Crowell, 1977), p. 267.

[9] This has been true of several reform periods. See Austin Ranney, *The Mischiefs of Faction* (Berkeley: University of California Press, 1975).

[10] Art Pine, "In Tax Cut Debate, the Democrats Are Where the GOP Used to Be," *Washington Post*, June 12, 1981, p. A–3.

[11] Everett Carll Ladd, Jr., "A Rebuttal Realignment? No. Dealignment? Yes." *Public Opinion*, Oct./Nov. 1980, p. 55.

[12] David H. Everson, "The Presidential Campaign of 1980," paper delivered

at the 1980 Presidential Election Lecture Series, Legislative Studies Center, Sangamon State University, October 22, 1980, pp. 18–19.

[13] Denis G. Sullivan et al., *Explorations in Convention Decision-Making* (San Francisco: W. H. Freeman, 1976), p. 9.

[14] For the two points of view, see Jeane Jordan Kirkpatrick, *Dismantling the Parties* (Washington, D.C.: American Enterprise Institute, 1978), pp. 5–9, versus Charles Longley, "National Party Reform and the Presidential Primaries," paper prepared for delivery at the 1981 Annual Meeting of the Midwest Political Science Association, Apr. 15–19, 1981, Cincinnati, Ohio, especially pp. 2–6. Also see Ken Bode and Carol Casey, "Party Reform: Revisionism Revised," in Robert A. Goldwin, ed., *Political Parties in the Eighties* (Washington, D.C.: American Enterprise Institute, 1980), pp. 16–18.

[15] Crotty, p. 267.

[16] See Dennis S. Ippolito and Thomas G. Walker, *Political Parties, Interest Groups and Public Policy* (Englewood Cliffs, N.J.: Prentice-Hall, 1980), p. 183.

[17] Kirkpatrick, p. 20. Of course, she also considers social trends such as technological change that contribute to party decline. Also see Everett Carll Ladd, Jr., "Party 'Reform' Since 1968: A Case Study in Intellectual Failure," in Patricia Bonomi et al., eds., *The American Constitutional System under Strong and Weak Parties* (New York: Praeger, 1981), pp. 81–95.

[18] This point is demonstrated conclusively by Jeane J. Kirkpatrick in *The New Presidential Elite* (New York: Russell Sage, 1976).

[19] Participation in the nomination process, caucuses, and primaries has increased, however. See William Crotty, "The Presidential Nominating Process in 1980," paper delivered at the 1980 Presidential Election Lecture Series, Legislative Studies Center, Sangamon State University, October 1, 1980, p. 19, table 3.

[20] "The Brittle Mandate: Electoral Realignment and the 1980 Presidential Election," *Political Science Quarterly* 96 (Spring 1981): 3.

[21] Ladd, p. 22.

Bibliography

Anderson, Kristi. *The Creation of a Democratic Majority.* Chicago: University of Chicago Press, 1979.

Axelrod, Robert. "Where the Votes Come From." *American Political Science Review* 66 (March 1972): 11–20.

Barber, James D. *The Pulse of Politics.* New York: Norton, 1980.

Bauer, Raymond A., et al. *American Business and Public Policy.* Chicago: Aldine, Atherton, 1972.

Bennett, W. Lance. *Public Opinion in American Politics.* New York: Harcourt Brace Jovanovich, 1980.

Bentley, Arthur F. *The Process of Government.* Chicago: University of Chicago Press, 1908.

Berelson, Bernard R., et al. *Voting: A Study of Opinion Formation in a Presidential Campaign.* Chicago: University of Chicago Press, 1914.

Berry, Jeffrey M. *Lobbying for the People.* Princeton, N.J.: Princeton University Press, 1977.

Broder, David. *The Changing of the Guard.* New York: Simon and Schuster, 1980.

Brody, Richard. "The Puzzle of Political Participation in America." In Anthony King, ed. *The New American Political System.* Washington, D.C.: American Enterprise Institute, 1978.

Burnham, Walter Dean. *Critical Elections and the Main Springs of American Politics.* New York: Norton, 1970.

Burnham, Walter Dean. "The Changing Shape of the American Political Universe." *American Political Science Review* (1965): 7–28.

Burnham, Walter Dean. "The 1980 Earthquake." In Thomas Ferguson and Joel Rogers, eds. *The Hidden Election.* New York: Pantheon, 1981.

Burns, James McGregor. *The Deadlock of Democracy.* Englewood Cliffs, N.J.: Prentice-Hall, 1963.

Calhoun, John C. *Disquisition on Government.* Indianapolis: Bobbs-Merrill, 1953.

Campbell, Angus, et al. *Elections and the Political Order.* New York: Wiley, 1966.

Campbell, Angus, et al. *The American Voter.* New York: Wiley, 1960.

Cobb, Roger W., and Elder, Charles D. *Participation in American Politics.* Baltimore: Johns Hopkins University Press, 1972.

Converse, Philip. "Change in the American Electorate." In Angus Campbell and Philip Converse, eds. *The Human Meaning of Social Change.* New York: Sage, 1972.

Converse, Philip. *The Dynamics of Party Support.* Beverly Hills: Sage, 1976.

Converse, Philip. "The Nature of Belief Systems in Mass Publics." In David E. Apter, ed. *Ideology and Discontent.* New York: Free Press, 1964.

Cotter, Cornelius P., and Bibby, John F. "Institutional Development of Parties and the Thesis of Party Decline." *Political Science Quarterly* 95 (Spring 1980): 1–27.

Crotty, William J. *Political Reform and the American Experiment.* New York: Crowell, 1977.

Crotty, William J., and Jacobson, Gary C. *American Parties in Decline.* Boston: Little, Brown, 1980.

Dahl, Robert A. *A Preface to Democratic Theory.* Chicago: University of Chicago Press, 1956.

Dahl, Robert A. *After the Revolution.* New Haven, Connecticut: Yale University Press, 1970.

Dahl, Robert A. *Pluralist Democracy in the United States: Conflict and Consent.* Chicago: Rand McNally, 1967.

Dahl, Robert A. *Who Governs?* New Haven: Yale University Press, 1961.

Dawson, Richard E. *Public Opinion and Contemporary Disarray.* New York: Harper & Row, 1973.

Downs, Anthony. *An Economic Theory of Democracy.* New York: Harper & Row, 1957.

Eldersveld, Samuel J. *Political Parties.* Chicago: Rand McNally, 1964.

Epstein, Leon D. *Political Parties in Western Democracies.* New York: Praeger, 1967.

Erikson, Robert S., et al. *American Public Opinion,* 2nd ed. New York: Wiley, 1980.

Everson, David H. *American Political Parties.* New York: New Viewpoints, 1980.

Germond, Jack W., and Witcover, Jules. *Blue Smoke and Mirrors.* New York: Viking, 1981.

Graber, Doris A. *Mass Media and American Politics.* Washington, D.C.: Congressional Quarterly Press, 1980.

Hardin, Charles. *Presidential Power and Accountability.* Chicago: University of Chicago Press, 1974.

Hartz, Louis. *The Liberal Tradition in America.* New York: Harcourt, Brace and World, 1955.

Hayes, Michael T. "Interest Groups and Congress." In Leroy N. Rieselbach, ed. *The Congressional System*. North Scituate, Mass.: Duxbury Press, 1979.

Hayes, Michael T. *Lobbyists and Legislators*. New Brunswick: Rutgers University Press, 1981.

Hayes, Michael T. "The Semi-Sovereign Pressure Groups: A Critique of Current Theory and an Alternative Typology." *Journal of Politics* 40 (1978): 159.

Hill, David B., and Luttbeg, Norman R. *Trends in American Electoral Behavior*. Itasca, Illinois: F. E. Peacock, 1980.

Holloway, Harry, and George, John. *Public Opinion*. New York: St. Martin's, 1979.

Hrebenar, Ronald J., and Scott, Ruth K. *Parties in Crisis: Party Politics in America*. New York: Wiley, 1979.

Hrebenar, Ronald J., and Scott, Ruth K. *Interest Group Politics in America*. Englewood Cliffs, N.J.: Prentice-Hall, 1982.

Ippolito, Dennis S., and Walker, Thomas G. *Political Parties, Interest Groups, and Public Policy*. Englewood Cliffs, N.J.: Prentice-Hall, 1980.

James, Judson L. *American Political Parties in Transition*. New York: Harper & Row, 1974.

Kessel, John. *Presidential Campaign Politics*. Homewood, Illinois: Dorsey, 1980.

Key, V. O., Jr. *Politics, Parties and Pressure Groups*, 4th ed. New York: Thomas Y. Crowell, 1958.

Key, V. O., Jr. *Public Opinion and American Democracy*. New York: Knopf, 1961.

Key, V. O., Jr. *Southern Politics in State and Nation*. New York: Random House, 1949.

Kirkpatrick, Jeane J. *Dismantling the Parties*. Washington, D.C.: American Enterprise Institute, 1978.

Kirkpatrick, Jeane J. *The New Presidential Elite*. New York: Sage, 1976.

Kornhauser, William. *The Politics of Mass Society*. Glencoe, Illinois: Free Press, 1959.

Ladd, Everett C., Jr., and Hadley, Charles D. *Transformation of the American Party System*, 2nd ed. New York: W. W. Norton, 1978.

Latham, Earl. "The Group Basis of Politics: Notes for a Theory." In H. R. Mahood, ed. *Pressure Groups in American Politics*. New York: Scribners, 1967.

Lazarsfeld, Paul, et al. *The People's Choice*, 3rd ed. New York: Columbia University Press, 1968.

Lindblom, Charles E. "The Science of 'Muddling Through'." *Public Administration Review* 29 (Spring, 1959): 79–88.
Lipset, Seymour Martin. *Political Man: The Social Bases of Politics*. Garden City, New York: Anchor Books, 1963.
Lowi, Theodore J. "American Business, Public Policy, Case Studies and Political Theory." *World Politics* 16 (July, 1964): 677–715.
Lowi, Theodore. *The End of Liberalism*, 2nd ed. New York: W. W. Norton, 1979.
Luttbeg, Norman R. "Political Linkage in a Large Society." In *Public Opinion and Public Policy*. Homewood, Illinois: The Dorsey Press, 1968.
McClosky, Herbert. "Consensus and Ideology in American Politics." *American Political Science Review* 58 (June, 1964): 361–82.
Mahood, H. R., ed. *Pressure Groups in American Politics*. New York: Scribners, 1967.
Mann, Thomas E. *Unsafe at any Margin*. Washington, D.C.: American Enterprise Institute, 1978.
Mayhew, David. *Congress: The Electoral Connection*. New Haven: Yale University Press, 1974.
Michels, Robert. *Political Parties: A Sociological Study of the Oligarchical Tendencies of Modern Democracy*. New York: Free Press, 1962.
Milbrath, Lester W. *Political Participation*. Chicago, Illinois: Rand McNally, 1965.
Miller, Warren E., et al. *American National Election Studies Data Sourcebook*. Cambridge, Mass.: Harvard University Press, 1980.
Miller, Warren E., and Levitin, Teresa E. *Leadership and Change: Presidential Elections from 1952 to 1976*. Cambridge, Mass.: Winthrop, 1976.
Miller, Warren E., and Stokes, Donald E. "Party Government and Saliency of Congress." In Angus Campbell et al. *Elections and the Political Order*. New York: Wiley, 1966.
Moe, Terry. "A Calculus of Group Membership." *American Journal of Political Science* 24 (November 1980): 629.
Monroe, Alan D. *Public Opinion in America*. New York: Dodd, Mead, 1975.
Mosca, G. *The Ruling Class*. New York: McGraw-Hill, 1939.
Neustadt, Richard. *Presidential Power: The Politics of Leadership from FDR to Carter*. New York: Wiley, 1980.
Nie, Norman, et al. *The Changing American Voter*. Cambridge, Mass.: Harvard University Press, 1979.
Olsen, Mancur. *The Logic of Collective Action*. New York: Shocken, 1968.
Ornstein, Norman J., and Elder, Shirley. *Interest Groups, Lobbying and Policy-Making*. Washington, D.C.: Congressional Quarterly Press, 1978.

Page, Benjamin I. *Choices and Echoes in Presidential Politics*. Chicago: University of Chicago Press, 1978.

Pareto, V. *The Mind and Society*. New York: Harcourt Brace, 1935.

Pateman, Carole. *Participation and Democratic Theory*. Cambridge: Cambridge University Press, 1970.

Patterson, Thomas E. *The Mass Media Election*. New York: Praeger, 1980.

Patterson, Thomas E., and McClure, Robert D. *The Unseeing Eye*. New York: Putnam, 1976.

Petrocik, John R. "Voter Turnout and Electoral Oscillation." *American Politics Quarterly* 9 (April, 1981): 161–80.

Petrocik, John R. *Party Coalitions*. Chicago: University of Chicago Press, 1981.

Phillips, Kevin. *The Emerging Republican Majority*. Garden City, N.Y.: Arden Books, 1970.

Pierce, John C., and Sullivan, John L. "An Overview of the American Electorate." In Pierce and Sullivan, eds., *The Electorate Reconsidered*. Beverly Hills: Sage, 1980.

Pomper, Gerald. "From Confusion to Clarity: Issues and American Voters, 1956–1968." *American Political Science Review* 66 (June, 1972): 415–428.

Pomper, Gerald, ed. *Party Renewal in America*. New York: Praeger, 1980.

Pomper, Gerald. "The Decline of Partisan Politics." In Louis Maisel and Joseph Cooper, eds. *The Impact of the Electoral Process*. Beverly Hills, California: Sage, 1977.

Pomper, Gerald M. "The Presidential Election." In Pomper et al., eds. *The Election of 1980*. Chatham, N.J.: Chatham House, 1981.

Pomper, Gerald. "Toward a More Responsible Two-Party System? What, Again?" *Journal of Politics* 33 (November, 1971): 923.

Pomper, Gerald. *Voter's Choice*. New York: Dodd, Mead, 1975.

Pomper, Gerald M., and Lederman, Susan S. *Elections in America*, 2nd ed. New York: Longman, 1980.

Prothro, James W., and Grigg, Charles M., "Fundamental Principles of Democracy." *Journal of Politics* 22 (1960): 276–94.

Ranney, Austin. *The Doctrine of Responsible Party Government*. Urbana: University of Illinois Press, 1954.

Ranney, Austin. *The Mischiefs of Faction*. Berkeley: University of California Press, 1975.

Ranney, Austin, and Kendall, Willmoore. *Democracy and the American Party System*. New York: Harcourt Brace Jovanovich, 1956.

Ripley, Randall B., and Franklin, Grace A. *Congress, the Bureaucracy and Public Policy*, rev. ed. Homewood, Illinois: Dorsey Press, 1976.

Robinson, Michael I. "Public Affairs Television and the Growth of Political Malaise." *American Political Science Review* 70 (June, 1976): 409–32.

Sanford, Terry. *A Danger of Democracy.* Boulder, Colorado: Westview Press, 1981.

Scammon, Richard M., and Wattenberg, Ben J. "Is this the End of an Era?" *Public Opinion* (Oct./Nov., 1980): 2–12.

Schattschneider, E. E. *Party Government.* New York: Holt, Rinehart and Winston, 1942.

Schattschneider, E. E. *Politics, Pressures and the Tariff.* New York: Prentice-Hall, Inc., 1935.

Schattschneider, E. E. *The Semi-Sovereign People.* New York: Holt, Rinehart and Winston, 1960.

Seymour-Ure, Colin. *The Political Impact of Mass Media.* Beverly Hills: Sage, 1974.

Simon, Rita James. *Public Opinion in America.* Chicago: Markham, 1974.

Stouffer, Samuel A. *Communism, Conformity and Civil Liberties.* Garden City, N.Y.: Doubleday, 1955.

Sundquist, James L. "Congress, the President, and the Crisis of Competence in Government." In Lawrence C. Dodd and Bruce I. Oppenheimer, eds. *Congress Reconsidered.* Washington, D.C.: Congressional Quarterly Press, 1981.

Sundquist, James L. *Dynamics of the Party System.* Washington, D.C.: Brookings, 1973.

Sundquist, James L. "The Crisis of Competence in our National Government." *Political Science Quarterly* 95 (1980): 183–208.

de Tocqueville, Alexis. *Democracy in America.* Garden City, N.Y.: Anchor Books, 1969.

Truman, David. *The Governmental Process.* New York: Alfred A. Knopf, 1951.

Verba, Sidney, and Nie, Norman H. *Participation in America.* New York: Harper & Row, 1972.

Weaver, David, et al. *Media Agenda-Setting in a Presidential Election.* New York: Praeger, 1981.

Wildavsky, Aaron. *The Politics of the Budgetary Process*, 3rd ed. Boston: Little, Brown, 1979.

Wilson, James Q. *Political Organizations.* New York: Basic Books, 1973.

Index of Names

Abramson, Paul R., 91
Alpenn, D. M., 93
Anderson, Kristi, 92, 93, 234
Arieff, Irwin B., 214
Asbell, Bernard, 189
Axelrod, Robert, 164, 173, 234

Bach, Stanley, 187
Bachrach, Peter, 40
Banfield, Edward C., 55, 176, 187
Barber, James D., 34–35, 39, 234
Bayh, Birch, 193
Beck, Paul Allen, 55
Bennett, W. Lance, 64, 71, 234
Bentley, Arthur F., 25–30, 33, 38, 234
Berelson, Bernard R., 70, 234
Berry, Jeffrey M., 93, 234
Bibby, John F., 91, 92, 235
Bode, Ken, 231
Bonomi, Patricia, 19, 231
Boyd, Richard W., 92
Brademas, John, 193
Brady, David W., 54, 56, 91
Braestrup, Peter, 117
Brock, William, 80
Broder, David, 93, 97, 101, 114, 139, 230, 234
Brody, Richard, 92, 234
Bullock, Charles S., III, 54
Burnham, Walter, Dean, 56, 81, 82, 92, 230, 234
Burns, James McGregor, 44, 54, 234
Bush, George, 101, 103–4
Butler, David, 19, 56

Calhoun, John C., 19, 22, 23–24, 38, 234
Califano, Joseph, 230
Campbell, Angus, 54, 70, 92, 139, 160, 172, 173, 234
Carter, Jimmy, 11, 50, 96–7, 101, 102–03, 104, 108, 114, 120, 165, 167, 170, 192, 198, 220, 223, 227, 237
Casey, Carol, 231
Chambers, William Nisbet, 92
Church, Frank, 193
Citrin, Jack, 91
Clark, Timothy B., 212–13
Clymer, Adam, 212
Cobb, Roger W., 116, 234
Cohen, Bernard, 109
Cohen, David, 93
Cohen, Richard, 214
Connolly, William E., 18
Converse, Philip, 166, 172, 173, 234
Conway, Margaret M., 55, 87, 93
Cooper, Joseph, 238
Coser, Lewis, 38
Cotter, Cornelius P., 92, 235
Croly, Herbert, 10
Cronin, Thomas, 187
Cronkite, Walter, 110
Crotty, William J., 20, 91, 93, 94, 114, 222, 230, 231, 235
Crouse, Timothy, 115
Culver, John, 193
Cutler, Lloyd, 11, 20

Dahl, Robert A., 18, 19, 20, 39, 70, 71, 235
David, Paul T., 20, 194, 211
Davis, Lanny J., 114
Dawson, Richard E., 127, 140, 156, 235
Demkovich, Linda E., 213
DeNardo, James, 166, 173
Devine, Donald J., 18, 71
DeVries, Walter, 106, 116
Dewar, Helen, 230
Diamond, Martin, 19
Dickinson, John, 13
Dodd, Lawrence C., 54, 55, 187, 188, 239
Dole, Robert, 211
Domenici, Peter, 211
Domhoff, William, 114
Downs, Anthony, 54, 235
Dreyer, Edward C., 55

Ebring, Lutz, 116, 117
Edwards, George C., III, 187, 188
Efron, Edith, 188
Eisenhower, Dwight, 43, 83, 182
Elazar, Daniel, 187
Elder, Charles D., 116, 234
Elder, Shirley, 237
Eldersveld, Samuel J., 54, 235
Epstein, Laurily Keir, 116, 117
Epstein, Leon D., 18, 54, 235
Erikson, Robert S., 70, 139, 140, 144, 156, 173, 235
Eulau, Heinz, 38
Everson, David H., 19, 55, 91, 92, 94, 116, 230, 235

Finifter, Ada W., 91
Fishel, Jeff, 115
Ford, Gerald, 97

Franklin, Grace A., 187, 189, 213, 238
Frankovic, Kathleen A., 194, 211
Fraser, Donald M., 225
Free, Lloyd, 127, 140

Garceau, Oliver, 28, 38
Garn, Jake, 211
George, John, 236
Germond, Jack W., 115, 235
Glass, Andrew J., 93
Goldman, Peter, 215
Goldwater, Barry, 162
Goldwin, Robert A., 55
Goshko, John M., 212
Graber, Doris A., 102, 114, 115, 117, 235
Gramm, Phil, 204, 205
Greenstein, Fred J., 70
Grigg, Charles M., 70, 238

Hadley, Charles D., 157, 172, 173, 236
Haig, Alexander M., 197, 212
Halberstam, David, 110
Hardin, Charles, 55, 235
Harmony, Rita, 96
Harris, Louis, 153–54, 157
Hartz, Louis, 18, 230, 235
Hawley, Willis D., 92
Hayes, Michael T., 35, 40, 235
Helms, Jesse, 54, 211
Hill, David B., 92, 236
Holloway, Harry, 236
Hrebenar, Ronald J., 91, 236
Hyman, Herbert, 70

Ippolito, Dennis S., 93, 231, 236

Jackman, Mary R., 156

Jackman, Robert W., 71
Jacob, Charles, 211
Jacobs, Andy, 206, 214
Jacobson, Gary C., 91, 93, 94, 235
James, Judson L., 19, 236
Johnson, Lyndon, 50, 97, 162
Jones, Charles O., 184, 189, 211
Jones, James, 203, 213

Kaiser, Robert G., 211, 213
Katz, Daniel, 70
Kaufman, Arnold S., 19
Kendall, Willmoore, 20, 54, 238
Kennedy, Edward, 104
Kernell, Samuel, 187
Kessel, John, 54, 92, 99, 236
Key, V. O., Jr., 54, 66, 70, 71, 79, 91, 92, 114, 156, 236
King, Anthony, 91, 188, 234
Kirkpatrick, Evron, 55
Kirkpatrick, Jeanne J., 54, 226, 231, 236
Kornhauser, William, 22, 24, 38, 236

Ladd, Everett C., Jr., 52, 93, 116, 157, 172, 173, 228, 230, 231, 236
Laffer, Arthur, 187
Latham, Earl, 38, 236
Latta, Delbert, 205
Lawrence, David G., 71
Lazarsfeld, Paul, 38, 115, 168, 173, 188, 236
Lederman, Susan S., 54, 188, 238
Lengle, James I., 115
Lescaze, Lee, 212, 214
Levitin, Teresa E., 172, 237
Lindblom, Charles E., 70, 188, 236
Lippman, Walter, 24, 38, 98, 114

Lipset, Seymour Martin, 91, 156, 236
Longley, Charles H., 20, 91, 231
Lowi, Theodore J., 33, 39, 139, 184, 188, 230, 236, 237
Luttbeg, Norman, R., 70, 92, 156, 236, 237

MacNeil, Neil, 211
McClosky, Herbert, 70, 139, 237
McClure, Robert, 107, 115, 116, 211
McCombs, Maxwell, 116
McCormick, Richard, 92
McGinniss, Joe, 107, 116
McGovern, George, 102, 103, 193, 195, 225, 227
McLuhan, Marshall, 107
Madison, James, 6, 18, 22–23, 38
Madron, Thomas Wm., 93
Magnuson, Warren, 193, 202
Mahood, H. R., 38, 236, 237
Maisel, Louis, 238
Mann, Thomas E., 65, 71, 237
Margolis, Michael, 55
Mathews, Donald R., 115, 187
Mathews, T., 94
Mayhew, David, 214, 237
Michels, Robert, 18, 70, 237
Milbrath, Lester W., 70, 71, 237
Miller, Arthur H., 91
Miller, Warren E., 70, 121, 139, 140, 156, 172, 173, 237
Mills, C. Wright, 188
Mineta, Norman, 214
Mitofsky, Warren, 93
Moe, Ronald C., 93
Moe, Terry, 39, 237
Monroe, Alan D., 142, 156, 237
Mosca, G., 70, 237
Moynihan, Daniel P., 19, 213

Mueller, John E., 114
Muskie, Edmund, 101–02, 115

Nader, Ralph, 87
Nelson, Gaylord, 193
Neustadt, Richard, 179, 187, 188, 237
Nie, Norman, 54, 56, 65–66, 71, 92, 139, 140, 237, 239
Nimmo, Dan, 115, 116
Nixon, Richard, 44, 50, 97, 107, 114, 171, 195, 227

Odegard, Peter H., 28, 38
Olsen, Mancur, 33, 39, 237
O'Neill, Thomas P., 204–05, 209, 214
Oppenheimer, Bruce I., 54, 55, 187, 188, 239
Ornstein, Norman J., 237
Ostrogorski, M., 86, 93

Page, Benjamin I., 237
Panetta, Leon, 214
Pareto, V., 70, 237
Parker, Joan A., 92
Pateman, Carole, 18, 237
Patterson, Thomas E., 107, 115, 116, 182, 188, 238
Peabody, Robert L., 188
Peirce, Neal R., 19
Perkins, Jay, 215
Petrocik, John R., 160, 172, 173, 237, 238
Phillips, Kevin, 172, 238
Pierce, John C., 71, 238
Pine, Art, 230
Plissner, Martin, 93
Plotkin, Henry A., 211

Polsby, Nelson W., 114
Pomper, Gerald, 54, 55, 92, 139, 173, 188, 192, 211, 238
Prothro, James W., 70, 238

Ranney, Austin, 19, 20, 54, 55, 230, 238
Reagan, Ronald, 44, 50–51, 53, 103–04, 108, 111, 139, 140, 165, 169, 171, 172, 176, 179, 186, 192–210, 211, 212, 213, 214, 215, 215–221, 223, 229, 230
Redman, Eric, 187
RePass, David E., 64, 71
Rieselbach, Leroy N., 40, 235
Ripley, Randall B., 187, 189, 213, 238
Robinson, Michael I., 117, 188, 238
Roosevelt, Franklin, 171, 210, 220, 237
Roosevelt, Theodore, 10
Roper, Elmo, 70
Rose, Richard, 92
Rosenbaum, David E., 207, 213, 215
Rosenbaum, Walter A., 55
Rossiter, Clinton, 18, 38
Rothman, Stanley, 40
Rowan, Hobart, 212

Saloma, John S., 91
Sanford, Terry, 238
Sartori, Giovanni, 18
Savage, Robert L., 116
Scammon, Richard M., 55, 173, 238
Schattschneider, E. E., 20, 28, 31–32, 38, 39, 44, 54, 164, 238, 239
Schubert, Glendon, 20

Index of Names

Scott, Ruth K., 91, 236
Seymour-Ure, Colin, 188, 239
Shafer, Byron E., 115
Shaffer, Stephen D., 92
Shapiro, Martin, 182, 188
Sharkansky, Ira, 187, 188
Shaw, Donald, 116
Sheatsely, Paul B., 70
Silk, Leonard, 214
Simon, Rita James, 140, 239
Smith, Hedrick, 212
Smith, Judith G., 93
Sontag, Frederick H., 91
Stacks, John F., 140
Stockman, David, 195–198, 212, 213
Stokes, Donald E., 70, 121, 139, 237
Stouffer, Samuel A., 70, 71, 239
Sullivan, Denis G., 20, 231
Sullivan, John L., 71, 238
Sundquist, James L., 55, 75, 76, 89, 91, 187, 239
Sulzner, George T., 187

Taft, Robert, 43
Tarrance, Lance, 106, 116
Thelen, David P., 19
Thurmond, Strom, 211

de Tocqueville, Alexis, 22–25, 38, 239
Toffler, Alvin, 19, 74, 89, 91
Tolchin, Martin, 204, 213, 215
Tower, John, 211
Truman, David, 18, 20, 25, 28–31, 33, 38, 40, 177, 239
Truman, Harry, 114, 165, 182

Ullman, Al, 193

Verba, Sidney, 65–66, 71, 239

Walker, Jack, 71
Walker, Thomas G., 93, 231, 236
Watson, Jerome R., 215
Wattenberg, Ben J., 55, 173, 238
Watts, William, 127, 140
Weaver, David, 239
White, Theodore H., 115
Wildavsky, Aaron, 114, 183, 188, 239
Wilson, James Q., 194, 211, 239
Wilson, Woodrow, 46, 187
Wirthlin, Richard, 230
Witcover, Jules, 115, 235
Woodward, Julian L., 70

Yankelovich, Daniel, 140

Index of Subjects

Abnormal politics, 184–85, 208, 218, 222–23
Attentive public, 64

Boll Weevils, 204, 205

Civil rights, attitudes on, 131–32, 149–51
Coalitions, electoral, 164–166
Congress, role in policy-making, 88, 178, 180, 200, 202–04, 210
Conservatism, 120–38, 151–53, 194, 219
Cycles in American politics, 49–51, 222–24

Decline of party, 48–53, 77–81, 170–71, 218, 224–26, 228
Democratic elitism, 63–64
Democratic rules of the game, 61–62
Democracy, 2–3, 5–11, 15–16, 63–64, 218–19
  classical view of, 2, 8–9, 16, 58, 63, 218
Direct participation in primaries, 15

Federal bureaucracy, 182
Foreign affairs, attitudes on, 125–31, 147–49
Four-party politics, 44
Fragmentation of American politics, 74–75, 90, 96–97, 112–13, 120, 176–77, 209, 218, 219, 223, 224

Governing coalition, 89
Group basis of partisan identification, 160–64
Group theory, 25–37
Group voting patterns, 164–70

Hyperpluralistic politics, 53, 171, 186, 218, 229

Incremental policy-making, 183, 218, 222
Interest-group liberalism, 33
Interest group theory, 22–37
Interest groups, 11–12, 85–88, 90, 218, 225
  role in policy-making, 34–35, 180–81
Iron triangle, 195, 200–02, 207, 212
Issue voting, 60–61, 66–67

Law of minimum effects, 105–06
Liberalism/conservatism, 136
Liberalism, non-economic, 151–54

Majoritarian parties, 45–48
Majoritarian view of democracy, 2, 5–9, 14–15, 31, 53, 218
Mandate, 192–94, 196, 219, 220
Mass media, 96–113, 181–82, 207, 224, 226
Mass media and political agenda, 109–10
Mobilization of bias, 32
Multiple group memberships, 29–30, 36

Index of Subjects

New Deal, 195, 221, 227
Non-incremental change, 194–95, 209

Particularized contacting, 66
Party identification, 160–64
Pluralism, classical, 22–25, 208
Pluralist parties, 42–45
Pluralist view of democracy, 2, 5–9, 13–16, 53, 218, 222
Policy
    distributive, 184
    re-distributive, 184, 221
    regulatory, 184
Policy dimensions, 121
Policy-making process, 176–86
Political action committees, 79, 87, 93
Political
    cynicism, 75–77, 111–12
    information, 59–60, 64–65
    organizations, 3–4, 13–15
    participation, 60, 65–66
    reform, 10–11, 16–17, 224–28
Political parties, 42–53, 180
    functions of, 11–12
Political party competition, effects on voter turnout, 81–83
President, role in policy-making, 178–80, 192

Presidential nominations and mass media, 100–04
Public interest, 13, 31, 33, 87
Public interest groups, 87–88
Public policy and mass media, 108–12, 219

Rational-activist model, 58–59, 64–69, 193
Reaganomics, 195–96, 196–200
Realignment, 48–51, 160, 170–71, 185, 219, 220, 222, 224, 228
Responsible parties, 11, 14, 45–48, 218
Rules of the game, 61–62, 67–68

Separation of powers, constitutional, 176–77
Single-issue groups, 86, 93
Social attitudes, opinion on, 132–35
Social welfare policy, attitudes on, 122–25, 142–47
Subgovernments, 201

U.S. Supreme Court, 178, 182

Voter turnout
    decline, 81–85, 218, 227
    of groups, 166–67